LAWRENCE GRASSI

From Piedmont to the Rocky Mountains

Lawrence Grassi was a trailblazer in every sense of the word. A working-class man of humble Italian origins who worked as a labourer and a coal miner for most of his life, Grassi had a deep passion for the Rocky Mountains. He was famous in the region for his commitment as a guide, a mountain climber, and a builder of greatly admired hiking trails. Today, in or near Canmore, his name graces a mountain, two lakes, and a school, and he is commemorated at Lake O'Hara in Yoho National Park.

In *Lawrence Grassi: From Piedmont to the Rocky Mountains*, Elio Costa and Gabriele Scardellato uncover the deeply private man behind this legend, from his birth in the small Italian village of Falmenta to his long and inspirational career in Canada. Using previously unexamined family letters and extensive information on Grassi's cohort of Italian immigrants, the authors reconstruct his personal and professional life, correcting myths and connecting his story to the long history of Italian immigration to Canada. The definitive biography of this Canadian mountain hero, *Lawrence Grassi* is essential reading for those interested in the history of immigration, sport, and the Rocky Mountains.

ELIO COSTA is a professor emeritus in the Department of Languages, Literatures and Linguistics at York University.

GABRIELE SCARDELLATO is an associate professor and the Mariano A. Elia Chair in Italian-Canadian Studies at York University.

Lawrence Grassi

From Piedmont to the Rocky Mountains

ELIO COSTA AND GABRIELE SCARDELLATO

UNIVERSITY OF TORONTO PRESS
Toronto Buffalo London

© University of Toronto Press 2015
Toronto Buffalo London
www.utppublishing.com
Printed in the U.S.A.

ISBN 978-1-4426-4849-4 (cloth)
ISBN 978-1-4426-2624-9 (paper)

Library and Archives Canada Cataloguing in Publication

Costa, Elio, 1939–, author
Lawrence Grassi : from Piedmont to the Rocky Mountains / Elio Costa and
Gabriele Scardellato.

Includes bibliographical references and index.
ISBN 978-1-4426-4849-4 (bound). – ISBN 978-1-4426-2624-9 (pbk.)

1. Grassi, Lawrence, 1890–1980.   2. Mountaineers – Alberta – Canmore –
Biography.   3. Italian Canadians – Alberta – Canmore – Biography.
4. Canmore (Alta.) – Biography.   5. Rocky Mountains, Canadian (B.C. and
Alta.) – Biography.   I. Scardellato, Gabriele Pietro, 1951–, author   II. Title.

GV199.92.G63C68 2015   796.522092   C2015-900828-X

University of Toronto Press acknowledges the financial assistance to its
publishing program of the Canada Council for the Arts and the Ontario Arts
Council.

    Canada Council   Conseil des Arts
                        for the Arts   du Canada

ONTARIO ARTS COUNCIL
CONSEIL DES ARTS DE L'ONTARIO
an Ontario government agency
un organisme du gouvernement de l'Ontario

University of Toronto Press acknowledges the financial support of the
Government of Canada through the Canada Book Fund for its publishing
activities.

Contents

Figures

Acknowledgments

A small financial contribution from the Mariano A. Elia Chair of York University was all the encouragement one of the authors of this book needed to help in the organization of an "Italian Homecoming" in Field, BC, in the summer of 2000. We owe Bryan Massam, a friend and colleague at York who has had a decades-long love affair with the Rockies, a great debt for introducing us to what in due course, and after repeated trips to the Rockies, coalesced into the idea for this book. The practical arrangements for the homecoming, which became the Field millennium project, were the work of two long-time Field residents, Randle Robertson and Irene Brook. Randle was then the executive director of the Burgess Shale Geoscience Foundation; Irene was the wife of Glen Brook, who had been chief warden of Yoho National Park. Both Glen and Irene were great friends and admirers of Lawrence Grassi. Irene, especially, called Lawrence a "great man." Glen, we later discovered, had hired Grassi as assistant warden at Lake O'Hara, where he would build some of his most noteworthy trails, including the one that leads hikers to Lake Oesa. It was on this trail that one of the authors first came across the name of Lawrence Grassi, inscribed in a bronze plaque installed by the Alpine Club of Canada. Regretfully, Glen and Irene are no longer with us and will not be able to see the publication of this book, to which they both contributed greatly. We are grateful to have known them and for the rare personal insight into Grassi's life and work that they provided. Randle, who in his younger years had been a park warden, has become a critical source of information and occasional guide for our all-too-rare excursions into Lake O'Hara and to some of its trails. Above all, he is a friend and exceptionally generous host.

We cannot imagine a more pleasant place to carry out research than the Whyte Museum of the Canadian Rockies in Banff, Alberta. There we found the "letters from home" in the Grassi fonds. This correspondence convinced us early on that Grassi's story could only be told by tracing his origins in Falmenta and the experiences of many like him who responded to economic and other challenges by emigrating. But the Whyte Museum yielded much more than the letters from home. We were fortunate in our visits there at different times to count on the wonderful courtesy and collaboration of all, even when the temperature outside plunged to minus thirty, as it did one recent February. We extend our warmest thanks to all who work there, from past executive director Michale Lang to the always helpful, knowledgeable, and cheerful Elizabeth Kundert-Cameron and to Lena Koon. You made our work both productive and pleasurable.

In Thunder Bay we are indebted to Roy Piovesana, the author of an important book, *The Italians of Fort William's East End*. The East End, in what was then the settlement of Fort William, is where the young Lorenzo joined Falmentine friends and relatives when he first arrived in Canada. Both Roy and his colleague, John Potestio, author of another important volume, *The Italians of Thunder Bay*, were welcoming hosts who took time to show us the world of Italian Canadians at the Lakehead. During our stay, our work in the Thunder Bay Museum yielded some useful materials, but it was one of Roy's suggested contacts, Joan Grassi, who produced tangible autobiographical, and pictorial, evidence of migration from Falmenta to the north shore of Lake Superior. In particular, Ms Grassi provided us with two photographs, both of which are reproduced in this book. One of these is a portrait of the members of the Club Novarese, essentially made up of Falmentines with names such as Bianconi, Tiboni, Cerutti, Testori, Minoletti, Zanni, Cantoni, and Milani, all of whom were part of the emigration network that included Lorenzo Grassi.

From Fort William Grassi moved on to the settlement of Jackfish, for which we could not have had a better guide than David Falzetta of Terrace Bay, Ontario. David was born in Jackfish, which was abandoned in the 1950s and is now a ghost town. He proved to be the ideal guide, and our visit there – an eerie, beautiful, and extraordinarily moving experience – was one of the highlights of our long retracing of Lawrence Grassi's life. The sight of a travel chest, abandoned in the silent forest steps from the awesome cold greyness of Lake Superior, struck a particularly sensitive nerve in both authors: we both made the Atlantic crossing many years ago with families that carried their worldly possessions in trunks similar to the one we now saw abandoned on the north shore. And to come across an abandoned cemetery, including a marker for the burial of Catterina Milani (8 September 1914–18 February 1915), daughter of previous Falmentine residents, or to enter David's own family home, now slowly being reclaimed by the elements, lent great emotional substance to the images of Jackfish we found in the local museum. Thank you, David.

Farther afield, and closer to Lawrence's home in the Rocky Mountains, we were greatly aided by the steady and solicitous support of Catherine McKinnon of Calgary and Nancy Wolfer of Medicine Hat. Catherine's links with all things Falmentine is rooted in her own family name of Minoletti. Her grandparents Amedeo and Caterina Minoletti, as well as other relatives, had migrated to Jackfish and resided there when Lorenzo arrived in 1912. We greatly appreciate Catherine's willingness to share family history and photographs. Her cousin Nancy Wolfer, another Westerner also with ties to Minolettis from Falmenta, was most generous in sharing the results of her dedicated genealogical research, including several photographs that we are pleased to include in these pages.

In the years since we conceived the idea for this book we have made a number of visits to Falmenta, and here too we could not have asked for a more welcoming atmosphere and enthusiastic support. Armanda Grassi, Lorenzo's great niece, and granddaughter of his sister Virginia, still lives in Falmenta with her sisters Marisa and Giulia and their families. Her warm reception of us and her generous sharing of a variety of family documents and other artifacts – above all her memories of life in the Cannobino Valley – provided a living link with Lorenzo Grassi's early life. It came as a revelation to us when she produced a pillowcase and bedsheet that had been embroidered by the very young Lorenzo, providing insight into an old Falmentine practice. In Oggebbio, not far from Falmenta, we were fortunate to spend a few days in the Hotel Belsoggiorno, overlooking Lake Maggiore. We were guests of Nunzio Vercelli, the grandson of Armandina Grassi, one of the twin daughters of Lorenzo's sister, who died tragically at the end of the last war. A wonderful host and great cook, Nunzio personified for us a resilience, renewal, and creativity that are in sharp contrast to the tale of hardship and suffering contained in Lorenzo's "letters from home."

We are greatly indebted to the mayor of Falmenta, Luigi Milani, and his wife Marilena for their generous hospitality. We are especially grateful to him for putting himself at our complete disposal, from arranging car rentals to facilitating access to the municipal archives and the parish records of the church of San Lorenzo. The Milani's strong interest in our project reflects their keen sensitivity to Falmenta's history of emigration. Aware of Lawrence Grassi's significance for Canmore, in 2006 Luigi Milani approached his Canadian counterpart about a possible twinning between Falmenta and Canmore. Nothing came of that initiative, but we dare to hope that this book will spark renewal of interest in the idea.

Other Falmentines to whom we are indebted are Emilio Cerutti, Marisa Grassi's husband, whose knowledge of Falmentine traditional stone construction techniques helped us to appreciate Lawrence's use of stone in his trails in the Rockies. It is a pleasure to express our appreciation to Silvano Dresti and his wife Ornella Ferrari, of Cannobio. Their gracious sharing of the knowledge they have gained in their study of emigration from the Cannobino Valley is proof, if any were needed, of the good will we encountered everywhere we went in this part of Piedmont. The same hospitality and willingness to share insights was exhibited by others we met in Falmenta, including residents Giuseppe Zanni and Janine Rohrbach-Grassi.

In Canmore, Bill Cherak generously shared important documents, photographs, artifacts, and personal recollections of his friendship with Lawrence Grassi. This friendship began when his father sold Grassi the log cabin in which he lived for almost his entire life in Canmore. Bill can be described as the most important living link with Lawrence Grassi, and we hope we have done justice to his memories of his neighbour and life-long friend. We are also grateful for the generous assistance of Edward van Vliet, then director of the Canmore Museum and Geoscience Centre, which by sheer chance managed to conserve some of the records of the Canmore Coal Company, Grassi's employer.

We first met Chic Scott through some of the many books that have made him Canada's leading mountain historian. He is also one of the country's great climbers, not only in the Rockies but also in the Himalayas and the Alps. His book *Pushing the Limits: The Story of Canadian Mountaineering* (2000), with a section dedicated to Lawrence Grassi, prompted us to contact him when we needed some expert advice in writing about Lawrence's mountaineering exploits. We met him in the

Whyte Museum, where he was giving a talk entitled "My Time in the Alps," and discovered that as a young man he had climbed not far from where we were born. Chic became one of our greatest boosters. He always made time to provide advice, unravelling complex mountaineering issues, and gave us names of others he thought would be useful. He also read large sections of the first draft and gave feedback of such scope that at times we almost felt obliged to add his name to ours as co-author. We will always be indebted to him.

Chic gave us Don Gardner's name when we were writing about Lawrence's trails, a topic fraught, as we soon found out, with all manner of hidden dangers. Don was involved in the design of the alpine ski trails that were built in Canmore for the Calgary Winter Olympics in 1988, and his knowledge of trails in and around Canmore, Banff, and Yoho Parks is encyclopedic. He was also a formidable climber in his youth, but for us he was a providential and all-knowing expert on the subject of trails. His minute descriptions of the ones built by Grassi (especially at Lake O'Hara), their history, their technical characteristics, and the changes to them over the years were as deeply useful to us as Chic's advice on mountain climbing. One incredible aspect of these two men was their willingness, when asked for information on a specific Grassi trail, to lace up their hiking boots and walk it, taking photographs for us. In thanking one we thank both for their selfless generosity.

Walter Odenthal was another providential benefactor, for his knowledge and appreciation of Grassi's work and his extension of the unfinished Skoki Lake trail, begun by Grassi in the 1940s. We are grateful for his technical insight and photographs and also for the hospitality extended to us in Banff by his parents, Freda and Heinz. Through Freda we met with Bini Fuhrman (née Albina Del Col), who reminisced with us about her encounter with Lawrence Grassi in Banff in the 1950s.

We are most appreciative of another first-hand technical account: Tim Wake's views on a famous trail originally constructed by Grassi when he was assistant warden at Lake O'Hara. Tim was an employee of the Lake O'Hara Lodge in 1975 and worked on the partial rerouting of the trail to Lake Oesa next to Seven Veils Falls. By 1976, when he became assistant manager at the lodge as well as president of the Lake O'Hara Trails Club, "the new trail was built and was controversial."

We also thank Franco Gaspari, who was instrumental in obtaining a contribution from Associazione INCA Canada towards some of the travel and research expenses involved in the writing of this book.

1 Jackfish, Ontario, 2009; abandoned trunk that once accompanied a traveller to the north shore village. Photograph courtesy of E. Costa.

Inevitably, others have been forced to accompany us as we traced the near-century of Lawrence Grassi's life and times. For their forbearance and for their good grace when asked to endure yet another fragment of a very long story, we thank our colleagues, friends, and families. Some of these were even willing to engage in the often humdrum work of archival research; in particular, we are grateful to Kathy Scardellato, who was a much appreciated and very able colleague during one of our research visits to the Whyte Museum.

Len Husband at the University of Toronto Press was from the start unwaveringly supportive of our project; thank you, Len. Thank you also to our anonymous readers, whose review of our work was supportive and encouraging. Our copy editor, Terry Teskey, was an engaged and thoughtful commentator, and her suggestions have helped us improve this book. Thank you also to Nick James, who produced an effective index in a timely and extremely competent manner.

We are, finally, extremely grateful for the financial support provided over the years by the Mariano A. Elia Chair in Italian-Canadian Studies, York University, including a generous contribution towards publication costs. The Elia Chair's mandate is to document the experience and significance of the Italian presence in Canada and to disseminate knowledge about that presence. We hope this study of the enduring accomplishments of one immigrant together with those who emigrated before and after him provides important new details to further the chair's mandate.

There is something almost uncanny in the fact that the trajectory of Lawrence Grassi's life paralleled the experience of one of the author's grandfathers a century ago, and even more so that of one of the authors in the 1950s. As well as an account of the achievements of one immigrant, then, this book is an homage to those others who, like Lawrence Grassi, were the trailblazers.

LAWRENCE GRASSI

From Piedmont to the Rocky Mountains

2 Lawrence Grassi, ascent of tower on Castle Mountain, c. 1930s. Sydney Vallance photograph, Grassi fonds, Whyte Museum of the Canadian Rockies, v240-660.

Introduction

Andrea Lorenzo Grassi came to Canada in 1912. He was born in the village of Falmenta in the province of Novara in the Piedmont region, in northwestern Italy, in 1890. Long before he died in 1980 in the Bow River Retirement Lodge in Canmore, Alberta, Lawrence Grassi, as he came to be known, had become a legend, a symbol of the mountains he loved, and an object of great affection and admiration to all who knew him.[1] A number of locations and structures in and around Canmore have been named after him, including a mountain, a lake, and an elementary school. What makes him an inspirational figure to this day, more than thirty years after his death, can be seen and experienced by anyone who hikes on some of the trails he built – for the most part single-handedly – in the Lake O'Hara area of Yoho National Park, in and around Canmore, and in Banff National Park. Grassi's fame is also based on his extraordinary mountaineering skills and achievements.

This biography of Lawrence Grassi emerges after a long gestation period that began with a visit to the Rocky Mountains in 2000, a trip that first brought one of the authors to the town of Field in the Kicking Horse Pass area of British Columbia. The occasion was a celebration of the homecoming of Italian emigrants and their descendants who, from the beginning of the last century, had formed a sizable enclave in Field. They originally came to work for the Canadian Pacific Railway (CPR) and, later on, for the building of the Trans-Canada Highway or for work in the national parks, but at the time of the celebration there were no Italians left in Field, the families having been drawn away by better job opportunities and schooling for their children. During the visit that author hiked to that most beautiful of destinations, Lake O'Hara, and amid the splendour of the Rocky Mountains first encountered the name of Lawrence Grassi. On the climb up to Lake Oesa and overlooking Lake O'Hara in its valley below is a bronze plaque dedicated to Grassi in 1971 by the Alpine Club of Canada; to the author it was a moving moment, as he made his way along Lawrence Grassi's beautiful trail. Meaning and historical context were gradually fleshed out by reading material on Lawrence Grassi that is easily found in guidebooks and on internet sites. Yet the figure of the Italian coal miner who had dedicated his life to the mountains, and who seems to have assumed the status of a sort of patron saint in the eyes of his adoptive town and mountain lovers – and the antithesis of the commercial exploitation to which national parks have been subjected in the more than thirty years since his death – remained an admirable but essentially iconic figure.

Grassi had come to be celebrated as a Paul Bunyanesque figure of "superhuman" strength, setting out from his cabin on the edge of town, pick and shovel on his shoulder, to build a trail, moving huge boulders aside; or with rope and ice pick for some lone ascent of a previously unclimbed peak. The numerous accounts of these and other feats in guidebooks and elsewhere certainly celebrate aspects of Grassi's life and elicit the admiration their authors intend. But in the end they provide only a one-dimensional portrait; they do not satisfy a desire to know more about Lawrence Grassi himself. Yet little had been written about his life other than the often-repeated commonplaces: born in the little village of Falmenta (frequently misspelled or geographically misplaced); emigrated in 1912; worked for the CPR before moving to Canmore, Alberta, in 1916; went to work for the Canmore Coal Company until he retired. But *who* was he, in essence? How did he live? Did he have family, friends? For those who, like the authors, come from an immigrant experience, other questions were equally important: did the twenty-one-year-old travel alone when he crossed the Atlantic, or did he leave his village in the company of others? Did he travel with specific economic goals in mind? How did he come to know about possible work opportunities at a distant labouring frontier? Curiosity about details like these eventually led, about two years after that initial discovery of Lawrence Grassi, to the germ of a project to revisit his life.

The project began to coalesce when we first viewed the Lawrence Grassi fonds, or archival collection, housed at the Whyte Museum of the Canadian Rockies, Banff, Alberta. The fonds would yield a considerable part of the material that forms the substance of this book. What opened our eyes were the letters from home that Lawrence had received and kept. This is a significant if incomplete collection – the

3 On Cascade Mountain, Banff, Alberta, Lawrence Grassi with King Gordon, son of Ralph Gordon, the renowned Canadian novelist who wrote as Ralph Connor. The fossils shown are now in the Banff Museum. Courtesy of Grassi fonds, Whyte Museum of the Canadian Rockies, v240/700(pa).

earliest letters, for example, are missing – of more than forty items of correspondence sent by his immediate family in Falmenta to Lawrence, dating from 1922 to 1956. These letters, and other items such as photographs and casual notes written by friends and acquaintances over the years, became extremely valuable in the effort to give flesh and substance to Grassi's life and times. Because of these materials his birthplace did not remain for us a nondescript village in the foothills of the Italian Alps; instead it became a place where his mother and sister, his brother-in-law, and his nieces struggled to eke out a living in the midst of abject poverty. Details about the family inheritance and tensions related to its disposition, financial responsibilities, his mother's sickness followed by his sister's, their deaths, other characters in the family's life, the war and additional tragedies arising from it, now could be used to give context to the story of Lawrence Grassi.

The letters also provided valuable information about other emigrants on both sides of the Atlantic. They provided significant clues about a complex social interconnection that eventually would point us to the movement across continents of a considerable number of Falmentines, going back to the 1880s and their destinations on the north shore of Lake Superior, first to Fort William and Port Arthur, or present-day Thunder Bay, where many of their descendants still live. But many of them initially found work and made their homes in Jackfish, a former railway section stop about 130 kilometres east of Thunder Bay that was abandoned in the 1950s. Much of this information was found within the famous and enormously valuable Ellis Island ships' manifest collection, available online since the early 1990s. We discovered that Lorenzo Grassi had been part of a significant migration from Piedmont, and more importantly from his native village, to northern Ontario. His story could now be inserted within a larger, and previously unknown, story of both Italian emigration and Canadian immigration history. Our work was not, of course, limited to archives and websites. We also embarked on a series of journeys to the places that were significant for our reconstruction of Grassi's life. A visit to Jackfish, for example, a ghost town now being reclaimed by the forest, turned into a fascinatingly eerie voyage into the past, where the immigrant presence, although long gone, is still materially evident in an abandoned chest once used for the Atlantic crossing, an infant girl's burial site, or the collapsed school and homes of a once thriving settlement.

It seemed not only necessary but crucial to explore the village where Lorenzo was born. The conditions we found on our two visits there were the reverse of what Lorenzo had left behind him almost one hundred years ago. While it still retains a great deal of its appearance as it must have been when Lorenzo Grassi emigrated, Falmenta is now an attractive and placid village. Some of the homes that in his time sheltered both the owners and their animals have become the comfortable summer retreats or year-round residences of well-to-do Italians, Germans, and others. Visiting the village and environs allowed us to speak with his relatives, direct descendants of those whose names appear in the letters from home that Grassi had received in distant Canmore. From these relatives we obtained copies of the very first letters Lorenzo sent to his family, and some of those who knew him, or knew others who knew him, helped us fill in various pieces of the

4 Lawrence Grassi, probably in 1935, on the announcement of the Canadian expedition (1936) to climb Mount Waddington in British Columbia's Coast Mountains range. Courtesy of Grassi fonds, Whyte Museum of the Canadian Rockies, v240-(pa)-645.

puzzle that was Lawrence Grassi. All of those we met welcomed us and were enthusiastic supporters of our project; many contributed valuable material, much of which has made its way into this book. The first two chapters of this study, in particular, are the result of these journeys both real and virtual, which have enabled us to construct a more detailed and organic account of the first part of Grassi's life than was previously available.

For the story of Grassi's long life in the Rocky Mountains, beginning in 1913, we employed much the same method. We initially thought our task would be made easier by the mere fact of his having resided in

5 Lawrence Grassi on the front verandah of his cabin, Canmore, Alberta, 1960s.
Courtesy of Grassi fonds, Whyte Museum of the Canadian Rockies, v240-643.

Canmore, the town where his name graces well-known local sites, and
by the fact that his name appears in guidebooks and local histories.
The available published material, however, as we document in chapters 3 and 4, is often fragmentary, repetitious, apocryphal, and sometimes simply wrong. Fortunately, much new information came to light
through a systematic search for evidence, and we were thus often able
to correct unfounded or mistaken assertions. Also fortunately, some of
the people who knew him are still alive and very helpful in providing
their recollections, documents, and photographs. Of course, the Whyte
Museum staff could be counted on to provide precious assistance, as
did the staff of the Canmore Museum and Geoscience Centre. It was at
the latter, by a stroke of luck, that we were able to find essential information about Lawrence Grassi's employment with the Canmore Coal
Company, which had otherwise disposed of the company books at the
bottom of a mineshaft. At the Whyte Museum our starting point was

always the Grassi fonds, where we one day found a recorded interview with Lawrence in his later years, a discovery that provided us with a live human voice for a man who until then seemed to have had none. For one of the recurring motifs of Lawrence Grassi's life, as amply illustrated in the letters he received from his family in Falmenta, was his aversion to writing (only fragments of which remain), and he was also sparing with the spoken word. It was important, then, in our search for the man to look in as many directions as possible for any documentable fact about his life in the mountains, particularly his mountain-climbing achievements and his trail building.

We are academics of a certain age, from Toronto; to say we were challenged by the task of presenting an account of Grassi's life in the mountains is to put it mildly. Apart from documentary sources, then, of necessity we also consulted experts in fields in which Grassi excelled (whose names are, with gratitude, listed in our acknowledgments). When possible we put on hiking boots and shouldered backpacks to experience the extraordinary evidence of Grassi's love of mountains. In metaphorically retracing his steps we have also made the acquaintance, in person or through correspondence, of some of those who knew him. All of them, it seems, had in one way or another tried to engage him in meaningful dialogue, but Lawrence Grassi was to the end an elusive interlocutor. Only a few rare friends succeeded. These saw qualities in the man that we hope have also come to light – and to life – in the following pages.

6 Falmenta on its hillside in the Cannobino Valley, 2010. Courtesy of G. Scardellato.

1 The Beginnings: Falmenta, the Cannobino Valley, and Emigration

Perched high on a steep hillside, in a narrow and verdant valley, present-day Falmenta could easily appear in a destination poster advertising the attractions of the beautiful alpine region in which it is located. The narrow but paved and well-maintained road that winds its way along the valley, following the course of the Cannobino mountain stream, begins near the shore of Lago Maggiore (the "major" lake) at Cannobio. Here, and all around the lake, the beauty of the scenery, the mildness of the climate, the centuries of human activity and culture, have created a sophisticated living environment that attracts tourists and visitors from Switzerland – only half an hour's distance by car – and Germany and beyond. From Cannobio the Cannobino Valley extends west towards Falmenta, located on its steep hillside at the point where the Cannobino forks and from where its main branch flows from the north past other settlements like Spoccia, Orasso, and Gurro, each in turn on their perch on the side of the valley, each with their own roots in a distant rural culture that is now mainly preserved in local museums, tourist itineraries, and scholarly books.

Falmenta itself, currently home to about two hundred inhabitants, shows in its built fabric the result of skilful and dedicated restoration recently carried out and meticulously maintained. Its houses, many of which are still roofed with large and heavy stone slabs, are clustered together as if they were holding each other up. Its streets – no more than narrow, stone-paved passageways – only occasionally open up to reveal a glimpse of the valley below or allow space for a piazza, as in front of Falmenta's parish church of Saint Lawrence, from where the view of the valley and surrounding villages can be enjoyed. The stone steps that lead up and down to the various levels contribute to the impression of a community life that, as we shall see, was characterized by an intricate system of relationships and produced a sense of intimacy that is reflected in a network of familial connections.

Only a fraction of the residents now live in town year-round, a symptom of the radical changes that have taken place in communities like this all over rural Italy. The houses are now in great part used as vacation homes by families who live in urban centres, often in or around Turin or Milan, or who have emigrated. Non-Italians, especially Germans and Swiss, also buy these homes, attracted by the reasonable prices, the mild climate, the beauty of the Lake Maggiore scenery, and the cuisine. This is a very different environment from that which existed during the heyday of Italian emigration at the beginning of the last century.

Falmenta and the Cannobino Valley

It was just over a century ago that a young Falmentine, Andrea Lorenzo Grassi, set out to cross the Atlantic to the New World. Many others had made the journey before him, and many continued to do so long after his departure. Falmenta, located in the province of Novara, in the administrative region of Piedmont, is one of eleven valley settlements, organized as four municipalities. In 2011 the total valley population was about 6,100. By far the largest number, 5,100, lived in Cannobio. Falmenta, by comparison, with its total population of roughly 200, was the second smallest of the four valley municipalities. Thirty years before – in the early 1970s at the end of a century of Italian mass emigration – Falmenta's population was 541. This was almost two-thirds less than what it had been in 1871, when Italy had just completed its process of national unification: at that time Falmenta's residents numbered 1,393. These figures alone provide graphic evidence of the precipitous decline of the population, in which emigration played a significant role and during which Falmenta experienced the most severe drop in number of residents of the four municipalities.

The population growth in the Cannobino Valley, which began well before unification in the 1860s and lasted until the first quarter of the twentieth century, could not be sustained. Efforts were made to provide for the ever-increasing number of inhabitants by subdividing family landholdings, for example, but these were unsuccessful: over time landholdings became too small to support a family, and emigration became necessary to escape from hunger and poverty. The Grassi family were no exception. Many of the letters Lorenzo received from his family contain detailed discussions about the problems involved in the fragmentation of properties when inheritances had to be settled.[1] Emigration, in part to nearby France and Switzerland, could help to alleviate some of the problems at home. Lorenzo's own father was part of an annual migration process that took him to France as a woodcutter. Lorenzo himself, from a very young age and before the decision to cross the Atlantic, also had been part of this seasonal migration.

The inhabitants of the Cannobino Valley, including Falmenta, had since at least the Middle Ages been dependent on a subsistence pastoral economy. They raised cows, sheep, and goats, and subsisted on them and on their byproducts. The town of Cannobio was home to spinners and weavers to whom valley residents would market wool that they had gathered from their animals. This pastoral economy is reflected in the life of the Grassi family, as recorded in the letters they sent to the absent Lorenzo. So, for example, his mother Caterina wrote to him that she had received interest on a loan she had made in the form of butter rather than cash.[2] On other occasions, when economic conditions were particularly difficult, Lorenzo's family reported that they had resorted to the sale of a cow, an animal that would typically provide a family with milk, butter, and other products. Valley residents also were skilled woodsmen and, somewhat unusually, they used cows as draught animals to move timber that they felled. The valley woodlands were an important component of the local economy, providing fuel for home use and heat in the winter, and offering employment as well as material for the production of charcoal. Beech, birch, chestnut, and walnut woods were used for the local manufacture of different types of implements. Not surprisingly, Falmentines exploited another obvious and abundant resource, stone. Wood and stone were the building materials of necessity in the valley, and its inhabitants became particularly adept masons who worked in drystone construction techniques, plying their skills locally and in more distant locales. Soon after Lorenzo Grassi established himself in Canmore, Alberta, in 1916, he began single-handedly to build trails in which this characteristic use of wood and stone, learned from past generations, is evident. His trail building in the Canadian Rocky Mountains, discussed in chapter 4, is an important link to his Falmentine origins and one that provides significant clues about his personality.

A Fort William Chimney Sweep in Falmenta

Subsistence in the Cannobino Valley required various forms of migration including, or starting with, the transhumance practiced in local agriculture. To exploit all of the scarce resources available, the peasants seasonally transferred their households and livestock to different elevations in the valley and into the subalpine and alpine regions above it. This was a form of seasonal migration that prepared those who practised it with the notion that their economic survival depended on their willingness to move short distances, or sometimes longer ones, even outside the valley. This type of local migration is mentioned in Lorenzo Grassi's letters from his family. In July 1926, for example, Lorenzo's mother wrote that his sister Virginia and her family "are in the mountains and I am at home."[3]

A second type of migration that was common in the valley took advantage of another local "resource." The villages of Gurro, Falmenta, and others were known for "renting out" the services of young boys to padrones who employed them as itinerant chimney sweeps – *spazzacamini* – in cities like Turin and Milan.[4] This experience, regardless of how difficult it might have been for the boys involved, prepared both them and their families for emigration and the attendant role as a migrant labourer it involved. A glimpse into this roving world is provided by a family from Falmenta who settled for a time in Fort William, Ontario.

Antonio (Tony) Minoletti was born in Fort William in 1897 to Pietro and Emilia Minoletti, who were among the early Falmentine emigrants to Fort William who travelled to the north shore in 1892, when Pietro was twenty-seven and Emilia was twenty-five. According to Nancy Wolfer, their great grandaughter, Emilia returned to Falmenta in 1898, with her four Canadian-born children, three daughters and her son Antonio, who became "a *spazzacamino* as a little boy."[5]

His father did not settle with his family in Falmenta but instead became a "sojourner," a migrant who undertook a number of journeys to Canada, in this case to northern Ontario. Pietro returned to Fort William in 1902, probably after accompanying his family on their return to Falmenta. He made a similar journey back to Canada in 1907 and another return in 1922. By this time he had become a Canadian citizen, and he named his wife Emilia as his next of kin in Falmenta. In Fort William he reported that his contact was a cousin, resident at "505 McPherson St,

Ft William, Ont.": the same address Lorenzo Grassi gave ten years earlier on his way through Fort William to Jackfish.

In 1913, when he was sixteen years old, Antonio Minoletti returned to Fort William, his place of birth. He named his mother, Emilia Minoletti, as his next of kin at his last residence in Falmenta. His father was his contact at Fort William. This return immigration by a native-born Canadian to his place of birth is unusual, but it is also part of the larger emigration history that linked this valley in Italy to a variety of destinations in Canada.

Very little information about Lorenzo's father Giuseppe Antonio Grassi is available to us. What we know is taken from a brief genealogy provided by one of Lorenzo's great-nieces and confirmed and expanded somewhat by a review of municipal records. Giuseppe was born in Falmenta on 7 January 1858. His father's name was Cipriano and his mother's was Catterina Albertazzi. Lorenzo's mother, born in Falmenta on 8 April 1856, was christened as Caterina Maria Testori. She was the last child of Lorenzo Testori (son of Giuseppe) and his third wife, Santina Ferrari (daughter of Filippo). Giuseppe and Caterina Grassi were married in 1881 when they were, respectively, twenty-three and twenty-five years old. Their first child was born in July 1883 and baptized as Rosalia Luigia on 22 July 1883. She died on 17 September, when she was one month old, and was buried the same day. Five years later, on 6 September 1888, Caterina gave birth to a second child, a son Cipriano, who died only a few hours later; he was baptized by the midwife shortly before his death. A third child, Giuseppe Luigi Giacomo, was born in September 1889 and died in May 1891. Before his death Caterina gave birth to a fourth child, reported by his father at the municipal office as a son "whom he has named Andrea Lorenzo." The child was called Lorenzo after his godfather, who was named in the baptismal record as "Lorenzo son of Carlo Grassi." Another child, Giuseppe and Caterina's last, was born two years later, in 1892. She was baptized on 29 July 1892 as Luigia Virginia but would be known as Virginia.[6]

The Cannobino Valley and its villages at the time of Lorenzo's birth, and for years after his departure in 1912, were very isolated. A road running along the narrow valley bottom, beside the Cannobino, was built in 1878 and received some upgrading after World War I. This did

7 SS *La Provence*, Compagnie Générale Transatlantique. Courtesy of Statue of Liberty–Ellis Island Foundation Inc.

not improve access to the settlements on their respective hillsides, which for many years could be reached solely by footpaths or cart track. Only in 1921 was a road to Falmenta constructed, and the last settlement in the valley was connected by road as recently as 1974.[7] Bus service to Falmenta from Cannobio was started in 1922. Clearly, access to and from the valley and its settlements improved over time, probably as a result of mass emigration not only from the valley but also from other provinces and regions of Italy, beginning in the last quarter of the nineteenth century and continuing well into the first decades of the twentieth.

In the course of this emigration Como and Chiasso, close to the Italian-Swiss border and not far removed from the Cannobino Valley, became important transshipment points[8] in the business of emigrant recruitment and travel. Chiasso, in the nearby Swiss canton of Ticino, contained the offices of a number of steamship companies actively engaged in the lucrative, and sometimes illegal, business of emigrant recruitment. One of these, the Compagnie Générale Transatlantique (CGT; also known as the French Line) was the company with which Lorenzo Grassi travelled; it appears to have been preferred by most emigrants from the valley.[9]

The travel documents with which he emigrated, including his steamship ticket, have survived, and with these we are able to retrace his journey to a distant worksite in northern Ontario.

Leaving Falmenta

From Falmenta Lorenzo travelled to the port of Cannobio, on the shore of Lake Maggiore, from where he crossed the lake to Luino on its eastern shore. At Luino he travelled south and west by rail to Turin en route to the French border at Modano (Modane) and then to Le Havre on the coast of Normandy. At least the first portion of this journey, the border crossing at Modano and from there to the vicinity of Grenoble in France, was a known quantity for the young Falmentine. From the age of twelve he had travelled it annually with his father to work as seasonal woodcutters in the forests near Grenoble.[10] Of course, his 1912 undertaking was different from his previous journeys, and his decision to emigrate farther afield to "America," at the time the term Italians used to describe emigration overseas, required different preparation. In particular, he required different travel documents; happily, the preservation of these records of his one and only transatlantic crossing helped us to retrace his steps in some detail.

The first document to consider is a passport issued to "Grassi Andrea Lorenzo." Unfortunately, it is not dated in the partial photocopy available, but it does include his birthdate and the names of his parents.[11] In this document Lorenzo reported his "station in life" (*condizione*) as "*boscaiuolo*" or woodcutter, confirming what one biographer would later write about him.[12] There is also a birth certificate contemporary with his departure, issued for "the purpose of emigration" and obtained from the local municipal records on 9 February 1912, a few weeks before his departure from Falmenta. These two documents, and others in his possession, show that the young Lorenzo was well prepared for his travels, perhaps because he could obtain advice from acquaintances who had undertaken the same journey. As we shall see, there is considerable evidence that several Falmentines – including relatives – who had travelled to or already established themselves in Canada, were present in the village and were able to provide advice to their cousin when he decided to leave for North America. In fact, the cousin whom he declared as his contact in Canada when he was registered in the ship's manifest was present in Falmenta before Grassi's departure.[13]

Il presente passaporto consta di venti pagine

N. del Passaporto

N. del Registro corrispondente

IN NOME DI SUA MAESTÀ

VITTORIO EMANUELE III

PER GRAZIA DI DIO E PER VOLONTÀ DELLA NAZIONE

RE D'ITALIA

Passaporto

8 Page from passport of Andrea Lorenzo Grassi. Copy courtesy of Bill Cherak.

The Compagnie Générale Transatlantique operated an extensive fleet of ships whose names appear frequently in the Ellis Island ships' manifests, and Grassi travelled on one of them, the SS *La Provence*. For his voyage he purchased a third class (steerage) ticket for a departure scheduled to leave Le Havre on 2 March 1912. His Atlantic crossing was scheduled to last for six days. His ticket listed him as being entered on page eighteen, line twenty-two, in the manifest compiled to document passengers.[14] The trip from Turin to Modane cost 4.40 liras; from Modane Lorenzo continued to his port of departure by means of the so-called transatlantic railway service that the Compagnie Générale Transatlantique had created to transport Italian emigrants to its ships at Le Havre.[15]

The price for the remainder of Lorenzo's journey from Modane (via Le Havre) to New York was an additional 200 liras. The ticket was paid at Cannobio on 26 February 1912 and was stamped at the Modane border crossing on 1 March. Advertisements from this period by agents of the Compagnie Générale Transatlantique promised that an emigrant's journey to New York would proceed without need of a stay in either Modane or Le Havre.[16] In addition to this all-important ticket, Lorenzo held other travel documents, including an "inspection card" provided to passengers for collection by immigration authorities in New York. On this his name was recorded as "Grassi Andrea," and it contained the date of departure from France and other details already reviewed. On its face the card was stamped on 10 March 1912 by the health inspection authorities on Ellis Island. According to its manifest, the SS *La Provence* did sail on 2 March 1912, so clearly the voyage took longer than the promised six days.[17] The delay may have been caused by weather conditions in the North Atlantic or the presence of sea ice in the shipping lanes, or both. Whatever the cause, the ocean crossing had a strong impact on the young Lorenzo: his relatives in Falmenta, despite now retaining only a dim memory of their kinsman, remember that he complained about the harrowing nature of his ocean voyage.

La Provence carried 539 steerage passengers on this voyage, well below its 808-person capacity in this class, as well as 48 first-class and 254 second-class passengers. The ship, which had been built some six years earlier, included "new" or improved third-class accommodations, so Lorenzo was spared the "revolting" conditions[18] typical of the earlier type of steerage travel, in which passengers were housed in "disgusting and demoralizing ... large compartments, accommodating as many as 300 or more persons each."[19] His berth was in a cabin with two

9 Compagnie Générale Transatlantique ticket for "Grassi Andrea," for departure from Le Havre on board SS *La Provence*, 2 March 1912. Copy courtesy of Bill Cherak.

10 The Compagnie Générale Transatlantique inspection card issued to "Grassi Andrea" for his 2 March 1912 voyage. Copy courtesy of Bill Cherak.

to eight others and with better lighting and ventilation than earlier travellers had enjoyed; dining and sanitation facilities were also improved. The French Line promised its passengers three decent meals daily during their voyage, including meat and fish dishes and with vegetables for both lunch and dinner.[20] Regardless of such improvements, however, the rough crossing, which may have resulted in seasickness and confinement below deck for the duration of a North Atlantic storm, caused Lorenzo to vow, according to his descendants in Falmenta, that he would return only "if a bridge was built across the Atlantic."

We are again able to follow Lorenzo Grassi's various steps after landing in New York because of the inspection card he carried with him. It was stamped "PASSED" by the Canadian government official in New York City responsible for medical examination, and the same stamp was applied for a "Civil Examination." A third stamp, dated

10 March 1912, appears for a journey by Canadian Pacific Railway from Broadway Station in New York City.[21] A fourth stamp, dated 11 March 1912, was placed by a Canadian immigration agent after the train had crossed from New York State into Quebec at Athelstan, some distance north of the international border. We thus have very precise information detailing Lorenzo's trip from Falmenta at least as far as the crossing of the border between the United States and Canada, a trip that took fifteen days from the date on which he purchased his French Line ticket in Cannobio.[22]

The names of two Falmentines – Edoardo Grassi and Francesco Milani, both twenty-one years old – appeared on the same manifest page where Lorenzo's passage was recorded. A review of the entire manifest for this Atlantic crossing, in fact, reveals the names of five others from the Cannobino Valley, four of whom were from Falmenta and a fifth from the valley settlement of Orasso. The four from Falmenta were also described as in transit for Fort William, and three of them specified a final destination of Coldwell, Ontario, further east of Fort William on the railway line. All four of these passengers bore the surname Zanni, but one of the four, Agostino Zanni, aged twenty-five, is of special interest because he named the same person, Stefano Zanni of 505 McPherson Street, as his contact as had Lorenzo Grassi.[23] Agostino declared that Stefano Zanni was his brother-in-law, married to his sister Martina, whom Agostino named as his next of kin in Falmenta. Lorenzo Grassi, therefore, was travelling with at least one member of his extended family; also like Agostino Zanni, he was travelling with the knowledge of family members and other fellow villagers[24] at the end of his journey.[25]

Even this discussion of a small group of Falmentine travellers illustrates the difficulties that the limited number of family and given names creates in tracking family relationships and similar information. At least one misreading of the date and circumstances of Lorenzo's voyage has resulted: another Lorenzo Grassi also travelled on the SS *La Provence*, but on a voyage that arrived at New York on 29 April 1911, a year earlier than Andrea Lorenzo Grassi. The two have been conflated in at least one account.[26]

Although Lorenzo Grassi declared his destination to be Fort William, we know from early letters that he worked for some time while based in or near Jackfish, Ontario, a small fishing village and coal port, and a railway section stop, located east of Fort William on the CPR line. In Jackfish and vicinity he worked for the CPR as a section hand, a railway navvy or labourer employed for track maintenance and similar work. (He was not the only Falmentine to make his way to Jackfish for this type of employment: for this group of emigrants, Jackfish was the second most frequently cited destination in Ontario.) While these are the facts of Lorenzo's early days in the new country, based on documentary evidence, what cannot be ascertained so readily are his motivation and goals.

When asked what had compelled him to leave his village, Lorenzo – by then Lawrence – replied, "I needed to get something to eat."[27] He made this comment in the late 1950s, a long time after he left his birthplace. The somewhat apocryphal answer does seem appropriate given the challenges of the pastoral economy of the Cannobino Valley. It is also supported by the information contained in letters from Lorenzo's family. But Lorenzo's laconic answer – which as we will see was typical of the man – provides only a partial explanation for his departure and the decisions taken following it. It does not tell us, for example, whether he left Piedmont as a sojourner, intending to return after earning enough money, or whether he intended to settle permanently in North America, as he eventually did. And even if it were possible to answer this question, others remain unanswered.

Lorenzo Grassi left Italy after having served a very short portion of his obligatory military service. Many of his contemporaries, in fact, chose to leave Italy in order to avoid conscription altogether, generally because of financial circumstances: as a conscript, they could not usefully contribute to their family's well-being. Lorenzo received notice of his conscription in March 1910, when he was just over twenty years old, and he actually began his service in August of the following year. At enrolment he was recorded as a woodcutter by profession and as being able to read and write. He was conscripted as an infantryman in the Twenty-Third Infantry Regiment, Ninth Company, based in the provincial capital of Novara, and as early as September of that year he also received some training as a rifleman. His military career, however, was very short lived: he was released from service on "*congedo illimitato*" (indefinite leave) on 6 November 1911 with a note that he was not granted a declaration of good conduct because he had served fewer than three months.[28]

Aside from this brief conscription, there are two other items of evidence that touch on Lorenzo's military service. The first of these was a postcard he received from his cousin Giovanni Testori, then based at Ripple, Ontario, on the north shore of Lake Superior, in 1916, in the middle of World War I. Giovanni declared himself pleased to have received news from Lorenzo; somewhat sardonically, he wrote that in the absence of news he would have assumed Lorenzo had returned to Italy "to kill Poles" on the Italian northeastern front. Testori may have been teasing Lorenzo about his brief stint as a military conscript.[29]

A second mention of Lorenzo's military service is contained in a 1925 letter from his mother Caterina, who wrote in part to advise him that she had received a visit from the *carabinieri*, the Italian federal police, to whom she "could not refuse" to give Lorenzo's address in Canada. The visit was important enough for Caterina to reiterate: "I repeat again that the *carabinieri* came to get your address. They told me that it is about military service – to regularize your situation."[30] Perhaps this "regularization" involved the indefinite "leave" or "discharge" he had been granted in 1911?

At about the same time as the news about the *carabinieri* arrived, his brother-in-law reminded him of his promise to return to Falmenta. The question of renewed military service might have played a part in his thinking about a trip to Falmenta: news that the authorities were investigating his whereabouts could easily have encouraged him to delay a return. But in the end, military service was only a minor consideration in a contemplated return; over time other and more complex reasons arose until the possibility finally ceased to have any importance for him.

One of these reasons was money. There is ample proof that Lorenzo sent some of his earnings to Falmenta. This is clear from letters written shortly after his arrival on the north shore, in one of which he enclosed 125 liras, 100 for his mother and 25 for his sister. He was also concerned about 50 liras he had sent two months earlier but they had not acknowledged receiving. In another letter he wrote that he had enclosed another 50 liras for his mother and sister.[31] Over the years he sent additional funds for deposit to his account that, by the late 1920s, had grown to a sizeable total. It is possible, even likely, that some of the monies he sent home were intended for Virginia's dowry. Contribution to a dowry was a traditional way for a brother to become sole heir to family property after his sister's marriage. This provision, recognized in Italian law, enabled a brother to establish his own family. It is possible that Lorenzo's being named godparent to his sister's firstborn daughter, Angiolina, apart from the bond it recognized and enforced between brother and sister, acknowledged his contribution towards her marriage. Both his provision for a dowry and his accumulation of considerable savings in Falmenta suggest an intention to return. Despite the

11 Front cover of Italian post office savings account booklet, made out to "Grassi Lorenzo ... represented by his mother Caterina Testori." Copy courtesy of Grassi family, Falmenta, Italy.

considerable savings he had accumulated in Falmenta, despite his share in the inheritance that awaited him, and despite the trousseau items he left behind, the young emigrant of 1912 became an immigrant. He was never reunited, even temporarily, with the kin he left behind. In this sense, as well as in other ways, Lorenzo Grassi's life followed an untraditional trajectory.

A notable aspect of Grassi's life, from early adolescence until his death at the age of ninety, is that much of it was lived in isolation, particularly from the company of women. From the age of twelve he spent part of every year with his father as a seasonal woodcutter in the vicinity of Grenoble, France,[32] living apart from the family and its domestic environment. This domestic isolation was obviously exacerbated when he emigrated across the Atlantic. Such migration was an overwhelmingly male phenomenon, involving both single and married men, most of whom were sojourners. They endured the attendant travails and privations because, as one of Grassi's 1912 travelling companions, his "most affectionate friend" Edoardo Grassi, wrote, they hoped to earn what was necessary to achieve traditional goals and expectations in their personal lives. In his own case twenty-three-year-old Edoardo, after two years in the blackfly-infested wilderness of the north shore of Lake Ontario, dreamt of marriage – but only after a further ten years "of this existence," or perhaps even longer "when our beards turn grey … [in] 20 years."[33] Some Falmentines, we know, fulfilled expectations like these. Sometimes those who were already married were able to bring their families to join them wherever they had been able to find employment and to settle. If that plan failed – as it seems to have for Pietro Minoletti, discussed in a text box above – their lives as sojourners continued and they contented themselves with occasional visits to families left behind, or they returned home. We do not know whether Edoardo achieved his goal of married domesticity or whether, like Lorenzo, he followed the less common path of the life-long bachelor who lived mostly in the company of other men.

This was Lorenzo's experience during his time in Ontario, and it continued after his transfer to western Canada. The conditions in Canada's labouring frontiers, in large part because of the absence of women, family, or any semblance of a private domestic sphere, were far removed from those imagined by sojourners like Edoardo Grassi.[34] Lorenzo's life as a coal miner, for example, was spent labouring underground in the company of men. Outside the workplace, as mentioned, he lived his entire life as a bachelor. Only occasionally during those years and after

12 Detail of an embroidered pillowcase, showing the initials *GL* for "Grassi Lorenzo," 1901. Collection of the Grassi family, Falmenta, Italy.

do we find references to contact with women, all of whom nonetheless remained distant from his private or domestic life. He encountered women as occasional fellow-climbers, as spouses who accompanied their husbands, or as adventurous and independent spirits (usually unmarried) who themselves lived untraditional lives in the almost entirely male world of the Rocky Mountains. Late in his life some of his contemporaries, of course all of them men, joked with Lawrence that he should have married one of these independent women and so settled himself properly. He himself was quoted as regretting his failure to marry because a wife would have encouraged him to keep active in his later years by forcing him to get out of the house;[35] this seems less a lament for a heterosexual domesticity never experienced than regret for a missed opportunity to maintain his good (manly) health for as long as possible.

Grassi's public life was presented as lived according to parameters that were well outside domestic constraints. Despite his relatively small physical stature, he came to be known as someone possessed of such remarkable strength that he earned the title of "little Italian superman" of the Rockies. Men praised his masculinity, and women felt secure at the end of his rope when they were assigned to him for the climb to earn their Alpine Club of Canada credentials.

One last observation may suggest the link between the strong and masculine Lorenzo Grassi and the young boy who first left his native village. When he left Falmenta to cross the Atlantic as a young man, Lorenzo Grassi left behind an embroidered sheet with the year 1901 stitched on it and a pillowcase embroidered with his initials, both his handiwork. As his descendants explained, such embroidery was part of the traditional training boys received. The decorated linen was created as part of his trousseau, to which his mother continued to add after he had departed.[36] We hear nothing of this skill in his adult years. Instead, after settling in Canmore, he developed a reputation for carving cribbage boards and walking sticks and making a variety of other items that he gave to friends or simply to those who passed by his cottage. Perhaps in this way the child's long-forgotten introduction to domesticity was sublimated and directed into the creation of more "appropriate" masculine artefacts.

2 "Dear Son Write to Me": Those Left Behind and Life on the North Shore

Lawrence Grassi died in Canmore, Alberta, in February 1980 when he was ninety years old. By the time of his death he had lived in Canada for almost seventy years, but long before the end he lost touch with his family. He also lost touch with other native Falmentines who had emigrated and tried to maintain contact with him. According to his collection of family letters – now preserved in the Whyte Museum – he stopped corresponding directly with those in Falmenta in the late 1930s, more than forty years before his death. But even when he did manage some correspondence, it is clear that Lorenzo Grassi was never one to take up pen and paper willingly or often. This frustrated, irritated, and angered his family and also complicated practical issues that the family was sometimes called upon to resolve.

The Grassi collection contains some forty-six letters that Lorenzo received from his family. They were written over a period of roughly seventeen years, from 1922 to 1939; to them we can add four letters sent by Lorenzo – in 1912, 1913, 1924, and 1928 – to his family in Falmenta.[1] We could stretch the time frame for correspondence to include the last surviving letter he received from Italy, written by his niece Angiolina, in May 1956.

Lorenzo's sister Virginia was married on 26 February 1914, almost two years after Lorenzo's departure overseas. She was then twenty-two years old. Her husband Enrico had the same family name as his wife and was also known in Falmenta by the nickname "U Giuvanun." He was twenty-four when they were married. Their first child, Angiolina, was born in March 1917; when she was christened her absent uncle Lorenzo became her godfather by proxy. Five years later, in 1922, Virginia gave birth to twin daughters, Maria and Armandina.[2] So, in the jach Fish 3 - 12 = 1912

Carissima madre padre e sorella

Vengo con queste due righe per darvi di mie notizie
io di salute sto benissimo come spero di voi tutti
Vi faccio sapere che ò ricevuto il salame e vene ringrazio
molto. Vi ò spedito lire 125 donde 100 lire li tiendrete
per voi e 25 li darete a mia sorella. Mi farete sapere se mio
padre e venuto a casa questanno. io ci o scritto due lettere
e non o ricevuto nessuna risposta non so se le mie lettere sono
andate perdute o se lui mi abbia scritto e che siano andate
perdute non e ricevuto niente. Due mesi fa io o spedito una
lettera contenente lire 25 ma voi nella vostra lettera
non mi dite che l'avete ricevuta et e segono che andata
perdute in viaggio. Altro non mi occorre piu niente che
salutarvi di verocuore e baciarvi di vero cuore voi e
i parenti tutti da parte mia e di mio cugino. augurando
vi buon natale buon fine d'anno e miliar principio del
nuovo anno. Ricevete i miei piu sinci saluti e baci
da vostro filio e tuo fratello
L. Grassi

Contraccambio cordiali saluti
da Ignazio Tibani
e Saluterete Bianconi Giacomo
e familia perme

13 Letter dated 3 December 1912 at "jach Fish" (Jackfish), Ontario, from Lorenzo
Grassi and addressed to his mother, father, and sister. Courtesy of Grassi family, Falmenta, Italy.

14 Photograph of Enrico Grassi, "U Giuvanun," standing centre back row, posed with a group of Falmentines, sent to Lorenzo Grassi by his mother in a letter dated 7 December 1926. Courtesy of Grassi fonds, Whyte Museum of the Canadian Rockies, M45 1/13.

early 1920s Lorenzo Grassi's family included his widowed mother Caterina (his father Giuseppe had died by then), his sister Virginia and her husband Enrico, and their three children.

There is no information in Falmenta in either municipal or parish records about Giuseppe's death but his descendants, as well as some who have written about Lorenzo, state that he died during one of his sojourns as a woodcutter in the vicinity of Grenoble. All such accounts are almost entirely devoid of details about the circumstances of his death, including when and how it occurred. We know that Giuseppe Grassi was alive at the time of his daughter's wedding, in early 1914. Following this event, on 28 August 1916, Caterina Grassi and her daughter Virginia signed a *procura speciale* or special power of attorney in the name of Enrico Grassi, respectively their son-in-law and husband, which empowered him to act for Caterina and Virginia "as heirs to the deceased head of household Grassi, Giuseppe woodcutter in France and to gather whatever his inheritance might be in the form of whatever amount there is to collect and whatever credit he extended to whomever for whatever purpose." The *procura* also referred to Giuseppe's employer in France, a certain "Sig. Faure."[3] The authority Enrico was granted over the affairs of his wife's family helps to explain some of the contents of his letters to Lawrence, about both the family inheritance and Lawrence's financial well-being in Falmenta.

In the first years of their marriage, as their family grew, Virginia and Enrico lived separately from Caterina Grassi. After the birth of their twin daughters, their residence became too small for them, and Enrico Grassi wrote to Lawrence on a number of occasions to establish whether he could move into the home occupied by his mother-in-law. Eventually, faced with Lorenzo's failure to respond, Enrico and Virginia decided to buy a different home. Caterina, Enrico, Virginia, and Angiolina as she grew older tried to maintain contact with Lorenzo, but their attempts became more and more unavailing with the passing of the years.

Family Letters and Other Record Keeping

The correspondence Lawrence received over the course of his long life in Canada is an extremely valuable part of his personal archive. The largest group of letters are the ones he received from his family, but there are also some from individuals and institutions in Canada and elsewhere. They form part of a large assortment of personal memorabilia – including an impressive collection of photographs taken by him and an eclectic range of personal papers, publications, and ephemera – that he accumulated during his life. Most of the material in the archive dates from the time after Lawrence established a permanent residence in Canmore, in 1918. For some six years after his arrival in Canada he lived an unsettled life as a labourer for the Canadian Pacific Railway, which explains why there is relatively little in his collection from this period. This somewhat nomadic existence ended when he became a coal miner in Canmore. There, after a couple of years, he purchased and moved into a cottage where he remained, without interruption, for almost sixty years.

As a bachelor he never had to accommodate others in his living arrangements, and so he never experienced the need to discard possessions that might have become superfluous. This might be why he "preserved" pay slips from the Canmore Coal Company, for example, or union membership cards from his early days as a railway navvy, together with other material that can be described, at best, as odds and ends.[4] On the other hand, it is possible that with the passage of time, as his achievements as a mountain climber, trail builder, or good Samaritan received the attention of newspapers even beyond Canmore or Calgary, he began to develop a sense of himself as a public figure. This would explain why he saved personal papers, newspaper clippings, and the like. His reputation in the mountains in turn led to invitations to make presentations, during which he used his extensive collection of personal photographs and slides, as well as fossils he had found.[5] Eventually, in 1967, when he was in his mid-seventies, he began donating some of his memorabilia, beginning with his photograph and slide collection, to the Whyte Museum. He was assisted and encouraged in this by close friends like Elizabeth (Lizzie) Rummel,[6] a near contemporary, and one of those responsible for the only interview recorded with him.

The materials in his archive, however, are so helter-skelter as to suggest that Lawrence acted more as a careless housekeeper than attentive chronicler of his own exploits. This in turn suggests that his personal papers were an accumulation or accretion over time rather than a systematic collection. Still, the preservation of his family correspondence for more than fifty years cannot be easily explained as the result of indifferent housekeeping. Nor can it be explained as a practical concern for tracking matters such as family inheritance, property rights, or the balance in his savings accounts. Lawrence had not expressed much interest in such concerns even while receiving correspondence from home. Nonetheless, the letters from home must have had a deeply personal – if ambiguous and unfathomable – significance for him.

Over time Lawrence Grassi became isolated, perhaps deliberately, from his family and others. Even when faced with events in his personal life that cried out for at least a sympathetic emotional response, such as the long and painful illness and eventual death of his mother in Falmenta, he seems to have been unable or unwilling to respond. He could not have been impervious to the difficulties, and even suffering, contained in his family's letters. It is hard to imagine that he did not feel some sympathy and distress, yet his silence over the years can only be deemed at best inconsiderate and at worst morally wrong. Why, then, would he donate them to a museum when they portrayed him in a less than flattering light? Had he simply forgotten about their existence when he agreed to donate his materials to the museum? Perhaps discarding these letters represented for him an irrevocable break with his past, a step that he was unable to carry out. An answer to this question would do much to enhance our understanding of the person who was Lawrence Grassi.

Those Left Behind

Between 1922 and 1933 Caterina Testori wrote a total of twenty-one letters to her son that are now part of his archival collection in the Whyte Museum. She was in her mid-sixties at the beginning of this period and in her late seventies at the end of it. She died in February 1935 at the age of seventy-nine. Her age alone might account for the frequent mention of one of three topics – her health – in her letters. There were specific references to serious problems with her eyes and to debilitating bouts of arthritis. That her condition worsened over time is not surprising when we consider the harsh conditions and extreme poverty in which she lived,[7] nor is it surprising that the second-most frequent topic was financial concerns. A letter from Virginia – whose role as correspondent with her brother is discussed in greater detail below – shortly before her mother's death acknowledged her brother's suggestion that the family use his savings in Falmenta if needed. Virginia responded that only their mother had access to his funds, so should "she close her eyes tomorrow no one can claim a thing, not even for the [funeral] expenses."[8] Virginia was frustrated because her mother had sole power of attorney for some of the funds that Lorenzo sent to Falmenta, while the rest were deposited in his name only. After Caterina's death Virginia returned to the topic of her brother's finances, pointing out that he alone now had access to his funds in Falmenta.[9] This is confirmed by notations on the cover of postal savings account booklets that have been kept by Lorenzo's descendants, his great-nieces in Falmenta: two of these, dated March and November 1922, were registered to "Grassi Lorenzo son of Giuseppe, *represented* by his mother Testori Caterina daughter of Lorenzo" (emphasis added).[10]

   In her letters Caterina showed herself to be a scrupulous, even overzealous, guardian of her son's finances. She reported all the expenses paid for out of his savings, including ones related to her frequent health problems. In 1923 her eye operation and stay in the Maggiore Hospital

15 Italian post office bond in the sum of five thousand liras, made out to "Grassi Lorenzo … represented by his mother Testori Caterina." Copy courtesy of Grassi family collection.

in Novara, for example, cost Lorenzo two thousand liras. On another occasion she reported that she had been bed-ridden "for 46 days" with arthritis, which required the visit of a doctor from Cannobio. Worse, she informed Lorenzo that she was no longer able to work. But in the same letter she asked his advice about buying for him a small woodlot being sold by "uncle Sciurino." Also reported was a request for a loan from her son-in-law Enrico, granted and then repaid. In another letter just a few months later, in May 1924, however, Caterina expressed her concern for Lorenzo's well-being in words that are mingled with a seemingly selfish rebuke about her need for money:

> I don't know what to think whether you are sick or what else *because you don't send money.* Are you sick or what? If you are not sick I tell you that I need it [money] so send me something if you can.[11]

The money, she added, was desperately needed for various house repairs: "I can't live in the house anymore because of the water coming through … I even had [to move] the bed because of the water coming down." It is difficult to assess the financial situation then affecting the Falmenta household. Lorenzo by this time had been in Canada for thirteen years, but we do not know how much of his earnings he had managed to send home. Caterina reported in the same letter that she had again loaned money to her son-in-law, which may have depleted her funds. The situation had worsened by December of the same year, when Lorenzo had not responded to her previous appeal. She had a grocery bill and a doctor to pay, and the municipality was also demanding payment of a tax owing on the Grassi property: "If you want to send me something [money] I really need it."[12]

That Caterina's financial situation had deteriorated when she wrote these two letters is clear. But Lorenzo was also struggling. His employer, the Canmore Coal Company, experienced a five-month-long strike in 1924–25. This was the longest of a number of work stoppages that occurred about every two years in the 1920s.[13] Lorenzo's ability to send money home was therefore impaired just when his mother's worsening arthritis had left her unable to work. But by October 1925 Caterina's financial situation had improved: her son-in-law Enrico repaid two loans, one for one thousand and the other for twenty-five hundred liras. There followed four years in which her letters contained no further mention of financial concerns.[14] The topic of money resurfaced only in 1929 when Caterina told Lorenzo that he had earned a "premium" of one thousand liras from his post office savings account.[15] In the same letter she informed him that Virginia and her husband had decided to buy the "marshal's house" and move out of the Grassi home and the Ginesco property (the portion of the family landholding where the family's *cascina* or summer dwelling in the alpine meadows was located). They obviously wanted better accommodation for their family, which by then had grown to five people. To be able to buy, however, they needed a loan of six thousand liras from Lorenzo, for which Caterina asked for her son's approval.[16] Lorenzo did not respond, but his mother decided to provide the loan on her own initiative. She informed him of this in a letter sent eight months later, in December of the same year. Her justification for the loan struck an uncharacteristically generous note that suggested concern for the family's well-being:

> I gave it [the loan] to them to finish paying for the house. I hope I will not be reproached. If you don't do good for each other I don't know who you can rely on.[17]

A long letter by Caterina a year later also dealt with a number of financial matters. In it she informed Lorenzo that she had had the Grassi house assessed and that it was valued at 50,200 liras with "a bit of land above it" being worth an additional 70 liras. The Ginesco property was estimated to be worth 1,600 liras. Caterina was concerned, however, because she could not arrange for the transfer of the property to Lorenzo: "by law it's no longer possible to buy for a third party and therefore the buyer must be present." In a long afterword she reported that she had transferred 50,000 liras of his savings to a different account to take advantage of more than three per cent over the interest he had been earning.[18]

After December 1929 there are three more letters from Caterina to Lorenzo that have survived, only one of which was directly concerned with financial matters. All three, on the other hand, described worsening economic conditions, as the effects of the Great Depression made themselves felt in Falmenta. In December 1932 Caterina informed Lorenzo that his funds had reached a total of 121,832 liras. They were divided almost evenly between his postal savings account (66,462.95 liras) and postal vouchers (i.e., post office savings bonds in the amount of 50,000 liras).[19] She described the "great hardship" or *miseria* that everyone was experiencing because of unemployment. Difficult economic conditions, she acknowledged, also existed overseas: "they [Falmentine emigrants] are also coming home from America because it's bad over there too." Locally, "all the men are home unemployed." We can assume that Caterina was here subtly (and perhaps desperately) trying to put the idea in her son's mind that this might be a good time to come home. Despite the terrible situation, she seems to be implying, his savings in Falmenta would provide a comfortable and worry-free living for a long time. If this was her intention, it fell on deaf ears. In the same letter, perhaps as further enticement, she also described for Lorenzo a new "elegant clock" that had been donated for the church tower and a new bell: "if you could see Falmenta is almost turned into a city."[20]

The third most prevalent topic in Caterina's letters, after her health and finances, was her son's failure to write home. It appears for the first time in May 1924, in the same letter urgently requesting money: "it has been a long time that I have not received any news from you." She continued: "you don't tell me anything anymore whether you want to come home or whether you don't."[21] The same complaint is repeated in December that year, even though she "had already written [to him] in the month of May."[22] Some ten months later, in October 1925, having received only a brief note from him the previous December that had crossed her own in transit, her appeal reached a level of desperation:

Canmore 4-12- 1924

Carissima madre

Eccomi con queste due righe per darti mie
notizie. Con piacere posso dirti ke io godo
buonissima salute. e spero pure che voialtri
tutti godrete buona salute. Altro per il
presente non mi occorre che salutarvi voi
tutti augurandovi buona salute buon natale
buon fine e milior principio d'anno.
                    Vosto figlio
                        L. Grassi

16 Three sentences from Lorenzo Grassi to his mother, Caterina Grassi, dated
at Canmore, Alberta, 4 December 1924, written on a twenty-by-twenty-eight-
centimetre lined sheet. Copy courtesy of Grassi family, Falmenta, Italy.

"I beseech you my dear son I beseech you to write more often to your poor old mother not only once a year."[23] Two months later she still had not heard from Lorenzo: "you haven't even answered. At least tell me something about what I told you."[24] In a letter in December 1926 she pleaded again "for more frequent letters from you for my consolation [and] I hope you will not delay coming home so that we can see each other again before I die because I am old and one can't live beyond old." The letter is made all the more poignant by her news that Aurelio Grassi "has returned from America." (Aurelio had emigrated to Calgary in 1914, shortly after her son moved to western Canada, and had sent "his friend" Lorenzo a photograph of himself.)[25] Almost a year passed after this letter, and apparently Caterina still had not heard from her son:

> I don't know why you don't write me anymore. After such a long time we await your news to no avail. Can you … not remember your mother and send a letter as a greeting? It would be so dear to me … Dear son write to me send me your news who you are with and what you do and I would like to see you home soon. I have now passed my 70th year and therefore I would be very happy to see you come home soon.[26]

She also told Lorenzo that she had received a newspaper article "sent by a woman from Falmenta who has been in America for about 30 years," from which she had learned of his rescue of a fellow mountain climber.[27] She feared he might have put his life in danger, and once more urged him to write. Despite receiving no answer she wrote again in December 1928 with a more moderate tone but still begging him to write "a little more frequently," and she renewed her plea for his return home: "You have been away for umpteen years and could easily take a quick trip to see me since I am so anxious to see you."[28] The less anxious tone is perhaps due to a rare – and very perfunctory – letter by Lorenzo dated 5 December 1928 to his sister and brother-in-law, in which he noted that he was writing "after a long time." After three more letters from his mother in 1929, one in April and two in December, all of them apparently unanswered, Caterina's letters resumed in August 1931; after this date another four letters survive, but none of them echo the earlier anxious and pleading tones. So, for example, despite complaining in August 1931 that "I haven't had any news from you in a long time," she nevertheless described herself as happy because "I have had your news from Emilia Zanni and I am very happy that I have learned about you."[29]

We learn in the same letter from Caterina that a number of other Falmentine emigrants from Canada, besides Emilia Zanni, were returning, a fact that Caterina attributed to economic conditions, equally bad abroad as at home. But at least they brought her news of her son, which helped to alleviate her anxiety.[30] We should also note that Lorenzo had written at least twice, in December 1931 and sometime later, probably in the middle of 1932. Caterina's last letter to Lorenzo was written in December 1933, after which she was physically unable to write.

Lorenzo's sister Virginia was his second most frequent correspondent. There are some fifteen letters, eleven written by her alone, two by her but signed for her husband Enrico, as well as two that included a message from her daughter Angiolina. The first was written in December 1923, but there may have been others before it, since an envelope addressed to "Signor Grassi Lorenzo, Canmore P o Box 234, Alta [Alberta] Canada" survived among Lorenzo's possessions. It was stamped at Ponte di Falmenta on 10 November 1918 and again at Canmore when it arrived on 6 December 1918 (fig. 17). These dates do not match any of the family letters, so it is possible that the envelope was used to send Lorenzo two photographs now preserved in the collection. One is of Angiolina, his niece and goddaughter, as a baby in her mother's arms with her father standing behind them and flanked by a young man, no doubt Lorenzo's proxy as godfather, Giovanni Zanni.[31] Angiolina appears too young, less than a year old, for the date on the envelope, so this photograph probably dates from 1917, the year of her birth and baptism. An intriguing detail about Lorenzo's stand-in is a pin in the form of a maple leaf stuck into the knot of his tie, which suggests he was one of many Falmentines who had connections with Canada. The other photograph also shows Angiolina, but as a toddler, in a white dress and standing alone on a chair (fig. 19). She looks about twenty months old; this photo could have been sent by her parents to her godfather in 1918, perhaps together with her photograph as a baby.

Only six letters from Virginia to Lorenzo survive for the period to 1934. They are generally brief season's greetings, with snippets of news about her family. Virginia, like her mother, never failed to remind her brother of how long it had been since his last communication; "three years" in 1923; "no news" in 1926; "no news for a long time" in 1927, which caused their mother's tears; "a long silence" in 1930. In her 1926 letter she warned her brother, as her mother had done, about the ruinous condition of the house, from which, she informed him, she and her family had moved. Her husband, she also explained, was away,

17 Envelope addressed to "Signor Grassi Lorenzo" of Canmore, Alberta, stamped at point of departure on 10 November 1918. Courtesy of Grassi fonds, Whyte Museum of the Canadian Rockies, M 45 1-1.

working in Switzerland. On this occasion she added a light-hearted and subtle invitation to Lorenzo to make his way back home by reminding him that it was chestnut season: "Raise your hand if you want some roasted ones!"[32] Virginia's appeals, in fact, seem to aim at Lorenzo's emotional and nostalgic side, pulling at whatever sense of family ties he might still feel. So, she reminded him that her little girls are curious about their uncle "in America" and that his goddaughter would soon be eleven years old.[33] Nothing but short letters from his sister reached Lorenzo in the three years after 1927, but a brief note from her and Enrico during this period is significant because it included the first detailed letter from Angiolina, emerging here with an already definable personality.[34]

After 1933 Virginia's letters show increasing anxiety about deteriorating circumstances, both within her family and more generally in Falmenta and elsewhere. It was Caterina's precipitous decline in health, however, that featured most prominently. In May 1934 she had been

18 Virginia, her firstborn daughter Angiolina, and Enrico Grassi (wearing cloth cap), with Giovanni Zanni, Lorenzo Grassi's proxy for his niece's godfather. Courtesy of Grassi fonds, Whyte Museum of the Canadian Rockies, v240-878(pa)022.

19 Angiolina Grassi as a toddler, c. 1918. Courtesy of Grassi fonds,
Whyte Museum of the Canadian Rockies, M45 1/1.

"bedridden for two months and 20 days and there is no improvement from day one to today." Ironically, she was grateful that her husband was out of work because he was available to help with her mother, and he would not be able to accept a job – even if one were offered – because she would not be able to cope without him. Seven months went by and she chided Lorenzo in heart-rending terms: "you were not up to write not ever even for a word of comfort because she is your mother too." Caterina, in fact, had been given the last rites and, she added, their mother asked that Virginia write to Lorenzo to tell him that "I greet him very very fondly from the bottom of my heart and that [barring a miracle] this is the last time that I greet him." "And she tells me," Virginia wrote, "to tell you not ever to forget Virginia who has nobody."[35]

While a month later Caterina's condition seemed to improve somewhat, by the time of the next letter, in December, Virginia's exasperation was profound. Caterina seemed to be only moderately unwell one day and dying the next. Worse, Virginia wrote, "she turns very mean and at times even soils the bed." By January 1935 her condition had deteriorated even further:

> She will not be able to get out of bed anymore she is totally infirm. One has to be by her bedside day and night. She is not really grave but certain days she does not even bother to [get up] for her bodily needs. She just lets herself go.[36]

Her family's financial situation also continued to be a grave burden for Virginia. While gratefully acknowledging the receipt of twenty dollars from Lorenzo, and the letter in which he informed her that she could use the money from his accounts in Falmenta, she also reminded him that, as we know, only Caterina had access to those funds. Also, Virginia wrote, their mother demanded to read Lorenzo's letter – twice! – and then announced

> that she could not in good conscience go and get your money. She is not at all afraid to withdraw from your accounts for her things but we have to take care of everything else ourselves. Despite all that I do she always tells me that I would love to live off someone else. She can't even move any more but there is nothing wrong with her tongue. If you yourself don't tell her she will not come up with as much as a cent … She says she is in charge of everything [and] she keeps everything under lock and key[.] The keys she keeps under her pillow.[37]

Sadly, but inevitably, two weeks later Virginia announced that Caterina had died:

She was beside herself in almost constant terrible pain for about three weeks. On the first night of the crisis she kept mentioning your name and continued speaking as if you were standing next to her bed. Try to give yourself courage as we are doing.[38]

In April, two months after Caterina's death, Virginia still had not heard from her brother, but she generously allowed that a letter from him might have been lost. She provided details of funeral costs and of the settlement of their mother's will, and then raised the topic of Lorenzo's savings, and the risk he ran of losing everything because "both types of accounts are in your name only." Should no one claim the funds after a prescribed period "the government takes possession."[39] She added that Caterina had set aside sixteen sheets and two pillowcases for him, and closed the letter with greetings and also with the news that "on 11 April the wife of Giovanni Zanni the *pecorino* is leaving again … I thought I would send a little salami if she can get it through customs."[40]

Whether Giovanni's wife delivered the salami to Lorenzo, or news from Falmenta, along with a reminder of Caterina's death, we do not know. We do know that Lorenzo was still not moved to write his sister, who was left to wonder whether letters were going astray, and whose own condition, as she related in an undated letter sent sometime in 1937, had by then deteriorated to the point where she herself was unable to work. Citing her failure to sell a cow, and the rising price of staples like bread and flour, made worse by chronic unemployment, she was forced to ask her brother to send her a "hundred dollars or more." She closed with a plea for his return home, as other Falmentines had done, including some who had been away for twenty and even forty years. In the next brief letter, written on 4 January 1938, she acknowledged receipt of a money order from Lorenzo, which converted to 1,887 liras. But no letter by Lorenzo: "I haven't a note from you in three years. I don't know what to say." Her health had improved, but she was under "strict medical care." She also announced that her daughter Angiolina was planning to marry.[41]

The last letter by Virginia, written almost a year later, on 25 February 1939, contained another request for money. In case Lorenzo had sent some, and it had gone astray, she assured him that she had managed,

Salmento li 6 Febbraio 1935

Caro Cognato e fratello e.

Noi Veniamo a te con queste due righe per darti le nostre notizie che noi stiamo tutti bene e ne speriamo di te che sarai in buona salute

Ma dispiacenti siamo ad annunciati la dolosa notizia della cara mamma che dopo un anno di acuti dolori e sofferenze e morta il giorno tre Febbraio e ci abbiamo fatto il funerale il giorno 5.
e stata circa tre settimane sempre quasi fuori di se del gran dolore. la prima notte che e venuta aggravata ti ricordava sempre te e continuava a parlare come se fossi stato te accanto al suo letto
Insomma guarda di farti coraggio come facciamo noi intanto ti lascio cosi e un po piu tardi ti sperando avremo messo un po tutte le cose a posto ti scrivero di nuovo e cosi ti faro alcuenta di letto altro ti lasciamo i nostri saluti e un bacio dalle tue nipote e siamo tuo Cognato e
sorella Virginia Grassi

20 Letter from Virginia Grassi to her brother, 6 February 1935, announcing the death of their mother Caterina. Courtesy of Grassi fonds, Whyte Museum of the Canadian Rockies, M 45 2/11.

but had been forced to sell a cow. The greater part of this letter, however, dealt with her brother's funds in Falmenta. The post office staff had been very critical of the "measly interests" being earned in the savings accounts in which the funds were deposited. Remembering her mother's zealous concern about her brother's money and suspicions about Virginia's desire for access to Lorenzo's accounts, she nevertheless told her brother she had been advised to request a letter from him authorizing her to deal with his accounts in a more profitable way: "If you trust me I am only trying to protect your interests and nothing else ... because leaving the accounts this way is not to your advantage."[42] So great was her concern that she posted this letter to her brother by registered mail at the considerable cost of 2.75 liras. The receipt for its registration has survived among the Grassi family papers kept by her descendants in Falmenta, but this last communication from Virginia to Lorenzo, like so many others,[43] was not answered. She died on 5 March 1946.

Enrico, Virginia's husband, also made several attempts to correspond with Lorenzo. But by the end of his life in 1954, he too had failed. It is likely that a first letter had been sent with the 1917 photograph of himself and his family – Virginia, his infant daughter Angiolina, and Lorenzo's proxy as her godfather. Even when not personally writing, Enrico is mentioned frequently in the letters from both his mother-in-law and wife, on various occasions as a borrower of money from Lorenzo. In some records he was listed as a mason, while in others he, like most of his contemporaries, was listed as a peasant.[44] Regardless of his occupation, he was the breadwinner of a growing family. Like many others, however, he found few opportunities for work in Falmenta and, in the mid-1920s, he too resorted to migration. He worked in Switzerland for a time but his sojourning would not last for long. With the precipitous worsening of Caterina's health and Virginia's inability to care for her mother by herself, Enrico's plight became ever more difficult, and he increasingly devoted himself to trying to settle the matter of the Grassi inheritance. This, Enrico decided, was best done with Lorenzo present, so he also joined his mother in law and his wife in urging for his return.

The house was in dire condition, as Caterina had many times pointed out, and restoring it enough to make it livable would cost a lot of money, which clearly was not available. In 1929, as Caterina had informed Lorenzo in one of her letters, Enrico and his family managed to buy another house and moved into it. In 1935 he once again asked Lorenzo what should be done with the Grassi house, where "at least a quarter of the roof" had to be rebuilt due to a broken joist.[45] In the same letter

21 The   Grassi   family
house in Falmenta, shown
in an undated photograph
and before modern resto-
rations. Courtesy of Grassi
family, Falmenta, Italy.

Enrico, as his wife had done, raised the topic of Lorenzo's savings, and
the money that was lost ("1760 liras" annually) by keeping his funds in
post office savings accounts rather than "government bonds." All told,
Enrico explained, Lorenzo could easily stay home and live on the "5 or
six thousand liras a year" that his savings would earn in interest if in-
vested as he recommended. It was advice his mother had also offered
in her letter of December 1932. Considering the conditions Enrico and
his family were experiencing, as described in the next letter, written at
the end of November 1938, he must have contemplated these sums
with a sense of incredulity, if not envy:

> [The price of everything] is going up especially the cost of food. Imagine
> bread is 2.10 [liras] a kilo when mixed with corn flour. The other kind made
> with wheat is 3.10 a kilo. Corn flour is 1.40 a kilo pasta is 3.30 and rice is
> 2.30 a kilo … jobs are scarce and even then salaries are miserably low …
> The hourly rate goes from 1.90 to 2.60 an hour but working for more than
> forty hours a week is not allowed.

Not surprisingly, at the end of this letter and almost as an afterthought, Enrico made a plea for another loan, "at least as much as you gave me last year if you can ... we are at the end of the year there are taxes there is the store in short things are coming to a head."[46]

Angiolina, Lorenzo's niece and goddaughter, appeared in the correspondence in its early stages. After the photographs of her as an infant and as a toddler, she was mentioned occasionally by her family, and over time it is possible to see the emergence of a distinct personality: bright, alert to the world around her, conscious of the misery that comes with poverty, and anxious to get to know her "American uncle." In 1925 her grandmother wrote to Lorenzo to tell him that his niece had expressed a desire for a pair of shoes "from America" despite having received a new pair from her mother (a hint perhaps of the "naughty" child that Virginia would later describe). In 1927 ten-year-old Angiolina began to write to her uncle, as part of a letter in which Virginia, with a mother's pride but feigning concern, had this to say: "Your goddaughter is already in the fourth grade ... She has a fine head on her shoulders but she is a very naughty girl. She is a devil."[47] For her part Angiolina's Christmas greetings to her uncle echo her mother's and grandmother's constant theme: "I write to you once in a while but you never answer me. I would be very happy to receive a greeting."[48] This was expressed more fully three years later, but not before the now thirteen year old proudly stated that she was "very tall for my age":

> You have been away from Italy for a long time. In fact you never saw me when I was born and yet you are my godfather. Now I am grown up. If you saw me you would say that I am a young woman.[49]

As she grew into a sensitive and lively teenager, Angiolina continued to write to her uncle in America, adding her earnest voice to the calls for his return: "Dear godfather you have been in America for almost nineteen years and it never occurs to you to come home for a little trip to Italy. We would be very happy if we could embrace you and grandmother would be happy too if she could see you one more time." The return of Emilia (Cerutti) Zanni, who had come home that year (1931), and the news that she gave about Angiolina's famous American uncle, gave more impetus to her plea: "[She] told us that you are very well and that you are quite fat and we were very happy to have your news." Sensitive to the wider reality around her, however, she ended by drawing a doleful picture of both the general and her family's conditions:

Many people from Falmenta came home from America for lack of work and because of the great hardship. My father also stayed home. There is great misery in Italy and we hear that it's like this everywhere.[50]

She wrote just a month later, thanking her uncle "because *nonna* bought me a gift in your name because she received your letter and I thank you but I can't repay you because I am too far away. I can't do more than thank you with all my heart." In the next sentence she could not refrain from once again turning her thoughts to the more general human privation: "I am still young but I see that there is hardship [*miseria*] everywhere and I understand there is probably hardship there too because there probably is no work."[51] A few months later, in August of the same year, "after a long silence" she sent her uncle a photograph of herself and her mother and sisters

although we came out badly because the sun was bright. I would appreciate it if you sent me your photo too. I would be very pleased to see you because I have not seen you yet.[52]

The long silence that followed this letter coincided with her grandmother's prolonged illness and eventual death. The next note from Angiolina came in the form of an enclosure in her mother's letter announcing that "my daughter Angiolina your goddaughter will probably get married," an acerbic reminder to Lorenzo that he had a goddaughter. Confirming her mother's announcement, Angiolina enclosed a photograph of herself and her fiancé, and added: "It is likely that next year I will get married. We were planning it for this year, but since mother has been sick we decided to wait until next year."[53]

The marriage that Angiolina and her mother had announced before the war did not take place: she never married. She left Falmenta in 1952, two years before her father's death; her departure may have been an attempt to distance herself from the pain and tragedy that her family endured, which she writes of in one last letter to her uncle sent many years later. World War II had long passed, and the woman who now signed herself as Angela wrote to Lorenzo in May 1956 from Cunardo, a town in the province of Varese in Lombardy, across the lake from Cannobio. She began her letter with the hope that, unlike the others she had written him, which had perhaps gone astray, this one would reach her "uncle Lorenzo." She promised more news in subsequent letters if she had some indication that this one had reached him. The brief

22 Portrait of Virginia Grassi and her daughters Angiolina, Maria, and Arman-
dina, one of two photographs sent by Angiolina to her uncle and godfather,
August 1932. Courtesy of Grassi fonds, Whyte Museum of the Canadian
Rockies, M 45-2.

account she provides of the events of the previous ten years is an un-happy tale of family misfortune:

> With great sorrow I inform you that on 5 March 1946 mother died and on 5 April 1954 father died too. So Maria and I are the only ones left. For the past 4 years I have been working as a maid with a family in a town near Varese and Maria is living in Falmenta and she is making do with a cow and a few goats.[54]

Then, after this sad accounting of what was left of her family, a shadow of the younger, more optimistic Angiolina breaks through, together with the longing that she had expressed many years before:

> Life is certainly not very easy but patience, as long as there is health ... We have always had a desire to hear from you especially now that we no lon-ger have our parents or any other close relatives except you. I will not make this too long since I fear that this too will be returned to sender ... I am anxious to receive a letter from you after so many years of silence and hoping to find you in good health I extend very affectionate greetings also on behalf of my sister Maria.
>
> Your niece Angela Grassi and Maria

What is immediately striking about this letter is that she did not men-tion her other sister Armandina, Maria's twin.[55] Her letter was a last desperate attempt to reach out to the uncle and godfather she never knew, and as so often before, Lorenzo did not acknowledge this final plea from Falmenta. She never wrote again.

Angiolina died on 14 January 1997, seventeen years after Lawrence. At the time of her death she was living in the town of Luino, on the shore of Lake Maggiore.[56] Oddly, as Lawrence's health deteriorated in the late 1970s, he asked his executors in Canmore to trace any sur-viving relatives in Italy. They found no one, and perhaps for this reason Lawrence overlooked his niece and goddaughter in his will and instead bequeathed significant sums to the Alpine Club of Canada and to the Canadian Youth Hostel Association.[57]

The letters from Falmenta that survive with Grassi's papers provide invaluable insights into the lives of those he left behind. What they do not provide is equal insight into the mind and heart of the man who received them and kept them all his life. *Why* was he so unable to re-spond to the frequent plea of his mother, "Caro figlio scrivimi" (Dear

23 Portrait of Angiolina Grassi and her fiancé sent to Lorenzo Grassi in January 1938. Courtesy of Grassi fonds, Whyte Museum of the Canadian Rockies, M 45 2/16.

son write to me), a plea echoed by others in his family? Would he himself have been capable of answering this question? We may find clues to the answers by retracing the path his life took after he crossed the ocean.

Lorenzo Grassi and the Falmentines on the North Shore

Andrea (Lorenzo) Grassi and the group of paesans who sailed with him in April 1912 were destined for settlements on the north shore of Lake Superior. They were part of a process that had begun more than twenty years earlier and would continue for many years after their journey. Although first settled by Europeans in the course of the fur trade of the late seventeenth century, the settlements that became the twin cities of Fort William and Port Arthur thrived after the completion of railway

24 Latest edition (1912) of the "newest" *Italian-English Accelerated Grammar*. Photocopy of cover from the Grassi fonds, Whyte Museum of the Canadian Rockies.

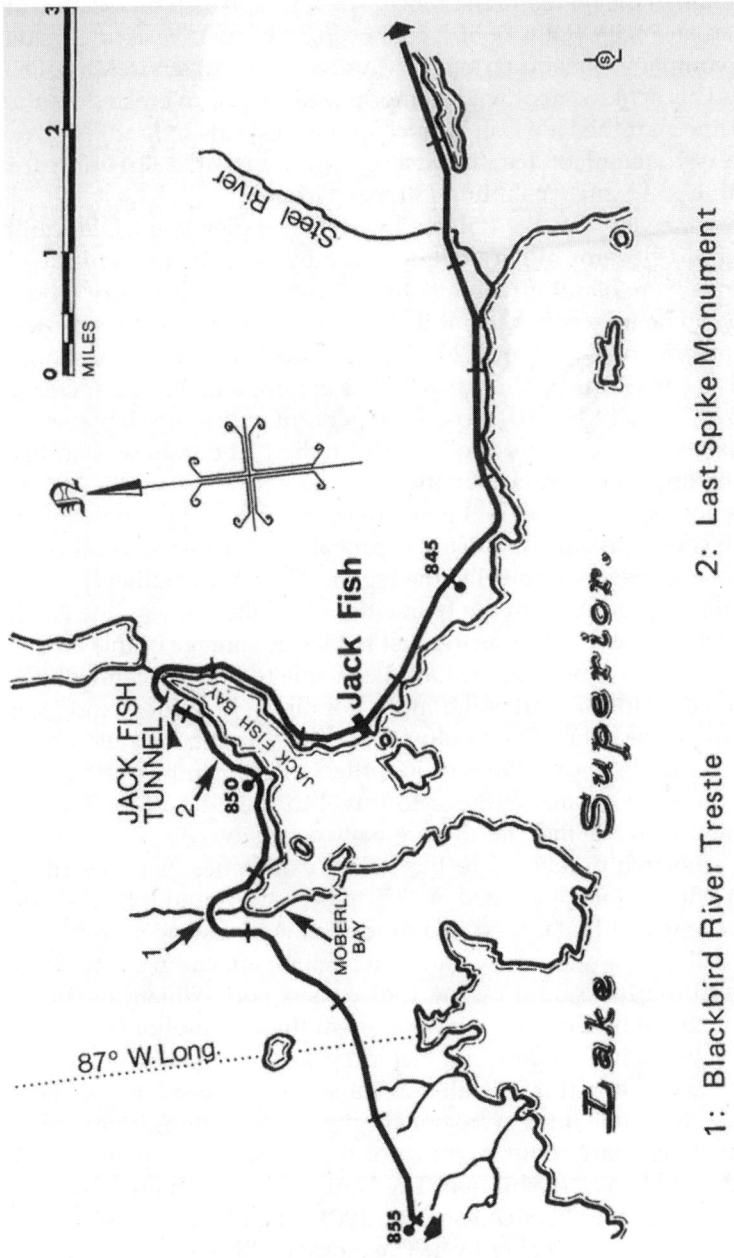

25 Location of Last Spike Monument at Jack Fish Bay, Ontario. Reproduced from Lavallée, *Van Horne's Road*, p. 183. Copyright Railfare Enterprises Limited. Used with permission.

1: Blackbird River Trestle   2: Last Spike Monument

construction in the region in the 1880s. The final spike on this section of the Canadian Pacific Railway line, connecting the line to eastern Canada and the company's headquarters in Montreal, was driven in May 1885 (fig. 25). This achievement was memorialized in a cairn erected on the railway line near the Jack Fish Tunnel on the west side of Jack Fish Bay, near the settlement of Jackfish itself, an important destination for Falmentine emigrants, including Lorenzo Grassi.

In the same year that the railway line was completed, the CPR built its first grain elevator in Fort William, and by 1891 the two Lakehead settlements were handling more than twelve million bushels of wheat annually. Some ten years later, at the beginning of the last century, the local population was roughly 7,200 and a decade later it had almost quadrupled to some 27,000. This growth was accompanied by an increase in cultural diversity. By 1901 close to 40 per cent of the population were of non-British descent, and the influx of Italian labourers was an important component of this diversity.

It was not long after the final phase of construction of the railway on the north shore – as early as 1888 and probably earlier – that emigrants from Falmenta began to travel to the region. They did so either to work for the railway company in the twin cities or on the railway line itself, but we cannot know who was the first to take advantage of this labour market. The earliest records we have been able to find for Falmentines in Canada date to 1873 (an emigrant to Winnipeg, Manitoba) and 1876 (in Montreal, Quebec).[58] Eventually, a significant number would chose either to settle in the twin cities or in settlements along the north shore of Lake Superior permanently or to travel to these locations for frequent sojourns while their families remained in Italy.

Local scholarship devoted to the Italian experience in Port Arthur and Fort William (amalgamated in 1970 to become Thunder Bay) sheds light on the world that Grassi and other Falmentines encountered on their arrival.[59] Emigrants from Falmenta begin to appear in the two settlements in the 1880s, and by the 1901 census Fort William included nine Falmentine households. Between them these households totalled about thirty-five individuals (not including seven Canadian-born children), or about one-third of all the Italian-origin residents of Fort William.[60] The Falmentines were only beginning to settle as immigrants at this relatively early date: just two of the households listed in 1901 included Canadian-born children. The family of Paul and Lucia Tiboni, for example, included six children by 1901, five of whom were born after their mother's arrival in 1891. The oldest child, a son, was born in

Italy and had immigrated with his mother. She had been preceded to Fort William by her husband in 1889.[61]

The local Falmentine population continued to grow and by 1911 it included about fifty-six adults and children who were born in Italy.[62] This number comprised fourteen families, ten of them husband and wife with children and four without children. Twenty-two of the children listed had been born in Ontario; six were Italian born. In total, those in Fort William who can be traced back to the Cannobino Valley, and directly to Falmenta, numbered almost eighty, including Canadian-born children.[63] By 1911 the majority of Falmentine-Italian households were concentrated on McLeod Street in the area of Fort William's East End, a neighbourhood located next to the CPR coal docks. This neighbourhood was even known in Falmenta where, by the early 1900s, according to local tradition, McLeod Street in Fort William's East End was colloquially known as "via di Falmint," or Falmenta Street.[64] An additional four Falmenta residences were located one block to the east of McLeod, on McPherson Street, which Lorenzo Grassi gave as his destination. That a relatively large number of Falmentine emigrants had preceded him to Fort William, and to other locations on the north shore of Lake Superior, meant that Lorenzo Grassi could rely on a well-established network of paesans when he arrived in 1912.

Before his arrival, for example, the Italians of Fort William had formed the Società Italiana di Benevolenza Principe di Piemonte (The Prince of Piedmont Italian Mutual Benefit Society). This society was created in 1909 to "provid[e] funerary and sick benefits for its members[,] and a few recreational activities," which is a strong indication of the appalling living conditions in which the majority of residents of Fort William's East End lived.[65] Those conditions also explain why families often were reunited – wife and children travelling to meet husband and father – in north shore settlements only to have the families return to Falmenta after a brief stay.

The Principe di Piemonte grew until it was able to purchase its own building in 1923. As a result, "Italians ... had a collective visible presence in the community. The building symbolized achievement and permanence; but, more importantly, it allowed the society to shed slowly its Savoyan and Piedmontese affiliation and acquire the more appropriate name, 'Italian Society of Fort William.'"[66] No information is available about the original membership of the Principe di Piemonte, but its name suggests it had an early "Piedmontese," and very likely Falmentine, affiliation before it developed into a pan-Italian association.

26 Executive and members of the Novarese Club, Fort William, Ontario, 1939.
Left to right, back row: James Zanni (secretary), Henry Tiboni, Attilio Cantoni
(from Crealla), William Tiboni, John Ferrari (president). *Front row*: Jean Cerutti,
Paul Tiboni, Aurelio Bianconi, Mella Zanni. Courtesy of Joan Grassi.

Some years later, in 1939, a group of Fort William residents formed
the "Novarese Club," perhaps in an effort to keep alive their links with
Piedmont and the Cannobino Valley. The province of Novara in the
Piedmont region at the time encompassed the Cannobino Valley, and
this organization brought together emigrants and their descendants
from the valley, in particular from the settlements of Falmenta and
Gurro. The founding executive of the club (fig. 26) included Paul
Tiboni, mentioned above and by then, at eighty years of age, one of its
oldest members. In the photograph he sits next to a somewhat younger
immigrant, Aurelio Bianconi, whose life on the north shore we will
trace in greater detail below. The photograph of the club executive is
accompanied by another taken to commemorate the first club picnic
(fig. 27),[67] attended by some 120 picnickers, presumably all of them
with roots in the Cannobino Valley.

27 The original caption superimposed on this photograph reads "First Annual Picnic Novarese Club July 9 1939." Courtesy of Joan Grassi.

When Lorenzo Grassi arrived at the Lakehead, the twin cities had become important migrant and immigrant transshipment or settlement points with a strong Falmentine component to their Italian-origin population. In 1911, a year before Grassi's arrival, the residence that he declared as his destination in Fort William was described as the home of Stefano and Rosalia Zanni, respectively thirty-five and thirty years old, who had immigrated a year apart. Stefano Zanni sailed to New York City in 1903 with three others from Falmenta; all four were in transit through the United States to Fort William. One of the four, thirty-six-year-old Giosue Zanni, was described as "Citizen of Canada" in the manifest, and he named his friend, Paolo (Paul) Tiboni, as his contact.[68]

Rosalia Zanni, a twenty-three-year-old housekeeper, sailed in 1904 to join her husband, but she did not travel alone: she was one of twenty-eight Falmentines on this voyage who, with two exceptions, were headed for Fort William. One of her fellow passengers, thirty-seven-year-old Antonio Zanni, also reported that his contact was his brother-in-law, Stefano Zanni. Both Rosalia and Stefano appear again in the passenger list of a 1913 voyage on board the SS *La Provence*, returning to Fort William after a visit to Italy. A few years after this voyage, however, Rosalia Zanni contracted influenza, the infamous "Spanish Flu" of 1918, and died in Fort William on 17 November. Ironically, the misfortune that struck the household at 505 McPherson Street in 1918 helps to explain an important relationship in Canada for Lorenzo Grassi. Stefano remarried in Fort William in 1920, and his marriage record reported his father's name as Giosue Zanni and his mother as Teresa Testori. Lorenzo's mother was Caterina Testori; she and Stefano's mother were sisters.[69]

We should also note that Stefano Zanni was present in Falmenta for some time immediately before Lorenzo's departure for the north shore. Stefano and Rosalia, as we have seen, returned to Fort William from Falmenta in April 1913. On that voyage Stefano declared that he had been in Canada before, during the years 1903–10. From these dates it seems that both Stefano and Rosalia were in Falmenta from 1910 until April 1913, which would have given their cousin Lorenzo the opportunity to learn about employment and other conditions on the north shore of Lake Superior and to arrange to meet his relatives there. What is curious is that, despite their being listed in the 1911 Canadian census, and despite Lorenzo Grassi and his paesan Agostino Zanni (who was on the same voyage) using their names and address as contacts, both Stefano and Rosalia must have been in Falmenta during the census as well as when the young men arrived.[70]

According to the 1911 census, the Zanni residence on McPherson Street was home to seven Italian lodgers, six of whom appear to have been from Falmenta. No information is available for either Lorenzo Grassi's or Agostino Zanni's time in the Zanni boarding house, where they might have lodged if their intention was to find work in Fort William. Certainly Agostino found work locally. Lorenzo, however, did not remain in Fort William; he was instead destined for work on what he and his contemporaries referred to as *la tracca*, or the railway track.[71] The destinations of those who worked on the track were spread out along the north shore of Lake Superior, and it was important that the newcomers arrive in northern Ontario in the early spring, preferably before the thaw and the beginning of outdoor work, when a railway company would be hiring.

Lorenzo Grassi – and many of his Falmentine paesans – was employed by the CPR as a "section man" or "section hand." CPR employee records used the terms "trackman" or "section man" interchangeably to describe workers employed for track maintenance and repairs.[72] The position required membership in a labour union, and Grassi joined the International Brotherhood of Maintenance of Way Employees in August 1912, a few months after his arrival on the north shore.[73] These workers, also known as navvies ("navy jacks" in British Columbia), were labourers supervised by section foremen, a position that several Falmentine Canadians on the north shore came to occupy. Grassi worked as part of a crew that moved up and down the track, sometimes travelling on a handcar, carrying the tools needed for maintenance and repair and probably under the supervision of a paesan foreman. While he was working for the CPR in this capacity in northern Ontario, together with other Falmentines, Lorenzo wrote at least once to his family and at least once to a cousin who was based in Switzerland, in Solduno near Locarno.

Information about that correspondence is contained in a letter to Caterina Grassi from a nephew, Domenico Grassi. In January 1913 Domenico wrote to his aunt from Solduno to let her know that he had received news from Lorenzo, who had advised him that if he intended to emigrate to Canada he should do so by the middle of March, and offered to send him the money for his journey. Domenico reported to his aunt that he had decided to leave and was waiting to hear whether "the brother in law of Giovanni" was also interested in the trip because

28 SS *La Provence*, ship's manifest page (part 1) recording the details of the passenger "Grassi, Andrea [Lorenzo]" at line 22, in March 1912. Courtesy of Statue of Liberty–Ellis Island Foundation Inc.

29 SS *La Provence*, ship's manifest page (part 2) with additional details for the passenger "Grassi, Andrea [Lorenzo]" at line 22, including his destination in Fort William. Courtesy of Statue of Liberty-Ellis Island Foundation Inc.

it would be good to travel with someone from Falmenta, and to travel together to the same place.[74] Domenico was uncertain whether he should make his travel arrangements from Switzerland and was seeking advice about what documents he might need and what clothing would be appropriate. It is not difficult to imagine that Lorenzo had posed similar questions to his cousin Stefano Zanni in preparation for his own departure. Others in Lorenzo's extended family also maintained contact, at least in these early years after his departure, both with him and with his family.

Another cousin, Giovanni Testori, in this case a relative on Lorenzo's mother's side, had emigrated about a year before Lorenzo. Like his cousin, he too was destined for Jackfish on the north shore of Lake Superior. Some two years after emigrating, Giovanni wrote an amusing letter to his cousin Virginia, Lorenzo's sister. Addressing his letter at "Jach Fisch, 6 Ottobre 1913," Giovanni announced to Virginia that he had found a suitable husband for her among the local native population. After a description of the life she might enjoy living in a tent in the forest on the north shore of Lake Superior with her new husband, he asked her to let him know immediately if she had already found someone in Falmenta. Given that he wrote a few months before Virginia's marriage, Giovanni clearly was teasing his cousin, and his letter also illustrates the network of connections that existed between far-flung locations in both Italy and Canada.[75]

A year earlier, in December 1912 – about eight months after his arrival in Canada – Lorenzo also had written (fig. 13) to his family from Jackfish, Ontario, in his own hand written as "jach Fish." In his typically brief note addressed to his mother, father, and sister, he extended greetings to another Falmentine with a history of sojourning to the north shore, Giacomo Bianconi, who might have been his foreman in Jackfish, and who was also part of the Falmentine network in northern Ontario.[76]

Jackfish

Bianconi was the oldest of four brothers and one sister from Falmenta who were either sojourners or settlers on the north shore while Lorenzo Grassi was based in Jackfish. Their experiences are typical of the lives and career trajectories of Falmentine emigrants on this labouring frontier. The world they created for themselves in a remote settlement like Jackfish provides important background for understanding Lorenzo's experience in this environment.

Fishing Village, Jack Fish, Lake Superior

30 Jackfish, Ontario, presented as a "fishing village" in a 1906 photograph postcard. The water tower in the background supplied water to the railway locomotives on the CPR line. Courtesy of Thunder Bay Historical Society, 973.13.316 N.

Giacomo Bianconi first travelled to the north shore in 1894, near the beginnings of Falmentine emigration to the area. On a voyage in 1907 he travelled with two of his brothers, Luigi and Salvatore, and all three men declared that they would contact their brother Aurelio, whose address they reported as "Jack Fish Fort William (Ont) Canada."[77] Some three years later, on a voyage in April 1910 but this time travelling alone, Bianconi reported a previous stay in Canada from 1906 to 1910[78] and declared that he was headed for White River, Canada, where his contacts were "[his] brothers Aurelio and Salvatore." In the following year Giacomo Bianconi, fifty-two years of age, was resident as a lodger in Jackfish, at the "Coal Docks Plant C.P.R."[79] His return to Ontario in 1910 might explain the greetings sent to him by Lorenzo Grassi from the north shore. In other words, like Grassi's cousin Stefano Zanni, Bianconi was also in Falmenta during the time Lorenzo was contemplating his own journey to the north shore, and he may have been present when Lorenzo reached Jackfish in 1912.

Giacomo Bianconi, although the oldest of the Bianconi brothers, was preceded to northern Ontario in 1891 by his brother Salvatore, then twenty-four years. This voyage may have been the beginning of the Bianconi family's connections with what became their distant labouring frontier. In 1891 Salvatore was one of ten emigrants from the Cannobino Valley travelling on board the French Line steamer the SS *La Bretagne*, three of whom, including Salvatore, were headed for "Ontario."[80] The record of a voyage he undertook some twelve years later, however, provides insights into an unusual aspect of this emigrant's life. The manifest entry from the voyage of SS *La Lorraine*, which arrived at the port of New York on 11 April 1903, listed "Mr Salvatore Bianconi … 36 [years old] married farmer" as a passenger who was travelling to Fort William. He also declared a previous sojourn of twelve years and stated that he was returning "home: Fort William Ontario." He was not travelling alone. His companion was his twenty-two-year-old wife "Mrs Matilde Bianconi" who was "accompanying husband [to] Fort William Ontario."

This is the only record, among the hundreds consulted to trace Falmentine emigration to North America, in which passenger's names are registered formally as "Mr" and "Mrs." The fact that their names are recorded in the first ten pages of this manifest, those reserved for saloon or first-cabin passengers, together with Matilde Bianconi's age, suggest that the couple were newlyweds, and in fact they had been married in Falmenta on 12 February 1903. Perhaps this helps to explain their accommodation, which is extravagant by the usual standards of Falmentine travellers headed for Ontario.[81] Some eleven months after this voyage Matilde gave birth to a daughter, Lucia Elena. Sadly, Matilde died of typhoid fever in March 1906 in Fort William, only twenty-four years old and survived by her husband and her two-year-old daughter.[82]

The 1911 census confirms Salvatore Bianconi's personal status. He was enumerated as resident in Jackfish, Ontario as a forty-four-year-old widower and his immigration date was given as 1899. Thereafter he made at least two trips to Italy;[83] and in 1925, on his last known voyage from Italy to Canada he was reported to be a section foreman for the "CP Railway" based at Peninsula, Ontario; his next of kin was listed as his "daughter Miss Helena Bianconi at Falmenta."[84] Clearly, he did not remarry after the death of Matilde; and at some point their daughter Helena returned to Falmenta while he continued his life in Canada, advancing in the CPR from "labourer" in 1911 to section foreman by 1925.

Aurelio Bianconi was the youngest of the four Bianconi brothers and the most prominent one in the CPR railway settlements along the north shore of Lake Superior. He first travelled to North America as a twenty-year-old in 1892 in the company of at least one other Falmentine. This journey was followed by another in 1899 during which he declared a previous stay from 1892 to 1899. Forty years later he appeared as an elder presence among the Falmentines in Fort William, as suggested by his inclusion in the photograph of the Novarese Club's executive and his attendance at that club's 1939 picnic (figs. 26 and 27). A few years before that photograph was taken Lorenzo's sister Virginia extolled him as an example to her brother of someone who had returned to Falmenta even though by then Aurelio had been away for "twenty years."[85]

Bianconi married Lucia Milani in 1899, the year in which he, then twenty-eight, made a second trip to northern Ontario. Lucia, about the same age as her husband, travelled a year later, in 1900, to join him in Fort William. She travelled with a Falmentine couple, husband and wife Francesco and Giovaninna Cerutti, who would become important in the lives of the Bianconis. When the Ceruttis travelled with Lucia in April 1900 they were recent newlyweds and related to her through marriage, as Giovaninna was her husband's sister.[86]

A Shipment of Murphys from

JACK FISH

1659

Reproduced from Photograph

31 Postmarked 27 August 1916 in Jackfish, Ontario, this light-hearted postcard showing giant potatoes – "Murphys" – purportedly shipped from the village was sent with "Best regard from yours truly P Grassi" to a "Miss J.J. Tiboni Port Coldwell C.P.R.," suggesting an extended community of Falmentines and their descendants on the north shore. Courtesy of Thunder Bay Historical Society, 973.13.316 M.

Some twenty years after his 1899 voyage Aurelio Bianconi undertook a very different journey. In November 1919 he was stopped at the international border on his way to Baltimore, Maryland, for a visit to that city's famous Johns Hopkins Hospital. The record of his attempt to cross into the United States does not specify his purpose in visiting the hospital. However, other details are suggestive. Bianconi was travelling with his son Marco, then seventeen years old, whose card was also stamped "REJECTED," and the reason given was "Epileptic." It seems clear that father and son were turned back in their attempt to reach Baltimore for treatment for Marco's epilepsy.[87]

By 1919, according to the same records, Bianconi was living in Jackfish with his wife Lucia. His occupation was recorded as "section foreman" (his son was employed as a "section hand") and he was travelling to Baltimore by means of a "C.P.R. [railway] Pass." Of interest is the information that Bianconi provided for the most recent voyage he had completed to North America. He had arrived in December 1913 at Halifax on board the SS *Empress of Ireland*, accompanied by his wife Lucia and their sons Frank and Marco. These four names appear with that of Aurelio's brother, the forty-year-old widower Salvatore, in the ship's manifest. All three Falmentines, and the two Canadian-born children, were travelling to Jackfish and were described as returning Canadians.[88]

Francesco Cerutti, Aurelio's brother-in-law, was one of the first emigrants from Falmenta to make his way to the CPR settlements of the north shore. According to the record of the April 1900 journey with his wife Giovaninna and Lucia Bianconi, the then thirty-three-year-old had been in Ontario for eleven years, from 1888 to 1899. Based on these dates he clearly preceded all of the Bianconi brothers as well as most other Falmentines. From the record of an 1894 voyage we know that he was previously married, as the name of his spouse was given as Virginia.[89] Virginia had been the sister of Aurelio's wife, Lucia, and had died accidentally of poisoning in January 1899 at White River, Ontario. Giovaninna was Francesco's second wife.

Cerutti returned to Italy shortly after the tragedy of his first wife's death, and in April 1900 was already on his way back to Ontario with his new wife, the twenty-six-year-old Giovaninna. In 1901 she gave birth to her first child, a daughter they named Virginia, no doubt in memory of Francesco's first wife. In the record of this birth the newborn's mother was given as Giovanna[90] Bianconi, and she can be traced in Falmenta's parish and municipal records as a sister of the Bianconi brothers. By 1911 the Falmentine family of "Frank" and "Anne Cherutti" were listed together with four children as Jackfish residents. By 1913, however, Francesco Cerutti might have resumed the life of a sojourner. On a return trip to Canada in that year he reported his wife Giovanna as his next of kin, resident in Falmenta, and he repeated the same information in 1923 when he declared that he had travelled to Italy to "see my family." By 1931, in his early sixties, Francesco himself had returned to his birthplace to join Giovanna and his family.[91] In other words, Francesco Cerutti's life on the north shore underwent an unusual transformation from sojourner to settler and then to sojourner again, after his immediate family returned to Falmenta.

That they were brothers-in-law was not the only connection between Aurelio Bianconi and Francesco Cerutti: their lives were intricately intertwined. Cerutti established himself as a CPR section foreman working from various north shore settlements like Jackfish, Heron Bay, and White River. Aurelio Bianconi also became a foreman on the north shore railway line and an important contact for paesans who were in search of work with the CPR. Cerutti named one of his sons for Bianconi, who was his godfather. And Bianconi on at least two occasions, swore declarations concerning the dates and places of birth of Cerutti's children, declaring himself to have been present at their births.[92] Bianconi, however, seems to have become the more prominent of the two. Beginning with references by his brothers in the early years of the last century, the first of which occurred in 1905,[93] he was named as the contact person on at least sixteen occasions by emigrants who were headed to Ontario (including six mentions specifically of Jackfish).

One of the contact references for Bianconi in Jackfish occurred in 1910 and connects in an interesting fashion with Lorenzo Grassi. In that year a labourer from Falmenta, Ignazio Tiboni, thirty-six years old and single, whose next of kin in Ponte di Falmenta was his sister "Bianconi Virginia," travelled to meet his "friend Aurelio Bianconi." For his final destination Tiboni reported both "Jack Fish" and "White River."[94] Little more is known about this Falmentine apart from a reference to him by Lorenzo Grassi. When Lorenzo wrote to his family in 1912 from Jackfish he asked to be remembered to Giacomo Bianconi, and he also asked that greetings from Ignazio Tiboni be passed on to the latter's friends and family in Falmenta. So for at least a brief period of time, while Grassi was based in Jackfish, he and Tiboni were close enough to share this exchange of greetings to their families back home. Equally important, after Lorenzo Grassi left the north shore for western Canada in July 1913, he received a brief message from his friend, "I. Tiboni." On the back of a photograph postcard dated 9 May 1914, and postmarked in Jackfish, Tiboni forwarded his best wishes both to Grassi and to "the whole gang" ("tutta la compagnia") on behalf of all the Falmentine friends Lorenzo had left behind. The photograph is one of two (figs. 32 and 33) that appear to have been taken on the same day and at the same location, though the subject matter of the two photographs is significantly different.[95]

Both show people posed on the side porch of the same house in Jackfish. The postcard photograph shows fourteen men and four children grouped in front of a room, the summer kitchen, at the back of the house.[96] Twelve of the men are positioned in the centre of the photograph and eleven of the twelve wore identical "party" hats. Aurelio Bianconi, of course here much younger than the elder statesperson of the Novarese Club executive portrait, is standing in the back row of the group, in front of the door to the house.[97]

In the second group portrait (fig. 33), although some of the men from the first photograph are easily recognized, the party hats have been discarded and the group has been expanded to thirty-two individuals: twenty men, including a couple of young adults or older adolescents, eleven children, and just one adult woman, Lucia Bianconi, almost hidden from view in the back row, standing on the right of her husband Aurelio. As in the scene with party hats, all of the men are well dressed and wear ties, waistcoats, and jackets, and with one exception all wear hats or caps. The girls wear what appear to be white dresses or "frocks"; one of them was probably Caterina Minoletti, daughter of Emilio and Geromina, who had emigrated with her mother and sister in 1908 to join her father.[98] The close-knit nature of this group of emigrants is underlined, in this case, with the knowledge that Elisa or "Elisetta," the second Italian-born child of Emilio and Geromina, eventually married another member of the group whose career we have already noted, the Canadian-born Falmentine chimney sweep Antonio (Tony) Minoletti.[99]

These two photographs gain more significance for our study if we juxtapose them with another that dates from almost the same time showing Lorenzo Grassi when he was twenty-three years old (fig. 34). In it he is wearing a fedora and is dressed in overalls over which he wore a heavy jacket. He is seated at a table or desk and on the wall behind him is a calendar for May 1914, which provides a date for this portrait. Below the calendar is part of a framed collection of membership cards for the International Brotherhood of Maintenance of Way Employees, a detail which suggests that the location was a union office.[100] It may be that Grassi had this photograph taken of himself to send to the friends and relatives he had left behind in Jackfish. What these exchanges reveal, besides the evidence of intertwining family relationships described above, is a wider, deeper, and mutually supportive social ambience. Lorenzo Grassi, at this early stage of his Canadian experience, was still very much a part of this collective reality, and it is

32 A portrait of Falmentine men in "party hats," Jackfish, Ontario, May 1914. Francesco Cerutti is seen in the back row of this photograph, standing behind a young boy (one of Aurelio Bianconi's sons) in a sailor's suit. His brother-in-law Aurelio Bianconi stands in the back row to Cerutti's left; unlike the latter, he is wearing a party hat. Courtesy of Grassi fonds, Whyte Museum of the Canadian Rockies, v240-886.

33 Falmentine residents of Jackfish, Ontario, in a group portrait, May 1914. Aurelio Bianconi is seen in the back row without a hat, standing next to his wife Lucia, while Francesco Cerutti is seated at the front of the photograph on the left, next to a toddler. Courtesy of Grassi fonds, Whyte Museum of the Canadian Rockies, v240-885.

34 Lorenzo Grassi after his transfer to western Canada, May 1914. Courtesy of Grassi fonds, Whyte Museum of the Canadian Rockies, v240-881(pa)025.

35 CPR station at Jackfish, Ontario, 1918. The man standing on the far right is Amedeo Minoletti, grandfather of Catherine McKinnon. The young girl in the background is Kay (Caterina) Bianconi, daughter of Aurelio and Lucia Bianconi. Courtesy of Catherine McKinnon.

not difficult to imagine him posed with his fellow navvies in Jackfish or in turn posing for a photograph that he would send to them.

The once prosperous village of Jackfish is now deserted. The site can be reached from the nearest major town, Terrace Bay on the Trans-Canada Highway, but only some cottages near to the lakeshore are maintained for occasional vacation visits. Otherwise, nature is reclaiming the settlement.[101] In its heyday, in the early decades of the last century, Jackfish included a one-room school with some forty to forty-five students, a general store, a Roman Catholic[102] and a Protestant church, the sizeable Lakeview Hotel, and extensive coal-handling facilities including a two-hundred-metre trestle dock built to receive freighters transporting coal from the Pennsylvania coal fields. In 1911 it had a population of 161, and more than one-half of its residents – ninety-eight

36 Falmentines in Jackfish, Ontario. *Standing, left to right:* Francesco Cerutti, Aurelio Bianconi, Aurelio Cerutti, Lucia (Milani) Bianconi, Pierina Bianconi, four unknown individuals. *Seated, left to right:* Frank Bianconi, Salvatore Bianconi, Caterina (Kay) Bianconi, unknown individual, Mark Bianconi, Adelina (Dee) Bianconi. *Standing at far right:* Lucia (Minoletti) Milani and her husband, Edoardo Milani, who lived in Jackfish from 1913 to 1919. Courtesy of Catherine McKinnon and Gene Milani.

37 Mobert, Ontario, 26 July 1914, five men in a canoe being eaten by blackflies?
Courtesy of Grassi fonds, Whyte Museum of the Canadian Rockies, v240-887.

individuals including Canadian-born children – were of Italian origin. Over one-third (35 per cent) of this Italian-origin population was from Falmenta; that is, thirty-four individuals were of Falmentine origin including their Canadian-born children.

There were four Falmentine households established in Jackfish before Lorenzo Grassi's arrival. Two, as we have seen, were the Bianconi and the Cerutti families; a third was that of Emilio and Geromina Minoletti; and the fourth was that of Amedeo and Angelina Milani and their two Italian-born daughters. In addition to these four families there was a Jackfish population of twelve Falmentine men who ranged in age from nineteen to fifty-two years (the latter being the elder Bianconi brother, Giacomo). Six of these "residents" were single, five were married, one was a widower (Salvatore Bianconi), and all were listed as lodgers in the settlement.

As previously noted, the sojourners and settlers from Falmenta (and other villages in the Cannobino Valley) made their way to north shore settlements other than Jackfish or the Lakehead. From the 1890s to the 1920s the most often reported destinations – excluding Fort William and Jackfish – were White River (nine), Coldwell or Port Coldwell (five), Heron Bay (five), Schreiber (three), and Rossport (two), but these figures probably underestimate the actual numbers of those from the Cannobino Valley. For example, the 1911 census reported fourteen residents at Rossport from the Cannobino Valley while another six were located at Peninsula (present-day Marathon) and other similar locations.[103]

In summary then, Falmentines could be found in virtually all of the north shore settlements on or near the route of the CPR, and this would include a location like Mobert, on the railway line to the east of Jackfish at about the midpoint between White River and Heron Bay. From that location, in the summer of 1914, Lorenzo Grassi received a photograph postcard of "five men in a canoe" sent to him by his "very close friend Edoardo Grassi."[104]

Edoardo was the twenty-one-year-old mason who in 1912 travelled with Lorenzo Grassi on their way to the north shore.[105] On that journey he specified Fort William as his destination but, like Lorenzo, Edoardo did not remain in the Lakehead settlement. Instead he moved on to a remote worksite where, as he complained to Lorenzo, he was being eaten by blackflies, a fate that he thought he might have to endure for another ten or twenty years. Like Ignazio Tiboni in his postcard to Grassi from Jackfish, written only a couple of months earlier, Edoardo also sent his greetings both to Lorenzo and to all of the companions with whom, we can only guess, Lorenzo was in contact.

It is difficult now to establish who those companions might have been and whether, for example, they preceded Lorenzo to the west, travelled with him as CPR employees to new worksites on the railway line, or travelled west after he did. From a number of sources we know that he was not the only emigrant from Falmenta to make his way to western Canada. What we cannot know with certainty is when, and under what circumstances, the Falmentines began to move westward after their arrival in Ontario. On the other hand, we know with some precision when Lorenzo moved west, although we remain uncertain about the reasons for his move.

3 Lawrence Grassi in the Mountains

Lorenzo (Lawrence) Grassi's move from the north shore of Lake Superior to western Canada would lead him eventually to great accomplishments and significant fame. In the west he settled finally in Canmore, Alberta, and from this base became a renowned mountain climber and climbing guide and a highly skilled and accomplished trail builder in the Rocky Mountains. Equally important, he gained the respect, admiration, and loyalty of a diverse range of people both locally and further afield. Until the 1960s – that is, when he was in his seventies – not much was written about him except for an occasional newspaper article that marvelled at some feat that had captured the public's imagination. Unfortunately, when he did begin to emerge onto a broader public stage some of the writing that was produced about him was careless and, though well intentioned, misleading. This is particularly obvious in what has been written about Grassi before his arrival in western Canada. In many cases, his move to the Rocky Mountains has been presented as a deliberate choice on his part, a choice that writers explain as rooted in a past in Italy that was mostly imaginary. Some clarity about this past is necessary before we can place Grassi's accomplishments in the mountains of western Canada within a meaningful context.

A general appreciation of Lorenzo Grassi's life began in the late 1960s with the appearance of an article written by Norman Wait, a retired school teacher. Wait had lived and taught in Canmore in the 1920s and so was in the vicinity when Lorenzo Grassi was in the midst of many of those activities on which his fame would be based. Wait wrote his piece in a style clearly intended to be heroic, and his respect for and admiration of his subject is evident throughout. He gave his biography the lapidary title "Grassi of Canmore"; his subtitle, embracing the popular

38 Lawrence Grassi on a peak overlooking the Bow River Valley, c. 1920s, possibly on a small sub-summit in the Fairholme Range (on the flank of Mount Lady Macdonald or Mount Princess Margaret) with Mount Rundle across the valley in the background. Courtesy of Grassi fonds, Whyte Museum of the Canadian Rockies, v240-646.

usage of the time, was "A Miner Who 'Did His Thing' and Gave Alberta a Heritage of Beauty."[1] After quoting a lengthy tribute to Grassi by the famous Canadian parliamentarian J.S. Woodsworth, Wait presented the details of Lawrence Grassi's life in a relatively straightforward, chronological sequence but including details not found in other, lesser-known accounts. According to Wait, Grassi

> attended school between the ages [of] five to twelve. His father was a lumberman whose work carried him into France, to a district near Grenoble. The young man worked with his father until his twentieth year ... Mr Grassi's father is buried in a small cemetery near Grenoble.
>
> A study of the geography of the district in which our young man spent the first twenty years of his life indicates and makes understandable the trend of his interests and activities during his entire life. An outdoor active life in the forested foothill country, adjacent to snowclad and glacier-covered mountains rising to heights of 12,000 feet [c. 3,700 metres] imbued the Italian youth with a love of the mountain peak country.
>
> Lawrence Grassi emigrated to Canada in 1912 and was employed by the CPR as a section man. During 1912–1913 he was located in the Lake Superior district east of Fort William. He obtained a transfer west to Hector to be in the mountains which were so much a part of his personality.[2]

The description of Lorenzo's father, Giuseppe, as a "lumberman" is fanciful. As already noted, Grassi senior was a migrant woodcutter who travelled seasonally to "a district near Grenoble." Perhaps in keeping with such embellishments, Wait also provided his readers with an interesting description of the geographical environment in which Grassi was raised. Falmenta itself is located at an elevation of some 715 metres in the Cannobino Valley, and the peak of the hill on whose very steep side it is perched rises behind the village to an elevation of 1,200 metres. Neither this nor any other hilltop in the vicinity, however, warrants a description of "mountains rising to heights of 12,000 feet." The highest summit nearby is Monte Zeda at 2,200 metres (7,200 feet), located about four and half hours on foot from Falmenta. Wait's references to "snowclad and glacier-covered mountains" are also questionable. There are only two peaks in northwestern Italy that might fit such a description: Monte Bianco/Mont Blanc (4,810 metres) on the Italian-French border and Monte Rosa (4,634 metres) on the border between Switzerland and Italy. Neither of these is within easy reach of the Cannobino Valley. We should also note that Wait does not include in his account the name of the "district near Grenoble" where Grassi worked with his father,

39 View across rooftops of modern-day Falmenta, to the forested foothills of the Cannobino Valley and beyond, and showing the older style of stone slabs used for roofing on some unrestored houses. Photograph by G. Scardellato, 2010.

making it impossible to know whether he experienced forested hill-sides and snow-covered peaks and glaciers while working as a migrant woodcutter.

The same imaginative leap was taken by another author who wrote about Lorenzo Grassi's early years. For the most part Edna Hill Apple-by, also a longtime resident of Canmore and former school teacher, repeated N.A. Wait almost verbatim, including his misspelling of Grassi's birthplace ("Felmenta") and similar idiosyncracies.[3] But not all of her account is simple repetition; she also notes that it was near Grenoble "in the glacier-covered mountains that [Lorenzo] became im-bued with love of the mountain peak country." In other words, she con-flates Wait's description of the environment of the Cannobino Valley (regardless of his accuracy) with "a district near Grenoble" even though Wait did not connect the latter with "glacier-covered mountains" and Grassi's "love of the mountain peak country."

Appleby then quotes, again almost verbatim, from Wait: "as a C.P.R. sectionman [Grassi] was located in the Lake Superior district, east of Fort William. He wished to be in the mountains and obtained a trans-fer to Hector, situated in the high Rockies."[4] For Wait the mountains were part of Grassi's personality, while for Appleby "he wished to be in the mountains," but both authors present the move west as Lorenzo's choice, a decision he made to relocate to a physical environment similar to one in which he had been raised.

In describing Grassi's youth both authors, as well as many who have written about Grassi after them, may have been influenced by their knowledge of his remarkable career in western Canada. That career naturally leads one to look for earlier hints of his later devotion to mountaineering or similar activities, and sometimes to overlook facts in the search for antecedents. One of the most detailed accounts of his early life, for example, names his birthplace as Falmenta but, inex-plicably, locates that village in Val Poschiavo, which is said to be near the Dolomites in Italy.[5] (It is in Switzerland, and a long way from the Dolomite Mountains, which lie on the Austrian-Italian border in Italy's northeast.) The Dolomites are famous for their climbing challenges, and that fame perhaps led another author to propose that Grassi learned his climbing skills in the Dolomites as an eighteen-year-old, from fa-mous Italian climbers, in the first decade of the last century.[6]

The motive for Lorenzo Grassi's move to western Canada, however, might be much more prosaic than has often been suggested. Certainly, the environment in which he was raised in the Cannobino Valley, with

40 Kicking Horse Pass, BC, looking east, 1887. Photograph William McFarlane Notman, VIEW-1647. Courtesy and copyright McCord Museum.

41 The CPR station of Field, BC, shown in the early 1900s. Mount Stephen rises behind the settlement, and the beginning of the approach to the Big Hill and the Kicking Horse Pass can be seen in the bottom-left corner of the photograph. Courtesy of Glenbow Archives, NA-1678–3.

its steep footpaths and challenging trails leading to the village meadows at elevations beyond the villages themselves, would have provided the young Lorenzo with ample opportunity to become familiar with life in an alpine world and to develop a keen appreciation for a well-constructed trail. There was also opportunity to engage in the climbing activity known in the world of mountaineering as "scrambling," that is, making unassisted climbs to the peaks of nearby hills (including the one that rises steeply behind Falmenta itself and separates it from the valley settlement of Gurro). To understand Grassi's move to western Canada, however, we need to ask questions that go beyond his early environment.

Grassi arrived in the Kicking Horse Pass area of Alberta and British Columbia from Jackfish, Ontario, in July 1913.[7] Most accounts report that he moved to Hector Station without mentioning where he actually lived. Field was the address he provided in a letter written a few months after his arrival in the west, but a post office box number is not very useful for establishing a person's residence. In short, we do not know what Lorenzo's accommodation might have been, nor where he stayed, during his time in the vicinity of the Kicking Horse Pass. Field is located on the western side of the Alberta-British Columbia border, in Yoho National Park, in the flat valley bottom immediately before the pass. Even in those early years Field was home to a small Italian presence, and it is possible that Lorenzo boarded with a family in the village. Or he may have been housed either in or around the CPR stations of Field or Hector: the distance between the two stations on the railway line is only twelve kilometres, an easy "commuting" distance by train, despite the steep challenge of the pass itself. At either location accommodation was available in company bunkhouses or in the specially built railway cars used to accommodate workers. Unfortunately, we can only speculate on the basis of a postbox address and a note of a dozen brief lines, with no specific information about either his work or his living arrangements:

Field, P. O. Box 161 B.C. Canada
10 November 1913

Dear mother and sister
With these two lines I bring you my news since I had not written to you in a long time. I enjoy very good health and I also hope that all of you are enjoying good health. I have received your letter but so far I have not written to my father. I hope you have received the Ł. 50 I sent in the month of June. It only remains for me to greet you and all relatives and friends.
And I am your son and brother

L. Grassi[8]

Other Falmentine emigrants in Canada, including Ignazio Tiboni, also wrote to Lorenzo at this post office addresss after his move west.[9] In fact, they sent greetings not only to Grassi but to "all of the companions," or to a group that we can only presume had also been transferred to western Canada, perhaps at about the same time as Lorenzo. A similar observation can be made from Edoardo Grassi's postcard from Mobert, Ontario, discussed in the previous chapter, which extended greetings "to the whole gang." Another postcard, from Giovanni Testori, was written at Ripple, Ontario, located 105 kilometres further west of Mobert. The area today is sparsely inhabited, and in 1916, when the postcard was written, it must have been just as dismal a worksite as Mobert and just as subject to frigid winters and mosquito- and blackfly-infested summers. The only access to the location was by train, and we can assume that the writer, like Edoardo Grassi, was stationed there as a navvy working for the CPR. The note is a reply to one Lorenzo had sent and is worth quoting in full.

Ripple August 14 1916[10]

After a long time I have finally received a card from you I had thought that you were dead or that you were there in the Trentino[11] to kill Poles now instead I see that you are still in Canada I realize you are still alive and that you still remember your cousin but if you wrote a little more often I would be much happier How are you getting on now? I have learned that you are no longer on the track[12] let me know where you are working? Here I regret that soon we'll have no beer or Wischi [whiskey] to drink but patience Nothing else to add except to return your greetings and hoping to receive your news often. Your cousin G.A. Testori.

Testori, as mentioned above, was the maiden surname of Lorenzo's mother Caterina. A Giovanni Testori had travelled to the north shore in 1911, where he named his friend Aurelio Bianconi as his contact.[13] The author of this postcard had, unlike Lorenzo, remained in Ontario and evidently was still working *sulla tracca*, or "on the track." Here, he expresses resignation at the prospect of prohibition, which, it is not hard to imagine, would soon remove the only form of escape from the conditions in which men like him were living and toiling.[14] Testori had learned elsewhere that his cousin had "left the track," and now the card he received from Lorenzo confirmed that the latter was no longer a CPR navvy; evidently Lorenzo had not conveyed many details about his situation.

These postcards, some from those who had made the transatlantic crossing with Lorenzo, others from those who worked with him or were relatives, make clear that Falmentine railway navvies often ended

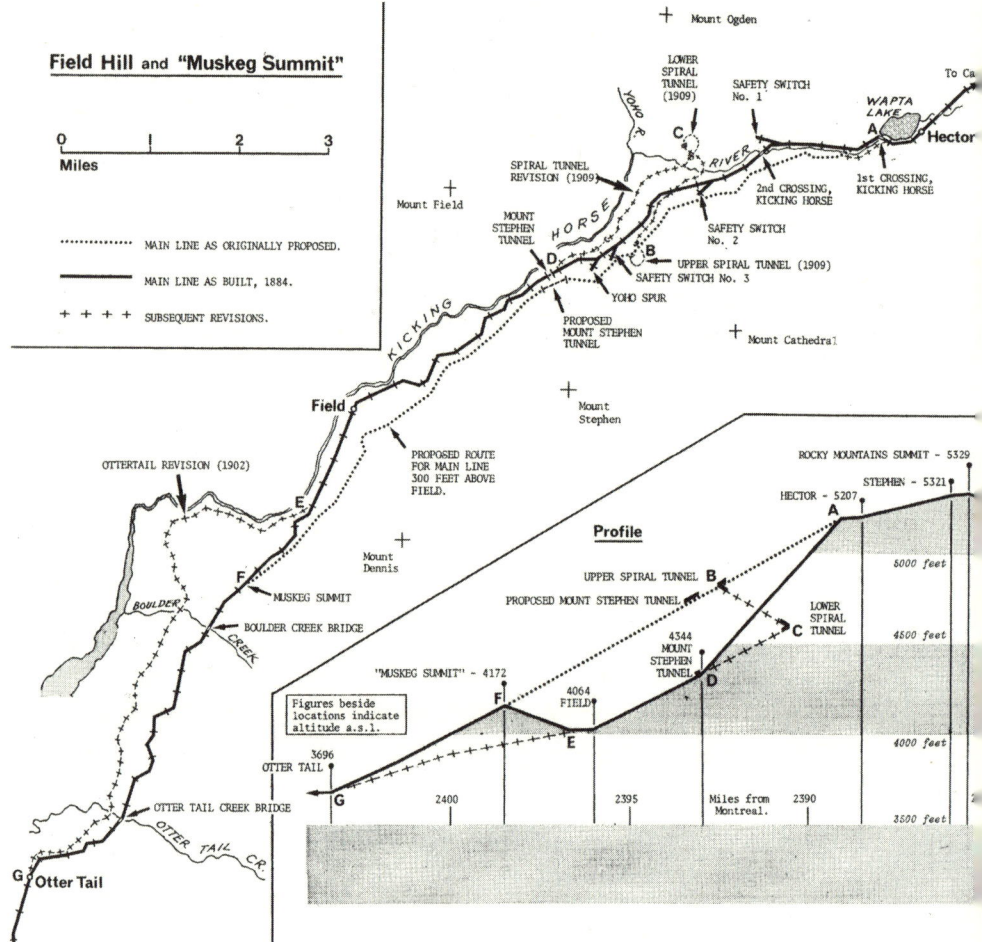

42 Map showing the location of Field, on the bank of the Kicking Horse River, in the flat valley bottom at the beginning of the Big Hill. Reproduced from Lavalée, *Van Horne's Road*, p. 191. Copyright Railfare Enterprises Limited. Used with permission.

up in very remote locations where living and working conditions were grim. Was Lorenzo's own move west motivated by the desire to avoid the wretchedness the letters describe, a desire to seek better working and living conditions? There is one piece of evidence that suggests Lorenzo's move to the Rocky Mountains may have been based on some knowledge on his part: his possession of a copy of a 1908 edition of Edward Whymper's *Chamonix and the Range of Mont Blanc*,[15] which carries on the reverse of its title page an advertisement for the Canadian Pacific Railway Company proclaiming its access to the "Finest Climbing in the World." We do not know when the book came into Grassi's possession, but it is the only evidence that suggests he had some previous knowledge of the mountains in western Canada. It might also be an indication that the mountaineering skills he would later display were based on more than trial and error. Grassi was not illiterate, and the Canmore house he bought and lived in for most of his life was, according to some, well stocked with books.[16] Volumes like Whymper's *Chamonix* could have provided him with information about mountaineering and similar pursuits.

There is some evidence, then, to support published claims that Grassi "requested" a transfer to the Rocky Mountains, but it is scant. N.A. Wait first proposed this idea, and he was echoed (in some cases with some elaboration) by those who published after him. Motivation for the move west, however, has been assumed: it has been read backwards from Grassi's eventual dedication to the mountains, which in turn has often been assumed to be rooted in the environment of his youth. If we posit instead that Lorenzo was simply transferred by his employer, this eliminates the need to explain whether he knew about the "the mountain peak country" in western Canada, or how, after only sixteen months of work as a navvy on the north shore, he was in a position to request a transfer, particularly in the middle of summer, the most important season for railway maintenance.

Another important question concerns whether Lorenzo Grassi travelled west alone or in the company of others, perhaps fellow Falmentines. We know that he was not the only emigrant from Falmenta to move to western Canada, but it is not clear whether these others preceded, accompanied, or followed him.

His move to the area of the Great Divide in the summer of 1913 is the first example we have found of Falmentines in Canada either temporarily or permanently settled outside of Ontario or Quebec. In fact, only in 1914, the year after his transfer, did destinations in western Canada

43 A photograph of a railway maintenance section gang sent to Lorenzo Grassi after he left Jackfish, Ontario. The worker standing in the front row, left, is foreman Aurelio Bianconi. Courtesy of Grassi fonds, Whyte Museum of the Canadian Rockies, v240-889(pa)028.

figure in the itineraries of a small number of Falmentines, ten of whom headed to Alberta between March and June. Counting those named as contacts, there were then at least fourteen Falmentines located in the province. There is no easy explanation why these Falmentines travelled directly to Alberta in the same year but only, apparently, in that year. They did not travel as a group, nor did they declare the same contact(s) at their destination, some of whom were relatives, in four cases either brothers or a cousin. Equally important, and also somewhat unusual, is the fact that at least two of these Falmentine travellers to Alberta – Aurelio Grassi and Agostino Grassi – would provide Lorenzo Grassi's family in Italy with a connection to their absent son (and brother and brother-in-law) in Canada.

Before World War I only a small number of Italian emigrants had reached Alberta. In the City of Calgary, for example, about 114 Italians, or roughly 3 per cent of the total population, were enumerated in the 1911 census. In other settlements in the area we can find at best an indirect link to Falmentines in the form of a number of emigrants whose origins were also in Piedmont, albeit not in the Cannobino Valley itself. This includes husband and wife Mario and Laura Trono, who emigrated from Piedmont and settled first in Canmore and then in the company town of Bankhead, Alberta, in 1904, a year after it was founded. The Tronos had four children: Mike, Dorothy, Anna, and Louis, who was born in Bankhead in 1909 and became a popular, well-known personality who performed as a musician at various venues in Banff and vicinity during a long and highly acclaimed life of performance.[17]

Evidence for a greatly increased presence of Piedmontese and other Italians in this area of Alberta, however, is provided by the 1916 census of Manitoba, Saskatchewan, and Alberta. In this source, and with the exception of Calgary itself, the highest concentration of Italian-origin residents was reported for the town of Banff, where most of those listed seemed to be employed in the service industry. Piedmontese, including various branches of the Trono family, were present in Banff and in a number of other settlements, including Canmore and Bankhead, but the now familiar Falmentine surnames also are well represented. The "West Calgary" district, for example, in 1916 included husband and wife "Peter and A. Zanni," their daughter Ida, and "Grassi, A.[,] ... lodger," who was a section hand for the CPR. Peter Zanni was listed as a section foreman for the railway. At "Eldon near Rocky Mtn Park [later Banff National Park]" the CPR was also the named employer for four Falmentines, two of whom were section foremen and the other two section men or navvies. The two section foremen were reported as having arrived in

44 Young navvies posing in a photographer's studio in Banff, Alberta, for a photograph to be sent home to Falmenta or to other friends, including Lawrence Grassi. Courtesy of Grassi fonds, Whyte Museum of the Canadian Rockies, v240-883(pa)027.

Canada in 1906, while the section hands had arrived, respectively, in 1910 and 1911. But we have no information to help us determine when they might have transferred to the vicinity of the Rocky Mountains, whether before or after Lawrence Grassi.[18]

The year of the census for the prairie provinces, 1916, was the year in which Lawrence Grassi moved to Canmore, but neither his name nor that of any other Falmentine is found in the enumeration for this settlement. There were, however, many other Italians in Canmore, and some of these, as noted, had emigrated from Piedmont. For example, this was the region of origin for the Massole family; husband and wife Ludovico

45 Members of the Mario and Laura Trono family and friends, c. 1915, on Muskrat Street in Banff, Alberta. Mario Trono is shown seated in the back of the automobile, with his daughter Dorothy in her mother's lap. Courtesy of Trono family fonds, Whyte Museum of the Canadian Rockies, v630/11(LC).

and Adelina were from Lessolo, close to the municipality of Ivrea. Their two children, Italo and Riccardo, were both born in Alberta. The Massole family, according to one local history, was the first from Italy to settle in Canmore, and this claim may be supported by Ludovico's 1902 arrival date in Canada followed by his naturalization in 1910.[19] Another Canmore family, that of John and Francesca Riva, were also originally from the Piedmont region, from Ribordone and nearby Sparone respectively, both municipalities located north and somewhat west of the regional capital, Turin.[20] Adolfo and Edirge Besso were also from Piedmont; he had emigrated from Lessolo, near Ivrea, in 1907 and in 1914 was returning to Canmore with his wife, who was from the municipality of Prazzo, located south of Turin.[21]

46 Photograph of Aurelio Grassi. Courtesy of Grassi fonds,
Whyte Museum of the Canadian Rockies, v240-877(pa)022.

Navvies and Coal Miners

Clearly, when Lawrence Grassi moved to Canmore he moved to a town that included a significant number of Italians, among them several families with origins in the same region of Italy as his native Falmenta. As we have seen, the postcards that Lorenzo received while based in the area of the Kicking Horse Pass or shortly after moving to Canmore strongly suggest that for a few years after he left the north shore he was not the only Falmentine employed by the CPR in western Canada. According to the 1916 census, other Falmentines were also present, working as railway navvies. At least at the beginning of his time in the west, then, he was part of a network of contacts, and this is confirmed by other correspondence preserved with his papers. For instance, in a letter to her son in 1926 Caterina Grassi reported that "Grassi Aurelio has returned from America": this was no doubt the same Aurelio Grassi, twenty-two years old, who had travelled in 1914 with his brother Giovanni to Calgary, where their brother Giuseppe had preceded them.[22] Lorenzo Grassi received a portrait postcard from "your friend always Aurelio Grassi" while he was still using his address in Field, BC, and by 1916 "A. Grassi," twenty-five years old, a CPR section hand, was a lodger in the household of Peter Zanni in Calgary West.[23]

A few years later, in April 1932, Caterina Grassi reported to Lorenzo the return of another emigrant, Agostino Grassi, who had visited Lorenzo "at his house," and who was returning to Canada with a salami she had sent for her son. This Agostino Grassi very likely was the same traveller who journeyed with his wife Maria and son Antonio to Calgary in 1914.[24] He was reported then as thirty-four years of age, one of the biographical details that connects him with Caterina Grassi's 1932 letter. In that year Agostino Grassi, by then listed as a fifty-two-year-old head of household, was recorded on board the Canadian Pacific's SS *Duchess of Atholl* on a trans-Atlantic crossing that began in Liverpool on 24 March 1932 headed for Halifax, Quebec City, and Montreal. His name was included on a manifest page for Canadian citizens, with place of birth given as Falmenta, Italy, and his address for his "previous" residence in Canada reported as Stalwart, Saskatchewan.[25] Residence in Canada was recorded as from June 1904 to November 1931. On this 1932 voyage Agostino declared that he was travelling to his employer, "C.P.R. Stalwart, Sask.," and he did so with a Canadian passport, railway pass, and one hundred dollars in his possession. Evidently, Agostino had been to visit Lorenzo Grassi in 1931, before his return to Italy in November of that year. He probably remained in Falmenta through early March 1932 and then returned to Canada.[26]

The surnames of these individuals who made their way to western Canada and were clearly in contact with both Lorenzo Grassi and his family in Falmenta raise the question of possible family connections. Regardless of Lorenzo's relation to Agostino Grassi, however, we do know that for a brief period beginning in 1931 and extending into August 1932 Lorenzo was in contact with his family. In fact, the visit by Agostino and the letter from his mother appear to have prompted Lorenzo to write, perhaps the last correspondence he would send to Falmenta. We know that he wrote home because in August of 1932 he received a letter from his niece and goddaughter Angiolina, in which she confirmed that they had received a letter from him. According to Angiolina, his family in Falmenta was pleased to learn from that letter that he was well and that he had received "the package that we sent you through Agostino Grassi" (presumably including the salami).[27]

Despite the Field postbox address that he used after his move west, Grassi probably was based at the CPR's Hector Station located at the top or eastern end of the Kicking Horse Pass, a station that no longer exists. Whatever explanation we accept for Grassi's relocation to this site, the fact is that Hector, at an altitude of 1,300 metres, was a notoriously bad place to be stationed. With snowfalls that were often several metres deep, winters there could be as brutal, if not more so, than on the north shore of Lake Superior, and the summers were even shorter. The railway line that ran west from Hector, close to the beginning of the "Big Hill" through the pass, was undoubtedly the most "treacherous" portion of the entire CPR main line. Men would be sent there "if they didn't measure up," according to some:

> Few returned unmarked, their tormentors would say, listing the grisly accidents, the cold and the endless deluges of snow that could bury a man in an instant. And the stories were mostly true. In 1885, the same year that Donald Smith drove the last spike, more than thirteen metres of snow fell on the Big Hill.[28]

Hector siding was located near Wapta Lake, some twelve kilometres distant from Field. A route for the CPR line had been surveyed orginally to follow contours through the pass to ensure that construction conformed with the 2.2 per cent maximum grade allowed for in the construction contract. This route would have required a considerable amount of time to complete, however, so an agreement was reached to permit the maximum grade to increase to 4.4 per cent. It was one of the epic chapters in the construction of the CPR. When first built, this railway tract was notoriously dangerous because of the steep grade over three miles of the line, which at 4.5 per cent exceeded even the newly negotiated maximum, with the remainder at a grade of 3.5 to 4 per cent. Although not the steepest in the world – a dubious honour held by the Central Railway in Peru – it was nonetheless the site of some horrendous derailments.[29] By the time Grassi arrived, the problem had been solved with the construction in 1909 of the Spiral Tunnels, which reduced the grade to an acceptable, government-imposed 2.2 per cent.[30] The decision to follow the route down the Kicking Horse Valley, however, provided access to what can justly be described as the most spectacular mountain scenery in North America. Lorenzo must have been awed when he arrived at Field, a feeling most likely tempered by thoughts of the job that awaited him.

Today passenger trains no longer stop in Field to let off or take on tourists and hikers as in Grassi's time, but it can be reached, if travelling west from Calgary, by driving along the Trans-Canada Highway past Canmore, through Banff National Park, and into Yoho National Park: an awe-inspiring experience for the first-time traveller through that part of western Canada. For a long stretch the highway runs parallel to the Bow River, which follows the majestic contour of the valley of the same name to Banff and Lake Louise. The drive from Calgary is a progression through the three fundamental geological elements of the Canadian West: the prairies, the foothills, and then the mountains. Between Lake Louise and Field itself is the Great Divide, the point at which rivers flow east in one direction, towards Hudson Bay and the Arctic, and west to the Pacific in the other. Field sits in the shadow of Mount Stephen, named after George Stephen, the Scottish financier who became the first president of the CPR and who was rewarded for his accomplishments later in his life by being named Lord Mount Stephen. The Kicking Horse River flows wide and shallow past the village here, in the flats, but fast and furious in the narrower canyons it has scoured through the mountains in its course down to the Columbia River.

When Field was chosen as a village site during the construction of the CPR line, it had an important function as a switching and refueling station before the trains began the steep climb up the Big Hill, or after their descent from Hector Station. A hotel, the Mount Stephen House, was built by the CPR in 1887 to accommodate the needs of travellers who disembarked at Field while the train locomotives were changed and serviced. It was much enlarged in 1901 to welcome tourists flocking to the Canadian Rockies, who would then venture out on hikes and excursions to a number of natural attractions in the area, such as Emerald Lake and Takakkaw Falls. Most of Mount Stephen House was torn down in 1953, and by 1963 it had disappeared completely.

A quiet little village now, Field is home to about 240 residents who live in town on the "need-to-reside" principle, that is, if their jobs somehow involve Parks Canada business. When Lawrence Grassi moved into the region in 1913, much of the town still had a "frontier-like" appearance, except for the "well-tailored grounds and old-world style" of the hotel.[31] Here he would have found himself in circumstances not entirely dissimilar from Jackfish. Like the latter, Field came into existence essentially as a CPR station and, just as in Jackfish, it had become home to a number of Italian immigrant workers, who had come to work for the CPR and in nearby mines. In time the Italian presence in Field grew, as the young men who had arrived in the area brought their brides from Italy and started raising families. A veritable Italian exodus occurred in the 1950s when the replacement of the old coal-fired locomotives by diesel engines made the Field stopover superfluous. Diesel-powered trains could travel through to Lake Louise and Banff without stopping – the same reason Jackfish and a number of other railway settlements were abandoned. Also, with the closing of mines in the vicinity, and the lack of school opportunities beyond the elementary level, families left Field and scattered far and wide through Alberta, British Columbia, and beyond.[32] Long before this dispersal occurred, however, Lorenzo had moved on both literally and in occupation, and possibly also in terms of his identity.

The decision to spend his working days in the dark bowels of the earth may appear an odd choice for a man whose love of nature and the mountains would become the defining aspect of his life. Perhaps Lorenzo had found his place in and near the mountains, and perhaps he wanted to avoid having another move imposed on him, if that was the reason behind his departure from Jackfish. Of course, the life of a section man was difficult, but coal mining, while it did not involve exposure to all kinds of harsh weather, was uncertain, subject to ups and downs, and was a more dangerous occupation. Given this danger, the shift from railway to mine could not have been motivated by a desire to obtain better working conditions. Perhaps of relevance is that a coal miner could earn considerably more than a railway navvy, especially during World War I, when mines were working at full capacity.

A Canmore Coal Company register of employees provides a precise date for Lorenzo's move to the coal mine: 12 September 1916 (fig. 47).[33] He was hired as a "helper," someone who worked alongside a qualified miner, a position which he himself assumed about five years later.[34] In his August 1916 postcard Lorenzo's cousin Giovanni Testori wrote that he had learned from Lorenzo himself that the latter was no longer working "on the track"; Lorenzo therefore had left his employment with the CPR at least a month before being hired by the coal company. The company register also specifies that Lorenzo had lived previously at "Staven," a place that does not exist on any map or in any historical atlas. This mystery – what or where is "Staven?" – has a plausible explanation. Throughout his life in Canada Lorenzo's speech was characterized by a heavy guttural accent that he never lost and that sounded more Germanic than Italian. This accent is evident in the interview recorded with him.[35] When asked where he had lived by an inattentive and not too inquisitive clerk, Grassi probably replied "Stephen," the name of the former siding in British Columbia, on the western side of the Great Divide and located next to Hector Station.[36] The recording clerk could easily have heard (and written) "Staven."

His new employer, the Canmore Coal Company, had begun operations in 1889. Canmore was a typical coal-company town of the Canadian West, but the settlement had been founded in 1883 as a division point for the Canadian Pacific Railway when it was constructed along the Bow Valley. By 1881, some time before the arrival of the railway, geological studies had revealed the presence of vast reserves of coal in the mountains west of Calgary and through most of southern Alberta. The first company to mine coal in the Bow Valley was the Cascade Coal Company, which began operations in 1883 at a location next to the Bow River, halfway between Canmore and Banff.[37] In 1887 it was the turn of the Canadian Anthracite Company (but based in Wisconsin) to open a mine at Anthracite in 1886, a few kilometres east of Banff, and at Canmore in 1887. This latter, called the No. 1 mine, was developed to exploit the reserves that sat astride the new CPR track. The Canmore location proved more promising than the Cascade and Anthracite mines, since its coal seams were thicker and less steep. Coal mining in the Bow Valley, however, was at a disadvantage in competing with coal produced elsewhere because of the steep angle of the coal seams, which made extraction difficult.

The method of extraction remained essentially the same throughout Lawrence's working life. It involved digging a tunnel near a seam, from which passages then branched out into the seams from which coal was extracted by men who usually worked in pairs. The passages they dug into the seams were widened into rooms whose ceilings were support-ed by pillars of coal, called the "room and pillar" method. The coal was removed from the rooms either by chopping it out with a pick – if it was soft – or blasting, which was set off by an electric charge. This, according to the information on Lawrence's pay slips in the 1920s, was part of his work, an indication of the high degree of expertise he had achieved as a contract miner after his start as a helper.

Once the coal was removed, the pillar or pillars were taken out and the "room" was abandoned and allowed to collapse. The men work-ing on the surface were responsible for the general maintenance of the mine. They delivered rails and timbers to the contract miners and they ran the machinery, such as the huge fans that pulled dust and gas out of the mines and forced clean air in, as well as the pumps that kept the shafts from flooding. They were "company" or "day men," who were paid a wage based on the number of hours worked. After being transported to the surface, the coal was weighed and checked for quality by a weighman who was elected by the miners them-selves. The content of the mine car was then dumped and the coal separated from the rock and passed over a screen, where it was sorted according to lump sizes: nut coal, pea coal, and slack (powder and small pieces). The coal would then be loaded into railroad cars and shipped to its destination. Miners were docked for "bone" (rock) or "slack," and sometimes fired if their coal was found to contain "bone" more than twice.

If the construction of a national railway linking the east and west of a country stretching from the Atlantic to the Pacific Oceans was a key plank in Prime Minister John A. MacDonald's vision of Canada, the presence of the coal deposits was a promising and providen-tially critical part of that vision. The CPR was the key means by which thousands of immigrant settlers would colonize the huge spaces ly-ing west of Lake Superior. An intimate relationship between the coal mines and the CPR was established when a coal-mining syndicate,

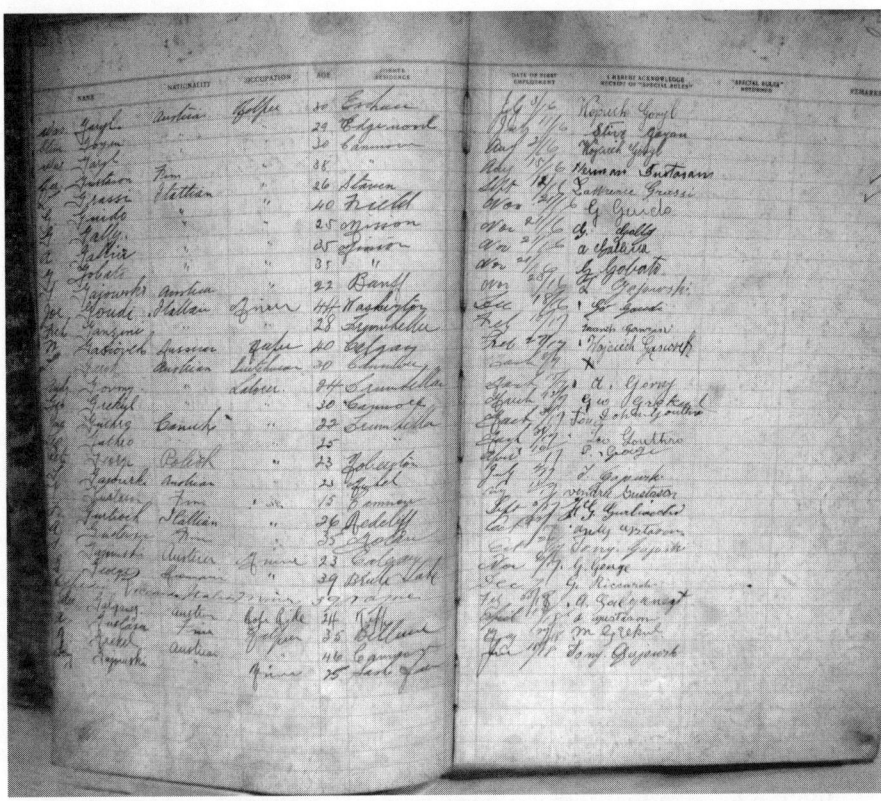

47 Page in the Canmore Coal Company employee register showing the entry for "L. Grassi," fifth line from the top, and the signature "Lawrence Grassi." He is listed here as twenty-six years old, Italian, and previously resident in "Staven." Courtesy of Canmore Museum and Geoscience Centre, Canmore, Alberta.

made up of British financiers and brought together by Sir Alexander Galt, one of the Fathers of Confederation and close friend of Mac-Donald, built a modern coal mine near present-day Lethbridge.[38] Despite the very generous government subsidies that had made the project possible, plus the building of a railway link to the main CPR line and a subsequent link to Great Falls, Montana, it was soon apparent that apart from the CPR itself, there simply did not exist markets for the coal produced by the many mines, large and small, that soon began sprouting in Alberta. Overproduction or, put another way, a limited market was just one of the chronic problems affecting Alberta coal. Another was that Alberta coal simply could not overcome the strong competition in the central Canadian market from Pennsylvania anthracite, since Canadian tariff policy was structured to keep fuel costs as low as possible.

As the CPR extended its line through the Crowsnest Pass from southwestern Alberta into British Columbia, beginning in the late 1890s, the huge deposits in that area also came on line. This was generally good bituminous "steam coal," with low ash content appropriate not only for steam engines but also for powering the smelters then being built in southeastern British Columbia. But even it had to compete with coal already being mined on Vancouver Island.[39] The coal produced in the Bow Valley, on the other hand, was of a poorer, lignite grade, with a high ash and moisture content, suitable for home heating, and was furthermore subject to deterioration when not handled properly.

In 1916, when Lawrence began working underground, Europe was in the middle of World War I, and Canada, along with other Commonwealth countries, had become a full participant on the side of Great Britain and its allies. The war effort by the Dominion of Canada resulted in a huge increase in coal production, and thousands of men were added to the labour force in the collieries. The fact that Lawrence became a miner at the height of the war was a reflection of a particular situation in an industry that otherwise was in a state of constant crisis. The sacrifices of the war, on the battlefields and in the factories, exacerbated a situation made even worse by the increase in the cost of living. Coalminers' unions, which had a tradition of radicalism, became even more militant in their demands for better wages and working conditions. One of these, District 18 of the United Mine Workers of America, to which practically all western miners belonged, called a strike in 1917 that brought production to a standstill for ten weeks. The strike was ended by the government's appointment of a coal commissioner, who had the authority to set prices and settle disputes, and peace was temporarily restored with a wage increase of 30 per cent. This brought a miner's wage to $4.50 for an eight-hour day, six days a week, and the rate for boys under eighteen to $2.00, for unskilled adult labourers to $3.50, and for powerhouse engineers to $4.70.[40] A special commission was also established by the Alberta government to look into and make recommendations to deal with the province's chaotic coal industry. The commission began its hearings in October 1919 and, at its public meetings in various towns and coal-mining communities, it brought to light a situation that was as bad as any in the world. What emerged in the testimonies of those who made their views known to the commission was the general squalor and poverty of the coal towns:

> Housing was generally poor, with families living in small frame shacks. Single men were often forced to pack their own blankets from camp to camp and live in overcrowded, unventilated bunkhouses. Indoor plumbing was unknown. Outhouses were allowed to overflow and foul drinking water. Water was sometimes supplied by cart or taken from dirty wells or directly from the nearest creek or river. Typhoid, cholera and other diseases related to poor hygiene were common. Company stores were accused of selling at outrageously high prices. School facilities for miners' children were poor and overcrowded at best, nonexistent at worst.[41]

Even while the commission was holding hearings, labour unrest escalated, with unions intensifying their demands for radical political and economic reforms. The Russian Revolution of 1917 and social upheavals in other European countries had their equivalent in North America. One manifestation of this increased radicalization was the movement to organize the One Big Union (OBU), a Marxist-inspired attempt to transform traditional labour groups into instruments for revolutionary change. Coal miners were generally supportive of the OBU. A strike called by District 18 in May 1919, against the directives of the United Mineworkers of America, who had the support of the mine owners, created a rift that caused the strike to collapse. The OBU movement lost that battle, but the struggle did not end there: unrest in the coal mines continued well into the 1920s. Strikes occurred regularly "every two years through the decade, the longest, in 1924–25, lasting for five months and resulting in a reduction in wages of thirty-three per cent – back to the 1917 level."[42] This was the general situation in which Lawrence Grassi found himself when he became a coal miner. There is no evidence that he participated in the labour struggles of the coal fields. Instead, he seems to have exploited the breaks provided by the strikes, and the frequent work stoppages, as welcome opportunities to explore and climb.

After switching jobs and during his first two years in Canmore, Lawrence boarded with an Italian family.[43] Then, in 1918, he bought a

48 Lawrence Grassi's home in Canmore, Alberta, long since demolished. Courtesy of Grassi fonds, Whyte Museum of the Canadian Rockies, v240-624(pd)1.

house from Steve Cherak in which he lived for the rest of his life.[44] "House" is a term that applies only loosely to what, from all accounts as well as many exterior photos, was a very modest dwelling, even in those days. It was built partially of logs, and Lawrence, as he now called himself ("Grassi" was an alternate signature), was content to live in it for the rest of his life. It was built on land owned by the coal company, a privilege for which he paid, according to company records, one dollar a month. This arrangement was a microcosm of life in Canmore, a typical example of a company town.

A Canmore Coal Company employee record for Lawrence Grassi dated 12 March 1943 lists his citizenship as "Swiss"; according to the same record, he had not been naturalized. How and why did Grassi end up being listed as Swiss? When he was hired in 1916 his nationality was clearly listed as Italian.[45] It seems likely that this switch in nationality occurred because attitudes towards Italians resident in Canada altered after 10 June 1940, when the Italian dictator Benito Mussolini entered World War II as an ally of Germany. In response Prime Minister Mackenzie King invoked the War Measures Act, as a result of which those of Italian origin in Canada who had been naturalized after 1929 (later changed to 1922) were labelled "enemy aliens" and came under the purview of the Defence of Canada Regulations. Individuals so labelled had their freedom of movement curtailed and were required, among other restrictions, to report monthly to their nearest RCMP headquarters. In these fraught circumstances it might have proven convenient for someone like Lawrence Grassi, by then almost thirty years in Canada but not natualized, to declare himself a citizen of Switzerland, which remained neutral for the duration of the war.

Lawrence's employment with the Canmore Coal Company lasted for some thirty years and, according to Jon Whyte, ended when Lawrence suffered an accident in 1945; the nature of the accident was not specified.[46] However, the employment card, originally compiled in 1943 but later updated, in which he was listed as a "contract miner," states that his employment ended in 1946. A later termination date also fits well with the facts about Lawrence's health and his financial situation in the late 1940s (see chapter 4). After his "retirement" he returned to work for the Canmore Coal Company for long enough to qualify for a company pension.

The Canmore Coal Company closed its mine in 1979, a year before Grassi's death. While most of its records were not preserved, some of

49 Pay slip for "L. Grassi" with the Canmore Coal Company, showing earnings and deductions for a twelve-day work period, March 1924. Courtesy of Canmore Museum and Geoscience Centre, Canmore, Alberta.

Lawrence's employment documents can be found in the Canmore Museum and Geoscience Centre, including a number of company pay slips in the name of L. Grassi.[47] From these it can be seen that as a contract miner Lawrence was paid by the cubic yard of coal he dug. The price is not always consistent. For example, a pay slip from 28 March 1924 shows that he was paid for eight yards at $10.28 per yard, and three yards at $9.99. Also listed is payment of $14.04 for twelve days' work, for a total of $126.25, which was then good pay for two weeks of labour. As well, the pay slip recorded some interesting deductions: blacksmithing (.25), powder (16.42), rent (1.00), water (1.00), wash house (.50), union (2.50), doctor (1.00), and check measurer (.50), an item not listed on any other pay slip. The net pay, therefore, came to $102.23, still a good sum for a working man in that era.

Of course, anyone who has not visited a coal mine, let alone laboured in one, can only imagine the working conditions. This is a topic not often mentioned in publications or oral stories about Grassi that focus on his mountaineering and trail-building exploits, glossing over what must have been a physically back-breaking, grinding existence. Sydney Vallance, a prominent member of the Alpine Club of Canada and its president from 1947 to 1952, started climbing with Grassi in the 1930s, and the two of them, the successful lawyer and the Italian coal miner, became good friends – an example of the unusual bond with people that Lawrence seems to have been able to establish. Vallance, according to Jon Whyte, described Grassi's career as a miner as "thirty years underground – 'often with water dripping on to his shoulders.'"[48]

As mentioned above, the story of coal mining in the West typically is one of boom and bust, and of frequent strikes, some of them long and bitter, particularly in the post–World War I period. This is reflected in Grassi's pay slips, which were not all as generous as the one previously cited. The 26 August 1927 pay for one day's work, for example, came to a total of $5.40 gross. After deductions for rent (1.00), water (1.00), light (.85), wash house (.50) and doctor (1.00), Lawrence took home $1.05. It must have been in such periods of little or no work that Lawrence set off for his outings or, with his pick and shovel and wheelbarrow, to build his trails.

The CPR and the Alpine Club of Canada

The working and living conditions, and perhaps the weather and much else besides, may not have been ideal for a section man working

50 Lawrence Grassi on unnamed peak. The climb likely took place after the
year 1918, which appears to have been painted on the rock in the foreground
and to Grassi's right. Courtesy of Grassi fonds, Whyte Museum of the Canadian Rockies, v240-651.

out of Hector and Stephen, but the Rocky Mountains apparently worked their magic on Lorenzo as soon as he arrived. As he himself remembered, he began his exploration of them from the very beginning of his stay in the area.[49] Whether he did so alone or in the company of others he did not say. In 1914 he went "into Lake O'Hara when I was working at Hector." The earliest photo of him from this period shows him in what appears to be a union office located perhaps in Hector itself, or in Field: a young railway man in his overalls looking at the camera with a rather bored expression (fig. 34). It's natural to speculate about his climbing activity in this early period: in the same interview he also declares that he took part in "only" four Alpine Club camps, the first of which, he remembered, was at Rogers Pass while he was still working at Hector station. This would place it between the summer of 1913 and that of 1916, and would establish the very significant fact that Lorenzo participated in the summer camps organized by the Alpine Club from the beginning of his move to the area. Yet Alpine Club records for camps in Rogers Pass contain no mention of his name until 1929.

It appears that Lawrence's memory was playing tricks on him, unless his participation in the camps was in some way related to his position as a CPR employee. It is possible that Lawrence was there as part of the considerable CPR contribution to the Alpine Club of Canada (ACC) camps after 1912. By coincidence, one of the two camps held in 1913 took place at Cathedral Mountain, in the Lake O'Hara Valley, on 15–25 July, roughly coinciding with his arrival in the area of the Kicking Horse Pass, and it is conceivable that this camp provided his introduction to the magnificent scenery of the area. In the following year the camp location was the Upper Yoho Valley, again quite close to Field and Hector, by which time, according to his own recollection, Lawrence had begun to explore and climb in the area. Not being a club member, he would not have taken an active part in the camp itself at this early date, but it seems possible and even probable that he was aware of the activities connected with it: the comings and goings of club members and the delivery of supplies, which were loaded on horses and delivered by packers. Given how close Hector station was to the Cathedral Mountain camp, we can speculate that he may have been deployed in a supporting role supplying provisions for the camp. It is highly unlikely that a CPR employee in the area, as Grassi was, would not have been involved in its activities in some way.

The 206 members who participated in the 1914 Upper Yoho camp arrived at the CPR station in Field. Arrangements were in place to take them to Takakkaw Falls, a journey of eighteen miles described in the *Canadian Alpine Journal* report as "the most beautiful part of the programme." Some members, however, preferred to walk from Field via Burgess Pass and the Wapta Highline Trail, while still others hiked to the site by way of Emerald Lake.[50] The number of those participating on this occasion, referred to in the report as a "small army," was average for an ACC camp. The camps were not very comfortable affairs: as described, they were spartan, with separate facilities for men and women and the two sexes meeting only for meals, afternoon tea, and, of course, climbing and hiking. The fact that women were allowed to become members and to participate fully in the club's activities was a significant departure from the practice of the English Alpine Club, on which the Canadian one was largely modelled. This feature was in great part due to the essential role Elizabeth Parker played in the ACC's founding, and in her tireless campaign for an autonomous Canadian organization.[51] The weather at the camps did not always cooperate, of course, and there are frequent references to rain and sometimes snow, as at the 1913 Cathedral Mountain camp. The camps were the occasions for new members to pass the test that formalized their entry into the club: to take part in the ascent of a peak under the supervision of either a professional Swiss guide or a volunteer guide.

In the 1914 Upper Yoho camp the two guides were Walter Schauffelberger and Conrad Kain. Kain was an Austrian guide who had conquered all the important peaks in the Alps and who was already a legend when he arrived in Canada in 1909. He had been invited to the Rocky Mountains by the founding president of the ACC, Arthur Oliver Wheeler, and took part in the annual camps for a number of years. One of his many first ascents, on 15 July 1916, was of Mount Louis, near Banff, a climb considered one of the most technically difficult in the Rockies, which he accomplished with another climber, A.H. MacCarthy. His words at the end of the climb have remained famous: "Ye gods, Mr. MacCarthy, just look at that: they never will believe we climbed it."[52] There is no evidence that Grassi and Kain ever met, but it is certainly possible that they crossed paths, in the relatively limited climbing community that existed in the years before and after World War I. It is striking, however, that Mount Louis became the mountain with which Lawrence Grassi's climbing fame is most associated: as we will see, he climbed it thirty-two times.

51 Mount Louis, view of the north face. Lawrence Grassi photograph. Courtesy of Grassi fonds, Whyte Museum of the Canadian Rockies, v240-624(2d)126.

The ACC was founded by Elizabeth Parker and Arthur Wheeler in 1906, and from the very beginning received support from the CPR as well as the governments of Alberta and Canada, all of which attempted in different ways to exploit the resources of the west, including tourism and mountain exploration. The CPR's contribution came in the form of mountain equipment such as tents and the services of two Swiss mountain guides for the camps.[53] The guides had been invited to Canada by the CPR, which of course had a vested interest in encouraging tourism and related activities such as hiking and mountaineering in the areas of the Rockies it had made accessible. The national parks system was inaugurated with Banff National Park (originally known as Rocky Mountains Park) in 1885 and Yoho National Park in 1886, in step with the building of the railway. At the same time the CPR, on the initiative of Cornelius Van Horne, had built or begun to build a series of hotels along the main line through the Rockies and the Selkirks to the west. These were modelled on the alpine resorts of Switzerland, and Mount Stephen House at Field was one of these. The Fraser Canyon Hotel at North Bend and Glacier House at the top of Rogers Pass were the others. They were followed by the Banff Springs Hotel in 1887 and Chateau Lake Louise, which opened as a chalet in 1890 and eventually became the most popular of all.

The Swiss guides began to arrive in 1899. The first two were Christian Häsler and Eduoard Feuz. From the beginning they tried to establish a certain tone: "Here were men in tweed jackets, with waistcoats and ties, wearing nailed boots and knickers with long wool socks."[54] Of course, not all local climbers adopted this type of mountaineering garb, least of all Lawrence Grassi. As the many photos of him show, Lawrence never went beyond the basics: hob-nailed boots, not infrequently common rubber boots, knee-high wool socks, denim pants held up by a belt (but not always) *and* suspenders over his rough woodsman shirt, and, of course, his rope and alpenstock.

The official organ of the ACC, the *Canadian Alpine Journal*, was first published the year after the club was founded. The lead article was written by Elizabeth Parker, who laid out the guiding principles of the club as follows:

By virtue of its constitution, the Alpine Club is a national trust for the defence of our mountain solitudes against the intrusion of steam and electricity and for all the vandalisms of this luxurious, utilitarian age ... It would be a great thing for young Canadians if all the automobiles vanished into space and walking for pleasure became the fashion.[55]

This idealistic vision, however, was somewhat at odds with that of the other founder of the ACC. Arthur Wheeler saw no contradiction between a desire to preserve the beauty of the wilderness and the CPR goal of attracting the largest number of visitors and tourists possible and of building high-quality hotels through the Rocky Mountains to provide its customers "with the luxury of an ultra, up-to-date civilization."

For its first few decades the ACC remained the preserve of "educated middle and upper-middle-class Anglo-Saxon urban professionals,"[56] practically polar opposites to those who peopled Grassi's world. A large number of its original members were born in England in the heyday of the Victorian era, and were imbued with imperialistic fervor, which spilled over into the pages of the *Canadian Alpine Journal*. For example, Julia Henshaw, the author of a popular book on the wildflowers of Canada, expressed herself in the following euphoric way in the inaugural issue of the journal: "There is no more beautiful, rich or varied alpine flora in the world than that of the British Empire and it is the proud boast of Canada that within her Western borders grow the choicest specimens of many mountain wildflowers."[57] Elizabeth Parker, in the same issue, expressed similar exalted patriotic ideas about mountain climbing and club membership, describing the latter as an "investment in nationhood, not of tears but of noble patriotic temper." The ACC, she added, "will, more than any national sport in the Dominion, weld together the provinces in the bonds of brotherhood; and furnish training in the more Spartan virtues of times of peace."[58] This noble-sounding patriotism was perhaps the reason, ironically, that membership numbers did not rise beyond a certain level, especially after the Great War. Patriotism was the heritage of the Victorian era, perhaps already out of step with the new social and cultural reality emerging in Canada.[59]

Despite Arthur Wheeler's tireless recruiting efforts and low membership fees of five dollars, businessmen, professionals, and civil servants persistently provided the bulk of the membership. Significantly, young people did not flock to the ACC, which continued to be governed by a uniformly middle-aged group. The conservative character of the ACC was reflected in its unabating reliance on traditional climbing methods after the war and into the 1920s and 1930s, ignoring and even consciously rejecting the revolutionary new techniques and equipment that had been introduced in Europe. Chic Scott goes so far as to declare, "While the world of mountaineering rapidly evolved, Canada was left in a time warp."[60] Grassi, although he remained a rather anomalous presence in the ACC once he became part of it, shared this disdain for innovation. The rope and ice axe remained the only tools he ever used in his climbs with, as we shall see, one exception.

By the second half of the 1920s the ACC establishment had come to recognize Lawrence as a first-class mountain climber and guide. His climbing had taken place over a number of years, probably ever since his days at Hector siding some ten years earlier. He had therefore honed his skills on his own before he was "discovered" and befriended by habitual participants of the ACC camps, who admired the Italian miner from Canmore and began to climb with him. It became apparent to them that, while he was in every sense of the word an "amateur" climber and guide, and thus fell outside the "norm" of the ACC, Grassi was the equal of the professional Swiss guides in the employ of the CPR hotels. Though no amateur guide was ever expected to be "as good as a good guide,"[61] Grassi would soon – and very dramatically – prove he was their equal.

The unassuming Lawrence was no doubt an unusual presence in the tradition-bound and generally middle-class cultural ambience of the ACC, but apparently he was well received. Over time he established relationships with some club members that continued for years, and in some cases a lifetime. The ACC camps usually lasted about ten days, and when he took part Grassi was given the task of guiding prospective members in their "graduation" ascents. Participants spent evenings around the campfire, an occasion for official speeches and reports by the officers of the club and prominent guests like provincial or federal politicians. There was also impromptu entertainment in the form of humorous commentary on the events of the day or week, readings, and other recitals. It is not easy to imagine Lawrence socializing on these occasions. It is more likely that he was busy preparing and coordinating the various aspects of the next day's climbing and guiding, an often frustrating task, but by all indications Grassi treated these responsibilities very seriously and was an absolutely trustworthy guide, as Margaret Fleming, Sydney Vallance, and others remembered.

The question of whether Grassi acquired his mountaineering skills before or after arriving in the area of the Kicking Horse Pass, as we have seen, is one that has not been settled with any certainty. What is certain is that the pass is located in ideal hiking and mountain-climbing territory, and Lake O'Hara – where, some years after Grassi retired from the Canmore Coal Company, he would be appointed assistant warden – is a stone's throw from the former site of Hector station. A 1926 article seems to be partly responsible for what would later become part of the Grassi mythology. According to this source "Mr. Grassi ... received his Alpine training among the Dolomites of the Italian Tyrol range." What exactly is meant by "Alpine training" is not clear. That the son of a poor peasant and migrant woodcutter who grew up in rugged foothill country could have had mountain-climbing "training" of some sort is not totally unlikely, but somewhat far-fetched if we understand this to mean some type of formal instruction. The reference to the Dolomites and Tyrol (parts of which were still Austrian territory in 1912, the year Grassi emigrated to Canada) can, on the other hand, be seen as a mistaken reference to Grassi's birthplace, Falmenta, whose surrounding terrain is quite distinct from the Dolomites. Further, these famous mountains certainly were not within easy reach for a poor boy from Falmenta, which is a long distance from the Dolomites.

This element of the Grassi mythology appears to derive not just from accounts of his life published in contemporary newspapers, as in this case, but also the accounts of individuals who knew him, for example, while he was assistant warden at Lake O'Hara.[62] One of these sources is credited with the claim that Grassi "occasionally spoke of climbing in the Italian Dolomites when he was a young man of 18 and 19 years of age. He said the rock there was very good – not the crumbling rock in the Rockies."[63]

The most likely supposition is that Grassi began serious mountain climbing after his arrival in the Rockies. According to Chic Scott, Grassi probably learned to climb in the Canmore area,[64] though to this we should add the time he spent in locations like Stephen and Hector before his move to Canmore. Grassi's own account of "going into" Lake O'Hara during this time could be considered the first step towards some type of tentative mountain exploration. And it is plausible to assume that his exposure to the ACC camps at Upper Yoho and Cathedral Mountain acted as stimulus to a more serious approach. It is worth noting that Grassi's reputation as a mountain climber was sufficiently well established by the time of his first ACC camp as to recommend him as an amateur guide for the club.

52 Sydney Vallance and Lawrence Grassi, summit of Castle Mountain, 1930s. Courtesy of Grassi fonds, Banff Museum of the Canadian Rockies, v240-712.

Louis Trono of Banff,[65] whose father got to know Lawrence soon after he "became a coal miner at the Canmore mine," refers to "another miner," Pete Ceruti (more correctly, Pietro *Cerutti*) from Canmore, who together with Grassi scaled "Cascade Mountain's vertical east wall where the waterfall can be seen." There is no mention of dates for this, or whether it was a first ascent, although that seems to be the implication. However, a brief note in the *Canadian Alpine Journal* attributes the first ascent of the east face of Cascade Mountain "just to the west of the waterfall" not to Grassi and Cerutti but to Grassi and Joseph Miskow, on 21 August 1934. As in other recollections of Grassi's exploits, Trono's account was faulty. Grassi's climbing with Cerutti had taken place years earlier, as we will see below.

53 Lawrence Grassi climbing the Eisenhower Tower on Castle Mountain, 1930s. Sydney Vallance photograph. Courtesy of Grassi fonds, Whyte Museum of the Canadian Rockies, v240-661. The same but hand-tinted photograph is claimed to have been taken by T.B. Moffat, according to the Moffat fonds, file no. S-20–5, Glenbow Museum and Archives.

"Mechanized Climbing" versus Traditional Mountaineering

Grassi's climb of The Finger in 1935, juxtaposed with Hans Gmoser's discovery some twenty years later of the cairn Grassi built on its summit, provides an opportunity to highlight a generational divide in mountaineering techniques. While Lawrence's achievements as a mountain climber were generally recognized, he also was part of a North American mindset that ignored and even rejected new techniques adopted by Europeans in the 1920s and 1930s. As Chic Scott states, "all the major summits had been climbed" in the Alps, and what remained were the more challenging "vertical walls of the Dolomites and the icy north faces of the western Alps," which, while more exciting, were riskier and thus required new techniques and equipment. In Canada the "mountain areas were wild and largely unknown," and mountaineering in the more traditional way satisfied the need to explore and "unravel the geography of wilderness regions rather than attempt the technical challenges of the period." In the middle and especially late 1930s it appears that this "time warp," as Scott calls it, was not just the result of a natural, organic evolution – or lack of it – but the product of a conscious cultural and even ideological position, and a reflection of a heightening political polarization as Great Britain and the western democracies faced the threat posed by the belligerent Axis powers, Germany and Italy.

A symptom of this situation is a review of a book by C.F. Meade titled *Approach to the Hills* (1940), in the *Canadian Alpine Journal,*[66] in which the new mountaineering techniques developed and practiced in Europe, with the proliferation of all manner of "mechanized" tools, are described as a war on the mountains in which the enemy "gives no quarter [and] all means are fair. Thousands of feet of rope, scores of hooks, clasps, pegs, wedges, stirrups, slings, hammers, pulleys, chisels, or anything else in the world that can be dragged or carried up a mountain, may be used; no manner of mechanical means may be rejected; this is the new spirit." Quoting extensively from the book, the reviewer summarizes the "absorbing drama" of the great ascents of "the gigantic cliffs of the Little Dru, the faces of the Matterhorn, the Grandes Jorasses, the Watzmann, each with its tale of defeat, death and final triumph culminating in horror ... on the north face of the Eiger in 1936" in a tone that increasingly emphasizes the almost fanatical "assault" on the mountain, even to the point of perishing in the attempt. The last paragraph makes explicit the ideological and political – and imminently military – significance of the conflict between the forces of "good" and "evil" facing each other, with the mountains as the all-important battleground:

It is important that the great exponents of mechanized climbing have been the Germans followed by the Italians. It has appealed only in a lesser degree to the French, and to the English not at all. At the moment of writing this, the forces that have engendered the art of living dangerously are in the ascendant, but to those to whom the mountains are friends, not to be defiled with hammer and piton, but approached with love and humility, there comes the words: "Blessed are the meek for they shall inherit the earth."

Did the position articulated here against the new "European" techniques by both the author of the book and its reviewer reflect the mindset of the British and Canadian mountaineering community? Resistance to innovation is suggested by the fact that Lawrence never used pitons again after the one he pounded into the face of The Finger in 1935. The Canadian Rockies had to wait at least another twenty years before young Austrian climbers like Hans Gmoser and others would spark a revolution in Canadian mountaineering with their training in this "mechanized climbing." Gmoser's rebuilding of Lawrence's cairn in 1956 seems like a symbolic and respectful bridging of an ideological divide that had been generated, in part, by tragic political events.

To prove how complicated these matters can sometimes be, especially in Grassi's case, there was another claim to a first ascent of Cascade Mountain in a letter to Jon Whyte dated 3 January 1990, seven years after the publication of Whyte's wonderful – but occasionally poorly documented as regards Grassi – book *Tommy and Lawrence*. In that letter the author provides a "snippet of information" that he admits "may or may not be of value": "Grassi's companion on the first ascent of Cascade's east face was a redoubtable Scot named W.J. Smith, who made many climbs with Lawrence in the late 1940s and 1950s."[67] The conflicting attribution is a symptom of the uncertainty surrounding Grassi's first or solo ascents over the years, the result of Grassi's own disregard for such things. According to some reports many of his solo climbs, "some of them undoubtedly first ascents ... were never recorded." One climbing partner states that, after reaching the top of Mount Charles Stewart, Grassi refused to sign the summit register, declaring: "I know I climbed it. That's enough."[68] Sometimes, however, the evidence of a previously unknown first ascent surfaces despite Grassi's lack of concern for official recognition. This is the case with a peak in the Sawback Range, twelve kilometres northwest of Banff, called "The Finger." Not a very challenging climb by the easiest route, The Finger, which is quite visible from the Trans-Canada Highway, was both named and climbed for the first time by Grassi in 1935. But this did not become known until two climbers, Hans Gmoser and Ken Baker, made it to the top in the summer of 1956. They thought they had just completed a first ascent, until they saw "a pile of rocks which might have easily been a cairn at one time."

The little mystery was solved in a 1963 *Canadian Alpine Journal* article that gives "amateur guide Grassi and party credit for the first ascent and the cairn." Based on a "1962 personal communication" with Lawrence Grassi, the author of the *CAJ* account also provides the exact route followed "from the high col on the east side," which he names "Route I." Grassi is also given credit for a second ascent, "this time from the southwest." This last climb, "though short, proved quite challenging," and is notable because it is the only occasion on which Grassi used a piton, an apparently isolated instance of experimentation with technique and equipment.[69]

According to Louis Trono, "Some time later [after Grassi's and Cerutti's ascent of Cascade Mountain] the duo made the first ascent to the peak of Castle Mountain."[70] This last climb is referred to in more specific terms in a *Canadian Alpine Journal* article by Ferris Neave entitled "Climbing at Banff." The "peak" in question was actually the southeast tower of Castle Mountain, and the ascent took place on 15 August 1926 according to Neave. Castle Mountain, in Banff National Park, is an impressive-looking massif, which rises on the edge of the Bow River valley, to the north and east of the Trans-Canada Highway halfway between Banff and Lake Louise. The massif was renamed Mount Eisenhower following the visit of the American general and future president in 1946, but was changed back to its original name in 1979. The southeast tower of Castle Mountain, however, somewhat lower in height than the mountain itself, retained the general's name, being called Eisenhower Tower. According to Neave, the Grassi-Cerutti duo "approached the peak via the amphitheatre to the north ... the final peak being thus climbed on the northwest side" (p. 90).

54 Lawrence Grassi on the peak of Mount Odaray, 1935, guiding an aspiring member of the Alpine Club of Canada, Ms Sadler of Calgary, one of many members who gained their membership under his guidance. Courtesy of Grassi fonds, Whyte Museum of the Canadian Rockies, v240-702.

Neave's article is a report on the 1929 ACC camp at Glacier National Park in the Selkirk Mountains, in which Grassi took part, as we also know from the membership card he preserved for that meeting. There is a fascinating account of that year's camp in the diaries of Margaret Fleming, another notable presence who was taking part in her first ACC meeting.[71] It is very likely that the route by which Grassi and Cerutti climbed Eisenhower Tower, described in Neave's article, was reported by Lawrence at the later camp in 1929. Jon Whyte's account of the event in *Tommy and Lawrence* adds a detail not mentioned elsewhere. Apparently a Dr J.W.A. Hickson and his guide "had long been intending the climb, but Mr. Grassi, without malice aforethought, and his companion knocked it off just days before the Hickson-Feuz accomplishment ... Dr. Hickson was certain his attainment had been usurped when he discovered the summit record, and Feuz could scarcely contain his client's anger."[72]

Pete (or Pietro) Cerutti was Grassi's climbing companion for some time in the 1920s. The surname alone connects Cerutti with Grassi's place of origin in the Cannobino Valley. Searching the records for an emigrant by this name who had travelled to western Canada by the mid-1920s, we find the most likely candidate was a twenty-one-year-old Pietro Cerutti who left Falmenta in April 1922, together with his sister Emilia (Cerutti) Zanni and her one-year-old son Pierino. They travelled on the SS *Dante Alighieri*, with their destination recorded as "Grand Coullee, S.C." where their contact was Giovanni Zanni, Emilia's husband. All three were designated as being "In Transit," that is passing through the United States, so their destination is best read as "Grand Coullee, S.C. [*sic* Saskatchewan]." Pietro Cerutti would have been about twenty-five or twenty-six when he climbed with Lawrence Grassi.[73] According to information provided by Falmentine descendants in Alberta, Giovanni and Emilia Zanni lived in Banff for some time; their two daughters were born there, and "apparently ... [the Zannis] were good friends with Lorenzo ... he used to pick them up [in his car] and they went on picnics together." The friendship no doubt extended to Emilia's brother, Pietro.[74] The friendship described between the Zannis and Lawrence is particularly important given that Emilia Zanni was one of several Falmentine emigrants who provided some type of link between Lawrence and his family in Falmenta. As we have seen, Emilia acted as liaison in the early 1930s during a visit to Italy shortly after the death of Lawrence's mother Caterina.[75]

Lawrence's participation in the ACC camps is an important element to bear in mind in piecing together his development as a mountaineer. By the time his participation in them was officially recorded, however, his achievements and his reputation had already been acknowledged by the climbing community. Lawrence's ascent of Eisenhower with Pietro Cerutti came about just a few days after a remarkable 1926 ACC camp during which his reputation took a leap forward. Up to that point he seems to have done a great deal of climbing alone or perhaps in the company of acquaintances like Cerutti or other local amateurs. But word soon spread about the Italian miner and his mostly solitary exploits. One of the tributes that appeared in the *Canadian Alpine Journal* after Grassi's death was written by Nan B.D. Drinnan, who briefly refers to the first contact between Lawrence and the Calgary

55 Pietro Cerutti, colour-tinted photograph portrait.
Courtesy of Nancy Wolfer.

section of the ACC community. It is typical of the tone of many personal memories of Grassi, and for this reason alone is worth quoting:

> I remember my late husband, Andrew Drinnan, talking about the Italian
> coal miner from Canmore who loved mountain climbing in his spare time.
> They started climbing together in the hills around Banff and Andy intro-
> duced Grassi to some of the Calgary ACC members. They climbed No 1 of
> the Three Sisters at Canmore (NE peak, first ascent, 1925, AW Drinnan,
> MD Geddes, TB Moffat,[76] L Grassi), some of the Sawback Range, Mt Edith,
> and made a traverse of the Rundle Peaks. Andy often laughed when he

told us how the day before the Rundle climb Grassi hid four bottles of Guinness in a small lake on Whiteman's Pass [perhaps one of the Grassi Lakes?] and then after the weary party returned from the long traverse he suddenly put his hand into the water and produced them. In the party were Alex Calhoun, and my husband and Grassi.[77]

If 1925 was the first ascent of the First Sister, it was not the last. Grassi would do it, alone or with others, many times after that. Glenn Reisenhofer quotes Don Gardner, who refers to Grassi's "wolverin-esque" enjoyment of climbing alone: "I do remember him talking fondly of his climbs on the First Sister and it seemed part of the attraction was that it could be done so fast and solo ... I forget how fast but remember being impressed that he would do this little climb with a 'before work' sort of feeling." Tim Auger, who knew Grassi and visited him in the Bow River Retirement Lodge, where he was confined, blinded by cataracts, in the last few years of his life, was impressed by how Grassi was able to describe "in detail the route on the lowest of the Three Sisters which Tim could see [through the window] as they spoke, but which for the aged man was only a dark blur. Later, when he made the climb, Tim found Grassi's description precise."[78]

The "Little Italian Superman" of the Rockies

Drinnan's introduction of Grassi to other Calgary ACC members was a sort of semi-official entry into the Canadian Rocky Mountains climbing community. In a newspaper report written on the occasion of Grassi's selection as a member of the expedition to scale Mount Waddington (discussed below), Andrew Drinnan is quoted as stating that he had met Grassi in 1923.[79] Whatever the date, the meeting was auspicious: the Drinnan "connection" was the beginning of important contacts and friendships that in some cases lasted a lifetime, and for Drinnan and Grassi a coming together of mountain enthusiasts that took on a special significance.

According to the same newspaper account, the "friendship ripened and in 1924 Grassi accompanied Drinnan to the Alpine Club summer camp, held that year in the Tonquin Valley." In fact, the Tonquin Valley camp took place in 1926; it was the first that Grassi attended, apparently at Drinnan's urging. The latter had passed the graduation test in 1921 during the summer camp held at the Lake O'Hara meadows. In July-August 1924 he and a small group of climbers that notably included the famed husband-and-wife team of Don and Phyllis Munday made an ascent of Mount Robson, the highest peak in the Canadian Rocky Mountains, guided by Conrad Kain, who had made the first ascent of the same peak in 1913 with Albert H. MacCarthy. This is clear evidence that Drinnan had become a very accomplished climber, given that, in Kain's opinion, Mount Robson was one "of the most beautiful mountains in the Rockies and certainly the most difficult."[80]

That Grassi had begun to climb with Drinnan and other members of the Calgary ACC is an indication of the respect and admiration he had earned. His climbing and guiding skills had led to his regular assignment as a guide for parties who undertook their initiation climbs for ACC membership during the camps he attended. He was moving in Alpine Club of Canada circles, and the extraordinary events of his first camp, held at Tonquin Valley in 1926, confirmed and indeed magnified his reputation.

The Tonquin Valley is located in Jasper National Park, near the border between Alberta and British Columbia, a rugged area over which looms the Rampart Range of mountains, which includes Barbican, Geikie, Turret, Bastion, Redoubt and Dungeon. The area is now a popular destination for backpackers and provides hikers with a series of spectacular views. Barbican and Geikie had been climbed for the first time two summers before, in 1924, by Val A. Fynn, a very skilled climber from St. Louis, and three others, including M.D. Geddes, who would scale the first of the Three Sisters near Canmore with Grassi in 1925.

In his description of the scaling of Barbican and Geikie for the *CAJ*, Fynn conceded that Geikie "does not present any serious difficulties ... There are many more difficult mountains in Canada. Among them is Mount Louis near Banff."[81] In fact, as we have seen, Grassi and Drinnan climbed Mount Louis together immediately after the 1926 camp, just one of the thirty-two ascents of the mountain accomplished by Grassi in his climbing career. Mount Turret, continued Fynn, "is without doubt the most difficult peak in the [Rampart] range, and I could see but one promising approach, i.e. from the southwest." The decision to scale Turret at the 1926 ACC camp was a response to a challenge by the president of the club, Arthur Wheeler. This is how Drinnan began his account:

On the afternoon of August 4th, 1926, after the annual meeting, Mr. Wheeler sounded a call to arms reminiscent of the Great Call to Arms twelve years earlier, by saying that he would like to have Turret or Redoubt

captured at that Camp and asked if Grassi and I had given the matter consideration. We both felt the honour keenly and had been turning the matter over in our minds but had not determined which to tackle.[82]

Wheeler's challenge to Drinnan and Grassi was issued because a few
days earlier they had given proof of their abilities by scaling Mount
Geikie. They accomplished this not by the southwest route used by
Fynn two years earlier, but the more difficult south-southeast route that
had been "suggested" by Fynn. Obviously, this ascent as well as other
climbs the two of them had been doing together brought them to
Wheeler's attention. That Grassi's presence was so prominently acknowledged by Wheeler seems on the face of it quite remarkable:
evidence that his mountaineering skills were now recognized at the
highest levels of the Rocky Mountains climbing fraternity. Wheeler
probably had heard of Grassi's exploits before the 1926 camp, but he
and the other members would have even more evidence of them on
this occasion. In fact, events during that camp would result in a much
wider public appreciation of Grassi than that provided by the *Canadian
Alpine Journal*.

Wheeler's challenge to scale Mount Turret, which Finn had referred
to as the "King-Pin" of the Rampart Range, was understood to involve
the first ascent of a difficult peak. Drinnan's personality, and the thrill
and pleasure of climbing with Grassi, are evident in his description of
the climb. He recounted all the joys that mountain climbers feel on the
occasion of a successful ascent: the perfect weather, the thrill of reaching the top, the enjoyment of the "substantial repasts" on the way and
back (no doubt prepared by Lawrence), the "magnificent appearance of
Mount Geikie, Turret and Bastion." He did not fail to make a passing
reference to his and Grassi's ascent of Mount Geikie a few days earlier,
not forgetting a sporting nod to "the genius of Val Fynn," who had
glimpsed a possible route to the top two summers before: "We looked
on Geikie and Bastion with a friendly eye, having had the happiness of
resting on their summits some days before and we hoped that Turret
too would be kind."[83] Mount Turret would be a successful first ascent
that took two days. This and other events at the 1926 ACC camp proved
to be the genesis of the "myth" of Grassi as the redoubtable mountain
climber, capable of extraordinary feats of strength and courage.

Two newspaper accounts of the 1926 camp in the Grassi fonds are of
particular significance. They were evidently clipped from newspapers,
perhaps by Lawrence himself, or they may have been sent to him. The

source of the first of these is clearly identified by its byline, "Special to the *Albertan*," a Calgary daily, and was published 5 August. It was this account that made the biggest contribution to the creation of the Grassi mythology. The second clipping had no identifying publication information, but we have been able to establish that it was published in the 5 August 1926 edition of *The Calgary Daily Herald*.[84] Both sources describe an achievement that would be included in virtually all subsequent accounts of Lawrence's life, but here we focus on the one published in the *Albertan*. The story was headlined "New Name Added to Roll of Honour of Alpine Clubs," and the subheading continued in a similar laudatory vein: "Lawrence Grassi, of Canmore Carried Injured Companion Two Miles Over Mountain Rocks. Deed Looked Upon as Great Achievement." The incident is best recounted in the words of the anonymous journalist:

> Tonquin Valley, Jasper National Park, Alta., Aug 5 – A new name has been added to the roll of honour of the Alpine clubs of the world, a roll already bright with many deeds of heroism, many examples of courage and fortitude. To this list is placed the name of Lawrence Grassi of Canmore, Alberta, who Tuesday evening carried on his back over two miles of treacherous rock and glacier, a companion who had been injured during a descent from the top of Bastion Peak, of the Rampart range.[85]

Near the peak of the mountain Robert Guy Williams from Calgary had suffered a compound fracture of an ankle, "under conditions which might have been serious had there not been present some one of such resources, strength and agility as Mr. Grassi." The danger consisted in the fact that the area is subject to unpredictable rock slides, and so to leave someone there while one sought help was to "court disaster." The story continued: "Mr. Grassi carried his unfortunate companion on his back down the steep slope, across the Drawbridge Glacier and beyond it to the foot of the rocks into timber line where he was met by the rescue party sent out from the main camp." The paragraph that follows is titled "The Full Significance," and elaborates on the dramatic aspects of Lawrence's action, stressing his daring and strength, especially in view of the

> type of country over which Mr. Grassi carried his companion ... The upper slopes are formed of shale and rotten rock, any piece of which is liable to give way at any time and precipitate the climber many feet down the

side of the mountain. Added to this is the always present danger of rock slides from above, slides that shoot tons of boulders down the slope with a sound like the discharge of field guns.

There follows further description of the terrain over which Lawrence managed to carry Dr Williams:

> The Drawbridge Glacier lies on a steep slope and is about a mile wide. Its face is seared with crevices into which any one but the most sure-footed could tumble to disaster. Below it again is a rock strewn slope of another mile or more, where boulders are heaped in great masses often higher than an ordinary house.

All this, the story continues, was done by Lawrence "with a speed that amazed even the most experienced members of the club ... It was a remarkable example of rock climbing that fully justified the reputation which Mr. Grassi has earned ... as probably the finest rock climber the club has ever seen."

The news of Dr Williams' rescue at the 1926 ACC camp reverberated far and wide, in fact reaching all the way to Falmenta and Lawrence's mother. In a letter dated 20 September 1927 (more than a year after the incident) she wrote to him: "I have learned that you have put your life in danger to save someone else. You have done a very admirable deed, though I regret it if you have put your life in danger too." The article, she adds, "was sent by a woman from Falmenta who has been in America for about thirty years[.] I was happy to get it to have news of you." This last is a sad and resigned comment by a mother anxious for news of her adventurous and now celebrated son, who was forgetful of his filial duties.The article, she added, contained his "portrait" (his photograph), and could not have been the one discussed above, from the *Albertan*, which did not include a photograph of Lawrence. This is further indication that the incident attracted attention, in that other papers probably also carried the story.

The story of Grassi's rescue of Dr Williams in 1926 on the descent from the peak of Mount Bastion was one of the central events defining the Grassi myth, although Lawrence played no part in the construction of that myth. As his mother's letter indicates, the story had a life of its own. Dr Williams, however, did significantly feed the mythology: in the years following the accident he continued to take part in the ACC summer camps, and around the campfire would frequently tell the story of the rescue, "never ceas[ing] to admire and praise as super-human the successful effort of Lawrence Grassi, who rescued him by carrying him on his back over a difficult section of mountain terrain."[86]

The same *Albertan* article is followed, if any further proof were needed of Lawrence's climbing skills, by a description of another "event of importance over the weekend, when, in association once again with Andrew Drinnan of Calgary and Hans Fuhrer, Jasper Park Lodge Swiss Guide, [Lawrence] made an ascent of Mount Geikie '10, 854 feet' in the record time of 15 hours. It was the second ascent of this peak." The first ascent, the reporter adds, had been made two years earlier in twenty-five hours. Significantly, Val Fynn, a member of the four-man team that made that first ascent of Geikie, was also a participant at the 1926 camp. Fynn had studied an alternative route, from the south-southeast, and advised Drinnan and Grassi, who followed that route successfully. The final paragraph of the article announces the planned ascent of Turret "later in the week by M.D. Geddes, Andrew Drinnan and Lawrence Grassi."[87]

Another article about the Tonquin Valley camp appeared in *The Calgary Daily Herald* of 9 August 1926, titled "Notable Climbs at Alpine Meet" and subtitled "Turret Peak Conquered by A.W. Drinnan, Calgary, and Canmore Man." It describes the just-ended camp as "the most successful" in the history of the Alpine Club of Canada, and continues with the description of "two outstanding climbs." The first celebrates the "conquest" of the "hitherto unclimbed" Turret Peak, "recognized as the most difficult of all the peaks of the Rampart range, and a climb comparable to any rock climb offered by the Alps of Switzerland." As in the previous article, here too Grassi is celebrated, and Grassi and Drinnan are described as "probably the finest pair of rock climbers the club has seen." Beating their record-breaking time, the report concluded, was "improbable."

The same article also mentions the achievement, during the camp, of the first woman to climb Mount Geikie, Esther Thompson of Winnipeg. It describes the departure from camp of most of the participants, who will "spend a few days at Jasper Park Lodge," while the "little Italian superman, who has distinguished himself throughout the whole meeting, is remaining in the Tonquin Valley for a few days in the hope of finding a partner to attempt with him the ascent of Redoubt peak, which up to the present has successfully resisted all attacks made upon it."[88] We are left to wonder whether Lawrence found a partner for an ascent of Redoubt. If he did, the attempt was unsuccessful, because the following year two climbers, "F.H. Slark and his inexperienced Swiss companion, Rutis Lauser," fell to their deaths in an attempt "to climb the virgin Mt. Redoubt."[89] What is not in doubt is that a few days later, on 15 August, Lawrence was back with Pietro Cerutti for the first ascent of the southeast tower of Castle Mountain, as described in Ferris Neave's "Climbing at Banff."[90]

The Calgary newspapers' celebration of Lawrence's deeds at the 1926 ACC camp is the apex of his life as a climber and all-round mountain man. This is the moment, one might say, when the Grassi myth is born, and while the praise might seem effusive from the perspective of today's alpinistic practices, it is clear that in the eyes of his contemporaries it was fully deserved. One might be led to wonder, however, why this should happen at this particular time, and what roles were played by the personalities involved in the creation of the Grassi myth. The answer can perhaps be found in another newspaper article in the Grassi fonds, worn and frayed almost beyond legibility, with two gaping holes in its middle and the last part missing. It was written before the 1926 ACC camp, and is titled "Two Amateur Alpiners Make a Daring Ascent." Its author was "Thos. B. Moffat," presumably, the same Moffat who wrote the Geddes obituary, but more importantly the same individual Nan Drinnan mentioned in her obituary of Grassi, published in the 1981 issue of the *CAJ*. The "Daring Ascent" in question is that of Mount Louis, described as "the most difficult peak to climb that one can find in our Canadian Rockies." As in the other two articles, the ascent is presented in language that borders on the epic: "These great slabs of rock rise almost perpendicular for 2,000 feet and one would think that even a fly would have a poor chance to climb on to part of this rock face." Mount Louis had been climbed before, of course, notably by Conrad Kain and Edouard Feuz (misspelled "Fenz" in the article) in 1916, and later by two others, including Val Fynn, who is quoted as stating that "as far as my experience goes Mount Louis is the hardest rock climb in the Canadian Rockies or Selkirks. Edouard thinks the same."

One might wonder, given the similarity of writing style, whether T.B. Moffat was also the author of the two articles discussed above, which elevated Lawrence Grassi from relative obscurity to the attention of a much wider public? Was this an honest effort on Moffat's part to give Grassi his due recognition? It appears that Moffat and Drinnan were promoting Grassi as a guide, but we know that Grassi did not accept payment for guiding, and so attracting more "customers," if this was the intent of the newspaper articles, would not have produced any tangible benefit for him.

Drinnan and Moffat were both members of the Calgary section of the ACC (as was another important Grassi booster and good friend, Sidney Vallance). Thomas Black Moffat was born in Fergus, Ontario, in 1870, and was therefore older than Grassi or Drinnan. At the time the articles were written he ran a jewellery and optician store with his brother in Calgary, but he had been trained as an engraver at the Chicago School of Engraving. He travelled extensively in the United States before returning to Canada, living in Toronto and Winnipeg and finally settling in Calgary. He joined the ACC in 1911 and served as its president in 1928, two years after the articles were published. He is mentioned in several of the official camp reports in the *CAJ* in the mid-1920s, and also published a number of articles in the *CAJ*. A photograph of him with some of the leading members of the ACC was published in the *CAJ* issue of 1916. Another one shows him standing in front of the Fay Hut, located in Prospectors Valley, in whose construction he participated actively – a very tall man, head and shoulders taller than Lawrence even though Lawrence is standing on a step above him (fig. 77).[91] In 1934 he and his wife "took a trip to Eastern Canada and the USA during which [he] gave illustrated lectures on the mountains of Canada and ACC activities."[92] Moffat died in 1939, and is commemorated in the name of Mount Moffat near Maligne Lake in Jasper National Park. He seems to have been a man who loved the mountains and spent a great deal of time in them.

Andrew Whitelaw Drinnan was born in Glasgow, Scotland, on 3 July 1888, and was therefore almost the same age as Lawrence. He emigrated in 1906, on board the SS *Sicilian*, which docked in Montreal. He was listed on the voyage as seventeen years old, single, and his occupation was given as "clerk." He travelled with a David Drinnan (forty-two), who was reported as "single" and so presumably was not Andrew's father. This may be an error, however, given that the first census of the prairie provinces carried out in 1906 contains an entry for a family consisting of George Drinnan and Catherine Drinnan, both thirty-nine, who had emigrated in 1904 and 1905 respectively; their six children; and David Drinnan (forty-four) and Andrew Drinnan, "son," then reported as eighteen years old. It appears, therefore, that the entry in the SS *Sicilian* manifest was wrong, and that David and Andrew were father and son. On 15 November 1915 Andrew enlisted in the Canadian army. His birthday on his enlistment form was given as 3 July 1888 and

56 Lawrence Grassi overlooking Lawson Lake, Kananaskis area, after a successful climb in the mountains he loved. Photograph, perhaps by Sidney Vallance, courtesy of Grassi fonds, Whyte Museum of the Canadian Rockies, v240(pa)667.

his next of kin as David Drinnan, but no relationship between the two was specified. His profession at this point was "purchasing agent." He died in Vancouver on 18 September 1976, where he and his wife had moved in the late 1920s.

The one common bond between Drinnan, Grassi, and Moffat was, of course, their love of the mountains and mountaineering. Drinnan continued to be connected with the ACC even after his move to Vancouver and to take part in ACC camps, and was club vice-president from 1930 to 1933. His patronage of Grassi was unceasing, and found official expression in the motion he put forward – seconded by Moffat – in a

57 Lawrence Grassi guiding a group of climbers on Mount President, Yoho National Park, BC, 1927. Courtesy of Grassi fonds, Whyte Museum of the Canadian Rockies, v240-726(pa)019.

report he gave to members during the 1931 camp in Prospectors Valley, Kootenay National Park:

> Mr Chairman, etc. I feel that all of us who have visited the Fay Hut could not but have been impressed by the fireplace which has been built there by our friend Lawrence Grassi. We appreciate very much all that he has done for us, not only in this particular instance but also around the Club House. We are very sorry that Lawrence is not able to be with us and I think we should send a letter to him expressing our appreciation of all that he has done and our hope that he will be at the next Camp.
> Seconded by Mr Moffat. Carried.[93]

Why did Lawrence not attend the 1931 camp? Attendance was generally poor during the years of the Depression, a fact that is mentioned in reports by both the president and honorary president of the ACC. Grassi could not have been exempt from the pressures felt by most working and middle-class individuals and families. The camp cost four dollars a day for meals and accommodation, and many people just couldn't afford it; for Grassi, who worked only a few hours a week when work was available, it must have been simply out of the question, although obviously he continued to climb. Perhaps his friend Drinnan would have hinted that in view of his volunteer work at the Fay Hut and the club house, discussed below, Lawrence should be extended a complimentary invitation. But the club itself had entered lean years: its general financial situation forced it to cut back on planned excursions, and even the journal suffered a cut of the thousand dollars the federal government had been providing for its publication. The CPR itself, the traditional supporter of the ACC's agenda and activities, found it necessary to rescind its special rates for travel to the camps. This latter alone probably would have prevented Lawrence from attending. At any rate, Lawrence would undoubtedly have refused a complimentary arrangement, just as he refused to accept payment for his voluntary services as a guide, whether at ACC camps or elsewhere: in the words of one writer, "Mr. Grassi would accept no reward for any special favour or deed."[94] Others had noticed the same: "If he had not saved sufficient money to attend camp, he would not go. Efforts were made at times to have him attend as a guest on account of his ability in guiding and climbing, but he would never go unless he paid his own way."[95]

A Mountain Logbook?

In his 1969 article "Grassi of Canmore," N.A. Wait referred to Lawrence's ascents of "many, many of the 'name' mountains in an area from the Rockies to the Selkirks" that were "listed in his *log book*" (our italics). This is a remarkable statement: there is no other reference in the literature on Grassi to a logbook, and if one existed, it would provide valuable, first-hand information that would fill the huge gaps in our knowledge of Grassi's climbing record as well as support his reputation as a leading climber of his time.

But did such a book actually exist? Put another way, is Wait a reliable source whose reference to a logbook can be accepted at face value? In his article Wait seems to have relied on his personal knowledge of Grassi in the heyday of his climbing and trail-building activity. (Wait was a resident of Canmore from 1922 to 1930.) He was able to obtain, no doubt through a personal interview, first-hand information about those years. While preparing his article he visited Grassi's home, where he observed "bookcases along the walls" and saw the life memberships awarded to Lawrence by the Alpine Club of Canada and the Sky Line Trail Hikers. It was probably during such a visit that he was also shown other materials in Grassi's possession, like newspaper clippings, and perhaps a logbook.

But if a Grassi logbook of mountain ascents existed, as Wait claims, why then was it not included with the other materials Lawrence donated to the Whyte Museum? We know that some of Lawrence's possessions did, in fact, go missing from his house over the years. People borrowed photographs or slides, for example, and never returned them. This was also the fate of one of his original cameras, so perhaps someone borrowed a logbook and never returned it. This is only speculation, however, and Wait's reference to a logbook can only be regarded as doubtful. We might, on the other hand, propose the existence of an alternative type of logbook. Lawrence was an indefatigable and accomplished photographer, and he produced a vast collection of images, including transparencies, of the mountains. In fact, he often entertained people with these images. His presentations, particularly of his slides, sometimes went on for hours, as Margaret Fleming for one recalls in her diary.

A Lawrence Grassi mountain logbook exists, then, if we shift our attention from a written record to a pictorial one; and some features of his mountain photographs support this suggestion. None of his photographs, for example, include people. This could mean that he took these photographs on his solitary outings, perhaps as deliberate records of ascents rather than as recording "views" as a conventional mountains tourist or hiker would.

The present arrangement of mountain photographs in the Grassi fonds at the Whyte Museum was established by Joe Clitheroe, a long-time friend of Lawrence, and Clitheroe chose to arrange them by individual mountain. As currently organized, for example, the collection contains numerous photographs of many of the peaks referred to above, from Cascade Mountain to the Three Sisters and from Mount Louis to Mount Waddington, and Mount Assiniboine, among many others. Unfortunately, the date of the photograph is rarely specified (probably because Grassi did not record this information). Nor does the present arrangement indicate the order in which they were organized when they passed from Lawrence to the Whyte Museum and Clitheroe. Massed together as they

58 Camera owned by Lawrence Grassi – a "Kodak 35 Anastigmat," model manufactured c. 1946–47 by Eastman Kodak – and now the property of Bill Cherak. Courtesy of E. Costa.

are, therefore, we are not able to compile an actual chronological sequence of mountains visited (and perhaps climbed) based on a photographic record composed by Lawrence himself. And because we do not know Lawrence's original arrangement, we cannot try to deduce the number of climbs from the sometimes multiple photographs of the same peak. For example, in Clitheroe's ordering there are thirty-nine photographs of Mount Louis, the peak that Grassi climbed thirty-two times, many of which no doubt were taken at different times, and thirty-four images of the first of the Three Sisters, which he also climbed multiple times.

If we discard Wait's claim about the existence of a logbook, therefore, we must fall back on the evidence, partial as it is, found in the *Canadian Alpine Journal*, newspaper articles, and other documents to trace Lawrence's climbing feats. The photographs and transparencies contained in the Grassi fonds are a precious resource that at the very least complement and support the written record of Grassi's mountaineering achievements.

Drinnan and Grassi were both immigrants from working-class or perhaps, in Drinnan's case, lower-middle-class backgrounds, with Drinnan's advantage being that he spoke English. By the time he met up with Lawrence he seems to have been well entrenched in the Calgary middle class. Might these two men have felt drawn together by their common immigrant experience, and by a sense of not belonging to the establishment? Another bond is perhaps evident in Nan Drinnan's memories of Grassi and her husband in her 1981 obituary of Grassi, which hints at an element of shared playfulness, and even mischievousness, between the two. This is also the tone found in the newspaper articles about Grassi, one and perhaps all of which were written by Thomas Moffat. It is obvious that Moffat and Drinnan were genuinely drawn to and admired Grassi and his mountaineering skills. What they perhaps admired even more was his down-to-earth quality, the day-to-day strength of character that from sheer love of the mountains propelled him from the hardship of a dark coal mine, and his simple cabin, and the loneliness he must have felt, to share the beauty of the mountains with those who followed him on the trails and who trusted his strength and his rope.

Ascents and First Ascents

Not all of Grassi's first ascents were recorded, as he was never overly concerned with such matters, except in the few cases in which he felt particular pride. And, as all mountain climbers know, not all first ascents are equal; no one was more conscious of this than Lawrence. Two first ascents that were recorded took place in June 1933, as reported in that year's *Canadian Alpine Journal* by anonymous participants on the climbs. The first of these was probably produced by Sydney Vallance, and describes the ascent of Mount Inglismaldie by its northwest face.[96] Vallance is listed among the group of climbers, all members of the Calgary section of the ACC. A photograph taken by him also accompanies the article. The group set out from Vallance's cottage located just east of Banff on Lake Minnewanka, which they crossed in a rowboat. Some time into the climb, while the group rested, Grassi "negotiated a possible route in his stockinged feet."[97] This outing was also the featured subject of an obituary note on Grassi, written by another member of the party, Margaret Wylie.[98] She describes the climb as "interesting … with some good bits, but nothing too difficult" since the participants "were not too experienced." The highlight of the outing, not mentioned in the 1933 version, was an encounter with a grizzly bear, which Wylie

59 Certificate of life membership in the Alpine Club of Canada, awarded to Lawrence Grassi in 1936. Copy courtesy of Bill Cherak.

remembered with humour: "Petrified, I thought, 'At least he has to eat Grassi first.' Natural not noble." As Nan Drinnan did in her obituary note, Margaret Wylie adds her fond memories of Grassi at Lake O'Hara and Lake McArthur in Yoho National Park.

The second of the 1933 first ascents was of Mount Ishbel,[99] in the Bow Valley east of Johnson Canyon, part of the Sawback Range that includes Mounts Louis, Edith, Norquay, and The Finger. This was also not a difficult climb, remarkable only for its loose boulders, scree, and rotten rock. On this occasion Sydney Vallance is not listed among the participants, although other members of the Calgary section were, and Grassi is recorded as having erected a "worthy cairn with a modicum of assistance" to mark the occasion.

Despite these clearly documented achievements, uncertainty remains about many of Lawrence's mountaineering activities, and this is not limited to the years *before* his introduction to the Calgary section ACC members. A number of first ascents are officially credited to him, but there are others that were never recorded, so that an official record of either first or solo ascents does not seem to exist. N.A. Wait mentioned Grassi's "log book" in which he kept a record of "many, many of the 'name mountains' in an area from the Rockies to the Selkirks" and of "many solo ascents of difficult peaks."[100] But as we have seen (see text box entitled "A Mountain Logbook"), there is reason to doubt that this logbook existed. Certainly some people who knew Grassi well – particularly Bill Cherak, who was closest to him in his later years – doubt its existence.[101]

That he did not keep detailed records is also implicit in the fact that there were times, according to Lawrence himself, when others claimed ascents that he felt belonged to him. During an interview in his later years, Lawrence commented on such a claim when discussing his first solo ascent of Mount Assiniboine in November 1925,[102] of which he was particularly proud. The mountain is located on the British Columbia-Alberta border and rises between Banff National Park and Mount Assiniboine Provincial Park. At an elevation of 3,618 metres, it is the highest peak in the Southern Continental ranges of the Canadian Rockies, as it rises a further 1,525 metres over Lake Magog. Its distinctive pyramidal shape has earned it the name "North America's Matterhorn." It towers five hundred metres above the surrounding peaks, and had been climbed for the first time in 1901 by a party of three. Even today, Assiniboine is not an easy mountain to reach; the guests of the lodge closest to it need to travel by helicopter from Canmore if they want to avoid a long hike to arrive within a few kilometres of its base. When Grassi reached the mountain he was not "figuring on climbing," as he said in the interview, and had only walked into the park alone "to see the country." That walk turned into a five-day outing. On the first day he walked from Canmore to Bryant Creek, a distance of some forty-five kilometres; he then walked to the base of Mount Assiniboine, where he made camp. On the third day he climbed Mount Assiniboine; "the next day to Sunshine [twenty-seven kilometres]; the next day to Banff [twenty kilometres] for a total of five days."[103] In the interview the elderly Lawrence makes a point of

60 Mount Assiniboine as photographed by Lawrence Grassi. Courtesy of Grassi fonds, Whyte Museum of the Canadian Rockies, v240-624(pd)487.

saying, with a tinge of resentment, that years later "somebody climbed alone, and they claimed it was the first time."

Grassi is generally credited with the first solo ascent of Mount Assiniboine. In the sometimes confusing and contradictory claims and counterclaims concerning such things, however, it is ironic that in one of the newspaper articles devoted to Grassi's selection as a member of the 1936 Mount Waddington expedition, his solo exploit on Assiniboine is denied him. The wording is a peculiar expression of admiration for what amounts to a failure: "Grassi's most spectacular achievement was a one-man expedition [sic] to 11,870ft. Mount Assiniboine, usually regarded as a difficult rope climb. He was turned back only a short distance from the summit."[104] This is the only instance we have found of a denial (notably, with no supporting evidence) of an exploit that is otherwise generally attributed to Grassi. The ascent was for him a high point in his climbing record and, while perhaps not exceptional by modern standards, it must rank as exceptional because of the matter-of-fact way in which he accomplished it. In fact he would climb Mount Assiniboine many times. In 1939 he did so with his employer, the president of the Canmore Coal Company, and on another occasion with James B. Conant, president of Harvard University, though he stated that on the latter expedition they did not climb all the way to the top. Certainly, Assiniboine is a mountain that Lawrence photographed time and again, as the many images in his collection show – a sign that it held a special place in his imagination.

By the 1930s, therefore, Lawrence had become one of the most skilled climbers in the Rocky Mountains. As well, the wandering and exploring that he had done on his own had given him a profound knowledge of the mountains around Canmore and Banff, and many sought him out as a guide. On this last point, however, Grassi demurred: "I was never a guide," he states during his interview. This is probably his way of respecting what he saw as the line that divided official guides from people such as himself who took on that role in an amateur way and were not paid for their services.

His disavowal of a guiding role does not stand up to testimonials from many sources, who sometimes refer to him as an "amateur" guide and sometimes simply as a guide. Although he did not have a guide's certificate, and never accepted payment for his services, the evidence very clearly suggests that he also excelled in this role. Sydney Vallance, in paying tribute to Lawrence, called him "one of the finest climbers and guides on this continent; the most modest and retiring of men."

Like others, he also praised him for qualities that went beyond skill, strength, and endurance: "for his expert guiding one had to resort to subterfuge to get his acceptance of even a token of appreciation."[105] One example of Lawrence's guiding ability, which inspired, in Vallance's words, "confidence [in] his firmness, authority and strength," took place in 1929 at the ACC camp at Rogers Pass, in Glacier National Park. In six days, Lawrence recollects, he "climbed" Mount Sir Donald five times.[106] The peak is the most prominent of the central Selkirks, and is described in the *American Alpine Club Climbers' Guide* as having the "ideal shape of a mountain, appearing as a towering obelisk with the great Northwest Ridge sweeping up from the left like a sublime balustrade." What Grassi either forgets or is too modest to mention is that these were guided ascents, and that as a guide he had to wake up at two in the morning to get gear and food ready to undertake a task that even today takes two days to bring off. In fact, a total of sixteen hours for the round trip today would be considered an achievement. Lawrence was able to do it in one day, but it meant coming back to camp late at night. Then he would do it again for the next day's climb, again rising at at two in the morning. What he does remember, as he recounts in the interview, is that he climbed Sir Donald a total of "ten to twelve times."

The Harvard President and the Miner:

James B. Conant and Lawrence Grassi

A "delightful trip together" was how the president of Harvard University, Dr James B. Conant, described his August 1939 two-day expedition with Lawrence Grassi to Mount Assiniboine in the Canadian Rockies. He did so in a letter to Grassi that included the scientific analysis of a fern fossil donated by Grassi to Dr Conant and Harvard University, an example of the way in which the humble miner sometimes crossed paths with figures of great historical significance.

James B. Conant (1893–1978) obtained a BA and PhD in physical and organic chemistry from Harvard (1914 and 1917 respectively) after graduating from Roxbury Latin School, the oldest boy's school in the United States, founded in 1645. After teaching in the Chemistry Department at Harvard, Dr Conant was appointed university president at the age of thirty-nine, a post he held for twenty years. During his tenure as president he transformed Harvard from a school that had traditionally catered to the New England elite to one of America's leading research universities, putting to an end a class system based on wealth and privilege. His aim was to provide equal access to education, a goal made critically important by the return to civilian life of eleven million young Americans after the end of World War II. This access was eventually achieved by the GI Bill, which opened the doors of colleges and universities to millions of people "and essentially created the post-war American middle class."[107]

At the outbreak of war Dr Conant had been called by President Roosevelt to serve as chairman of the National Defence Research Committee. He played a key role in the Manhattan Project and in the development of the first atomic bombs. With Fermi, Oppenheimer, Teller, and others he witnessed the first atomic bomb test at Los Alamos, New Mexico, on 16 July 1945. "The enormity of light quite stunned me," he wrote, leading him to fear momentarily that the explosion had triggered the thermal nuclear destruction of the planet, and which Oppenheimer commented on with the famous words from the Bhagavad Gita, the Hindu scripture: "I am become death, the destroyer of worlds."

The gift of the fossil fern was not an isolated gesture by Grassi, though no record of it exists anywhere except in this letter. When interviewed in 1971 Grassi simply said that he and Conant had climbed Mount Assiniboine, although not to the peak.

Dr Conant's visit is remembered by Nancy Lyall, manager of the ACC clubhouse in Banff from 1926 to 1943, in a long and moving note dated 29 October 1963, in which she reminisced about Lawrence's many kind and thoughtful deeds. She wrote of that visit: "I remember especially Dr. Conant, the President of Harvard University who told me on his return [from Mount Assiniboine] that it was the most enjoyable and worthwhile trip he had ever had."[108]

The letter from Dr Conant was written on 9 October 1939, two months after the hike: Conant apparently delayed writing until he had the scientific report on the fossil rock Lawrence had given him, which he enclosed. In his letter the Harvard president addresses his guide simply as "Dear Grassi," implying familiarity but also respect, and with a tone of genuine pleasure in the recollection of their time together, one of the more notable instances of the way in which the Canmore miner touched people.

If there are any dominant and common elements to emerge from these episodes in Grassi's mountaineering, they are the qualities of strength, steadfastness, and reliability, which is why people sought him out as a guide. No job was too big or too small for the little superman of the Rockies. This modest, unassuming coal miner knew he did not belong to the world of the rich and educated upper classes; they lived in separate universes. There were, of course, exceptions, but they were rare, as we have seen. His participation in the ACC camps was certainly considered useful, and occasionally also officially acknowledged. One such piece of recognition came on the occasion of the Mount Sir Donald camp in 1932, which took place on what was once the lawn of Glacier House, the first of the hotels built by the CPR in the Selkirk Mountains in 1887, just below the summit on the west side of Rogers Pass. Glacier House, now gone, was Canada's first mountaineering centre. The first Swiss guides had resided there when they arrived, but it had closed in 1925. In the president's annual report of that camp, Lawrence was given credit as a member of a "special party consisting of Mr. L. Grassi and Mr. C.A. Richardson" who had been assigned to prospect the feasibility of holding the 1932 camp at Mount Assiniboine.[109] (Their report was unfavourable because of the "great amount of overhead expense" necessary in the middle of the Depression.) The camp report contained another reference to Grassi (and also misspelled his name): "An outlying camp was established on the slope of the Dawson glacier, thanks to the heroic back-packing of Laurence Grassi and some of the camp boys ... From this camp Mount Hasler and Selwyn were climbed via Dawson glacier."[110]

This meeting in 1932 was addressed by Arthur Wheeler, president of the ACC from its founding until 1925, when he resigned that position and became honorary president, a position he held until his death in 1945. He was a much-respected figure, who had devoted his considerable energies and enthusiasm to the ACC, and whose members sometimes jestingly referred to him as "He who must be obeyed." It must therefore have been gratifying for Lawrence to hear Wheeler praising him to the assembled members at the 1932 meeting for "the very valued expert knowledge of Mr. L. Grassi [who along with guides Rudolph Aemmer and Ernest Feuz] have insured a full programme of climbing for all who desired it,"[111] particularly since Lawrence was all too often given credit solely for his "superhuman" strength. There is no overt indication that he minded the praise meted out simply for brawn, but the generosity that characterized his whole life, and his willingness to serve even in the humblest of ways, stemmed from an otherwise unexpressed desire to belong.

Grassi's name is also linked to Mount Waddington, once known as Mystery Mountain, which at 4,019 metres is the highest peak in the Coast Mountains of British Columbia. It had been spotted for the first time by Don and Phyllis Munday in 1925 from the side of Arrowsmith Mountain on Vancouver Island, about 225 kilometres away according to the Mundays' calculations. This was the beginning of an obsession that lasted a decade in the lives of this remarkable husband-and-wife team of mountaineers and explorers who "ushered in ... the golden age of coast exploration."[112] A few kilometres inland from the heads of Bute and Knight Inlets, the remoteness of the mountain made it extremely difficult to reach; once reached, it seemed impossible to conquer. The weather and the route conditions defeated the Mundays' first attempt, which required an "epic bushwhack" up the Homathko River.

Subsequent attempts involved the conquest of a variety of obstacles posed by the terrain, the long glaciers, the ice and snow, and the frequent and sudden storms that lasted days and increased the danger of avalanches; these also failed. Despite several expeditions over ten years, the Munday's most successful effort saw them reach the summit of the mountain's northeast peak, which they had mistaken for the main summit. They gave up after a last attempt in 1934.[113] In that year a young and promising twenty-six-year-old climber from Vancouver, Alexander Dalgleish, was killed in another attempt on Waddington organized by the British Columbia Mountaineering Club (BCMC). In 1935, the year after the Munday's last unsuccessful attempt, Richard M. Leonard, who took part in a Sierra Club of California expedition that also met with failure, asked what seemed a natural question: "Can Mount Waddington be climbed?" His answer was, as it was perhaps bound to be, a conditional yes: "given reasonable weather conditions it can be climbed ... It is the snow and ice on every ledge, the falling ice from far above, and the sudden storms that make Mount Waddington a problem that may only be solved in some season of extraordinarily long periods of clear weather."[114]

Then, in 1936, after various other unsucessful attempts following that by Leonard, Lawrence Grassi was given his chance to be among the first to scale Mount Waddington. He was invited to join a seven-man expediton that combined the efforts of the American Sierra and the British Columbia Mountaineering clubs; the invitation carried with it a very public recognition of Grassi's position at the top ranks of North

American mountaineering. (The offer had first been made to Don Munday, who was incorrectly quoted as having declared Waddington "unclimbable," but he declined because of what one newspaper referred to as "an earlier engagement.")[115]

Lawrence Grassi had been nominated by the Alpine Club to take part in the attempt to conquer Waddington, and his personal papers include a number of articles from Calgary and Vancouver newspapers that assign Grassi a prominent role in a venture that one of the newspapers referred to, hyperbolically, as "second only to that of [scaling] Everest." An article in the Calgary *Albertan* provided an extensive profile on Grassi that not only recapped the rescue of Dr Williams on Mount Bastion ("'Grassi is a superman,' Dr. Williams told the *Albertan*") but also made much of his many selfless trail-making efforts in the area of Canmore and Banff. Andrew Drinnan and Sydney Vallance were also quoted in praise of his exceptional mountaineering ability on rock and ice.

Upon arrival on the Franklin Glacier, at the foot of Mount Waddington, Grassi and the BCMC group met another headed by the Americans Bill House and Fritz Wiessner. Wiessner was a very experienced climber, who had honed his skills on some of Europe's most challenging peaks and had come to Mount Waddington with the latest European equipment: pitons, carabiners, "almost 100 metres of light rappel line for the descent," and "state of the art Eckenstein crampons."[116] Wiessner and House graciously allowed the BCMC climbers to go first, but what had promised to be the crowning achievement of Grassi's career ended just short of the summit. The climbers were turned back by the same obstacles of bad weather and difficult terrain encountered by all those who had preceded them. Ironically, the Wiessner and House duo, who had stepped aside just a few days earlier for the BCMC climbers, made it to the top of Waddington on 20 July shortly after the BCMC attempt.

Mount Yamnuska (officially Mount Laurie) was, according to Don Beers, Grassi's "favourite solo climb,"[117] but it is probably best described as his favourite solo scramble. An impressive-looking mountain whose south face is a steep and long (3.5 kilometres) limestone wall rising 350 metres over its base, it creates a strong first impression at the beginning of the Front Ranges of the Canadian Rockies. The south face is certainly a favourite of rock climbers today, as the many pitons embedded in it attest, but this face, insurmountable to ordinary people, can be circumvented and the summit reached via a reasonably easy hike or scramble. There is no reason to doubt that Yamnuska was Grassi's favourite solo climb, but we can also assume that, as a first-rate rock climber he probably circumvented the wall in favour of the scramble up the back of the mountain.

When asked what mountain he most loved to climb, Grassi never gave a clear answer. Without question, however, Mount Louis, the great spire first climbed by Kain and MacCarthy in 1916, was the one that Grassi most loved to share with people. Grassi climbed Louis a total of thirty-two times, as he states when interviewed by Elizabeth (Lizzie) Rummel and Ken Jones. It is a feat made extraordinary not so much for the technical difficulty involved, but for the sheer physical effort required. Louis was long considered a difficult climb, and even today it is not a mountain for amateurs, but many people who otherwise would not have had this thrilling experience were willing to place their lives in Grassi's hands. Such appreciation of Grassi's generosity in this respect is conveyed in a letter by Nancy Lyall, long-time manager of the old ACC clubhouse on Sulphur Mountain in Banff. Writing to Grassi when he was in hospital in Calgary for cataract surgery, she speaks in the name of "many members you guided up Louis & gave them the thrill of a life time ... there should be a medal for the few people like you but I suppose part of your reward was that you enjoyed the outings as much as your guests."[118] Her words clearly reflect the spirit with which Lawrence gave of himself by sharing his love for the mountains.

Lawrence Grassi's first ascents (even considering the questions and doubts about them that we may never be able to resolve) and other remarkable accomplishments such as his numerous climbs of Mount Louis made him in his day one of the most outstanding climbers in Canada, if not in North America. And as we have seen, the stories of his physical strength and skill as a climber abound. But neither of these appear to be the aspect of his life remembered best by those who knew him. What prompted the many personal tributes and accolades he received both while a mountaineer and later was his total experience of the mountains, the way in which he seemed to live it in all its manifestations, including both climbing and guiding. There is ample testimony for this in the many cards and letters from a variety of people, especially in his later years, which he kept to the end of his life and which are often moving acknowledgments of his expertise and generosity. People intuitively liked this simple, rough-hewn man who seemed to have been born to the mountains.

61 An older-looking Lawrence Grassi, posed in front of Mount Louis, which he climbed thirty-two times in his career as a mountaineer. Courtesy of Grassi fonds, Whyte Museum of the Canadian Rockies, v240-662.

But if Lawrence Grassi has an important place in the collective memory of residents and visitors to the Canmore-Banff-Lake Louise-Lake O'Hara region of the Rocky Mountains, it is his trail building that has to take pride of place. A solitary man all his life, whose passion for the mountains appeared to overshadow everything and everyone else, he nevertheless felt a deep desire to share their beauty with as many people as possible. When he was not climbing or working he was building trails, and one outstanding authority on Grassi's trails, Don Gardner, himself a Canmore resident, suggested an interesting comparison: "Every inch of his trails reads like a novel."[119]

4 The Trail Maker

Like his mountain-climbing exploits, Lawrence Grassi's trail making is not always easily documented. Even accounts by people who knew him and who witnessed or took part in his projects do not often provide exact dates, or provide only approximately remembered ones. Written accounts, published or unpublished, are sometimes strikingly and frustratingly misleading or else fragmentary. This is especially so in the case of his first major trail-building project, leading to Grassi Lakes on a ridge overlooking Canmore, as we will see. Much of his work has survived to the enduring enjoyment of Canmore residents or of tourists and hikers at Lake O'Hara in Yoho National Park and elsewhere. Much, however, has also disappeared, obliterated by time and the advance of modernity, or by bureaucratic decisions. What is left reveals much about a man who was complex and multifaceted, and whose withdrawn and solitary life revealed little beyond an almost total dedication to the mountains.

Such was Lawrence Grassi, coal miner and world-class mountain climber and guide, who generously led people to places they would otherwise never have reached, and when that was not enough he built the trails that eased their way there. The man whom Sydney Vallance called "one of the finest, if not the finest, rock climbers and guides of this continent" felt ill suited to play that part, or to exploit his talent for personal gain. Instead, he lived alone and modestly in the cabin he purchased in 1918, until he could no longer look after himself and moved into a retirement home for his final years. He was modest to the point of reticence as a chronicler of his own deeds, an attitude that reflected the nature of mountaineering in his day, as compared to the competitive sport it sometimes is today. It is instructive to consider the

62 Grassi Lakes, on Lawrence Grassi's trail from Canmore, Alberta, 2010.
Courtesy of E. Costa.

parallels with Conrad Kain (1883–1934), the great Austrian guide who
arrived in the Rocky Mountains just a few years before Grassi, in 1909.
Kain was also born in poverty and forced to find his way in the world
by dint of fierce determination. *Where the Clouds Can Go*, his autobiog-
raphy/biography edited by his great admirer J. Monroe Thorington,
depicted his life as a work of art dedicated to his love for the mountains. The book is also a detailed record of his every ascent of note on
three continents. But Grassi was not so fortunate as to find his own biographer, a fact probably attributable to his inability – and here he is
very unlike Kain – to overcome what could be called pathological shy-
ness, or a deep feeling of personal and cultural inadequacy that

63 Lawrence Grassi at work at the intersection of the Adeline Link Lake O'Hara Memorial Trail and the trail to Lake Oesa. Courtesy of Grassi fonds, Whyte Museum of the Canadian Rockies, v240(pa)626.

prevented him from feeling at ease in society. Also, and in this instance very much unlike Grassi, Kain had literary ambitions and had wanted all his life to be a writer.[1]

There is no evidence that Grassi and Kain ever met. Unlike Kain, as we have seen, Grassi left no record of his many first ascents, summing up his indifference in the lapidary statement "I know I climbed it; that's all I need to know," or words to that effect. The same can be said, regrettably, of his trail building.This indifference to fame had deep cultural roots; it sprang from generations of people for whom the mountains are not the arena for bravado or sporting competitions but the place where one is born and grows up, where the wood and rock they provide are basic elements of life itself. "Elemental" is in fact a characteristic that comes to mind when considering Grassi's life. All manner of sophistication or refinement, on the surface of it, seems to have been removed from him. Yet – lest one conclude that he lived a life devoid of artistic redemption – the Grassi trails, as we shall see, are the physical, material evidence of a deeply ingrained aesthetic vision that sustained him throughout his life. Not to be forgotten in this connection is his great passion for photography that he displayed from his earliest years in the Rockies. Hundreds of his photographs, of remarkable quality – significantly and uniformally devoid of any human presence – can be found in his personal archive in the Whyte Museum of the Canadian Rockies in Banff. It is always risky to resort to psychological speculation, but on this occasion there is little else on which to base an opinion, and so we will speculate, plausibly we hope, in an attempt to shed light on Lawrence Grassi the man and the trail builder.

The interview with Grassi recorded for the Whyte Museum by Lizzie Rummel and Ken Jones tells us little about Grassi himself, as if the interviewers were stumped by his seemingly stolid responses to the few questions they asked. Listening to it today, one can only feel frustration at the opportunity lost. Perhaps most galling is that nothing in the encounter engaged with what had been a major aspect of his life's work, his trail making. This is all the more surprising because when Lawrence carried out his trail work at Skoki Lodge in the 1940s, the lodge was run by Lizzie Rummel herself. And not long after the interview the bronze plaque that is now on the Lake Oesa trail and that honours Grassi for his trail work at Lake O'Hara was unveiled with Rummel and others in attendance.[2] Their friendship, in other words, gave her a great opportunity to delve into his life story for the record and for the benefit of those who would be interested in the future.

64 Lawrence Grassi and Elizabeth (Lizzie) von Rummel, Lake O'Hara, 1971. Courtesy of Rummel fonds, Whyte Museum of the Canadian Rockies, v554-1759-pa.

65 In the Durone district of Falmenta, a drystone-constructed baita or shed for storing hay and sheltering animals and their owners under a stone-slab roof. Courtesy of G. Scardellato.

Arguably, he was not an ideal subject for an interview. It is tempting to hypothesize that Grassi, who was not gifted in the expressive use of language, and who drove his mother and sister to despair with his silences, resorted early on in his life to expressing himself by means of the most elemental of materials: stone and wood. One of the people perceptive enough to grasp that words were not his forte was Dr George K.K. (Tommy) Link, who left his mark on the topography of Lake O'Hara with his own design and construction of trails over many years.

One could not find two more different men: the American academic and the Italian peasant turned coal miner, each of them living an intense, life-long experience with the mountains. "They respected each other," Whyte wrote, "but they weren't friends."[3] According to Whyte, Grassi's close friend Tim Auger described Link as "just a little envious of some of Lawrence's engineering" and reported that he commented on Grassi's trail work in a "slightly acrimonious" fashion: "Grassi comes from Northern Italy, and you know they make everything of stone there. No wonder he's so good with stone. In the Piedmont they make even clotheslines out of stone!"[4] In this light-handed reference to Lawrence's preponderant use of stone in his trails at Lake O'Hara, Tommy Link may intuitively have captured the essence not only of Lawrence's method, but also of his cultural identity; he had perceived that Lawrence had brought Falmenta with him, as a sort of deep memory of technique and practice passed on from generation to generation. Link was right that in Falmenta almost everything in the built environment was made of stone; and what was not made of stone was made of wood (as for example the Grassi home, before a recent restoration; see fig. 21). Stone was used for everything from the weight-bearing walls to the roofs, whose heavy stone slabs are a Falmentine characteristic. The letters his family wrote Grassi bear witness to the heavy financial outlay required when this type of construction requires extensive repairs.

At least as significant is that Falmenta's narrow streets and the pathways that branch off to reach the houses perched at a steep angle overlooking the Cannobino Valley are also made of stone, as are the many stepping stones, retaining walls, and trails leading to the outer limits of the village and to its neighbouring settlements and the world beyond. Street paving in Falmenta served both a structural and a practical-esthetic function, and was made up of stone slabs of various dimensions. Steps were sometimes dug right into the rock in the most difficult portions, with protective barriers in the dangerous spots. These were more often than not made *a secco*, that is, using the drystone wall technique that can be seen on the trail to Grassi Lakes as well as, even more famously, on the Lake Oesa trail. Falmenta's links with the other villages in the Cannobino Valley had only been made possible through the centuries by an extensive network of trails and pathways. But trails were also necessary to move animals up or down the very steep sides of the valley, according to the transhumance practised as the seasons changed. The majority of these trails have been abandoned because they no longer serve a practical purpose. But some trails – roughly 250 kilometres of them – are still maintained, because they have been deemed to have historical and cultural significance. They are clearly marked, and maps are provided for the benefit of weekend hikers and tourists.[5]

It does not seem forced, therefore, to propose a connection between the Falmenta tradition of stone and woodwork and trail building that Grassi had grown up with – and with which he probably had some practical experience – and his use of such materials in the Rockies. Many of the Falmentines who landed at Ellis Island declared their profession as "mason," which, given the topographical character of their territory of origin, included engineering practices that Lawrence himself might have absorbed and applied in his work, both in the coal mine and in his trail building. This became evident as he left his mark in the mountains of Banff and Yoho National Parks.

Grassi Lakes, Canmore

Lawrence's trail-building work extended over more than thirty years. The first evidence of it is a letter dated 9 September 1924 and signed by H. Price, secretary of the Canmore Advisory Council (for Geographical Names), expressing the council's "appreciation of the services you have rendered to the residents of Canmore by your untiring efforts to increase the comfort and pleasure of those who visit the sulphur springs." The letter also refers to benches and a table "personally erected" by Lawrence on the site of the spring, located not far from his cabin. The members of council, the letter continues, "hope to still further improve the grounds by making a bathing pool there." His "services will be very much appreciated," it continues, if he took it upon himself to undertake that task. Evidently Lawrence accepted the invitation: according to Edna Appleby, the bathing pool was built "under the leadership of Mr. Grassi," but was soon closed to the public "due to interference of government officials who declared it unsanitary … No pool being available, the children are still swimming in the backwash of the river."[6] In

66 Falmenta, Piedmont, staircase built using drystone technique to scale a steep hillside in the valley. Courtesy of *Atlante Toponomastico del Piemonte Montano*, facing p. 200.

67 Facing-stone work on Lawrence Grassi's drystone staircase, Lake Oesa trail, Lake O'Hara. Courtesy of G. Scardellato, 2010.

Don Beers' account of this work, Lawrence "dug a swimming hole, six feet down at the deep end. He trenched the effluent a mile to the Bow River so it wouldn't pollute the town's drinking water. Beside the pool, he fashioned a picnic table and benches ... When authorities in Banff found out what he'd done, they made him fill in the pool." In fact, Lawrence was officially informed in a letter signed by the park superintendent at the time, R.S. Stronach, who began by complimenting Lawrence "on the improvements you have made at these Springs." "The work done," he continued, "is certainly very beneficial and you deserve a great deal of credit for the public spirit and initiative in undertaking it." He added, however, that the resident engineer would be making a survey of Grassi's work and would "report concerning the question of the overflow from there mingling with the Mining Townsite water supply," after which Stronach would "take this matter up with the Canmore Advisory Council."[7] At the time Canmore was still within

68 Remains of bench built by Lawrence Grassi, Grassi's Lookout, Sulphur Mountain, Banff, Alberta.

Rocky Mountains National Park boundaries (which were moved a few kilometres west of the town in 1929 before the name was changed to Banff National Park). That the Canmore Advisory Council and park authorities had very different reactions to this work highlights how approaches to environmental issues in and around national park sites can conflict, which as we shall see is no less true today.

Lawrence was apparently undeterred by the setback, because the work at the sulphur springs was only the first stage of a more ambitious project: a trail that started behind his cabin and would eventually lead hikers to Twin Lakes, two crystal-clear and azure-tinted tarns hidden below Whiteman's Pass, between Mount Rundle and Ha Ling Peak, a distance of three kilometres from his cabin. He constructed this trail the following year, in 1925, with help from other miners, according to both Beers and Appleby. The chronology can be established on the basis of correspondence exchanged in 1960 between the Canadian

Youth Hostel Association, Mountain Region (CYHA) and other similar groups, on the one hand, and the Canadian Board on Geographic
Names in Ottawa. A letter dated 17 March 1960 from the CYHA requested an official name change of Twin Lakes to "Grassi's Lakes" for
the two little lakes to which Lawrence had provided access some thirty-
five years before.[8] The letter included a separate letter "by Mr S. Vallance
in support of this application" – which would appear with some varia-
tions as an article in the *Canadian Alpine Journal* in 1977 – describing
Grassi's work in glowing terms:

> Grassi saw that if these lakes could be made accessible to the people of
> Canmore, the miners and their families, a picnic place would be made
> available to many who might otherwise never see a beauty spot equal to
> it, and he set to work to make them accessible. But he was not satisfied
> with merely making the lakes accessible. The place must be made attrac-
> tive to the picnickers. The sheer cliffs of Mt. Rundle close to the higher of
> the two lakes heavily over-hung. He built dry-rock walls beneath the out-
> er edge of the over-hang, making open "caves," smoothed the floors and
> built stone fire-places, so that there were several good picnic shelters.
> Then he made seats, permanent fixed pole benches, for the picnickers.
> Week-ends and holidays saw them all occupied by groups from Canmore.[9]

Replying to the Vallance letter on 6 April, the Canadian Board on
Geographic Names noted that "the name Grassi Lakes, named after
Lawrence Grassi, well-known mountain climber and guide, had been
submitted to the Board for approval in a letter dated 9 March 1927 from
Mr. E. Mallabone, President, and Mr. W.M. Ramsay, Secretary, Canmore
Advisory Council for Geographical Names." To this the CYHA replied
on 16 May that these "lakes are known locally as Grassi Lakes, but since
the name may be confused with Grassy Lakes there appears some merit
in the name Grassi's Lakes or Lawrence Grassi Lakes." The last letter on
this issue, from the Canadian Board on Geographic Names to the
Geographic Board of Alberta, seems, despite some ambiguous wording, to decide the matter by endorsing the local use of "Grassi Lakes":
"In view of the mentioned local use, and board principles, possibly the
adopted name [that is, the name already accepted in 1927] could be retained. If acceptable to your office, we will advise the mapping office
that they might show the name on the next edition of the map." By
1927, then, because of a request submitted by the Canmore Advisory
Council for Geographical Names, Twin Lakes had become Grassi Lakes
both locally and officially.

69 Picnic site built by Lawrence Grassi (shown tending a pot over the fire) so that hikers from Canmore could find a place to shelter at Grassi Lakes. Courtesy of Grassi fonds, Whyte Museum of the Canadian Rockies, v240-809(pa)020.

These are the main facts and chronology concerning the naming of Grassi Lakes. But a new and significant element made its way into the Grassi narrative with the 1969 publication of N.A. Wait's article, and was continued in Edna Appleby's 1975 account of Grassi's life. Wait claimed that the naming of Grassi Lakes was due to no less a figure than J.S. Woodsworth, the charismatic first leader of the Cooperative Commonwealth Federation (CCF), and the prime mover and promoter of the name change.[10] As proof Wait quoted a lengthy tribute to Grassi given by Woodsworth in Parliament, which he attributed to the 1938 issue of the official Canadian parliamentary record *Hansard*, and followed by a motion of name change from Twin Lakes to Grassi Lakes.

This version of the Grassi Lakes story was repeated by Edna Appleby and picked up again by Jon Whyte, who also cited *Hansard* as a source.[11] The Grassi-Woodsworth encounter was certainly a significant one, because it gave the minister-turned-socialist "prophet" (he had been a Methodist minister) – an opportunity to create the image of the selfless, lone-immigrant worker who gave of his time and sweat for the good of the community. But it did not take place in the way these three authors imagined it, and certainly not in 1938 but eleven years earlier, in 1927, soon after the building of the trail and the subsequent renaming of Twin Lakes.

Woodsworth's account of his meeting with Grassi, as we shall see, became an opportunity for a social-political parable, and was presented as such in two separate newspaper articles. These in turn became the basis for a series of erroneous accounts of the naming of Grassi Lakes.

Woodsworth's first account was published in the July 1927 issue of the *Weekly News*, the newspaper of the Manitoba Independent Labour Party. Woodsworth had helped to found this party soon after the 1919 Winnipeg General Strike, and under its banner he was first elected to the House of Commons in 1921. In his article, titled "Study Groups and Holidays," he described his experience in Canmore, "a mining town in the midst of the mountains," where he spent a fortnight "under the auspices of the Miners' Union [conducting] a little school in history and economics and public speaking." At the end of the two-week course, he wrote, he and his family stayed on at the local Memorial Hall for "a fortnight's clear holiday."[12] He described "tramping up through Whiteman's Pass, then following the Spray River down to Banff" and "winding up with hot baths in the Sulphur Springs and a couple of miles more walking to and from railway stations." Of greatest interest to us was his conclusion:

> One of the most interesting men there is a miner, an Italian who came to Canada as a boy.[13] He lives alone in a vine-covered cottage surrounded by flowers and filled with books and pictures and mineral specimens. He is an ardent mountain-climber. Last year [he] rescued a man who had met with an accident, and has been honoured by the Alpine Club.
>
> Above all he is a trail builder. During a long strike some few years ago he went up into the hills ... and day after day made and cleared trails ... his fellow miners and villagers refused to follow his lead, but nevertheless honour him. Despite his modesty, they have renamed one of his favorite haunts after him, "Grassi Lakes."

70 Photograph by Lawrence Grassi of Twin (now Grassi) Lakes, from the trail in Whiteman's Pass. Canmore can be seen in the far distance. Courtesy of Grassi fonds, Whyte Museum of the Canadian Rockies, v240-624(pd)14.

71 Lawrence Grassi with visitors at his "vine-covered cottage." Courtesy of Grassi fonds, Whyte Museum of the Canadian Rockies, v240(pa)675.

Although Woodsworth does not overtly say that the trail that he and his family hiked through Whiteman's Pass was built by Grassi, it is clear that he is referring to this path, as the longest of the mining strikes was in 1924–25, lasting for five months,[14] which nicely dovetails with the time at which Grassi was building that trail. That Woodsworth described Grassi's cottage as "filled with books and pictures" is noteworthy. By "pictures" he probably meant photographs of the mountains, taken by Lawrence himself, a feature that other visitors had noticed. Others also mention his collection of books, though not in sufficient detail to determine what Lawrence's interests, besides mountain climbing and trail building, were. It is wholly in Grassi's character that he should open his house to Woodsworth. Sydney Vallance in his 1960 tribute to Grassi stressed his hospitality: "few people took the walk without calling at the little cabin of the man who had made it [the trail to Grassi Lakes] possible," adding that "in his lonely winter evenings he made walking sticks from saplings he gathered during his summer walks, and if a caller was without one he was invariably given one."[15] He may well have given Woodsworth and his family this type of gift, in addition to the one represented by the trail on which they hiked.

The second account of Woodsworth's 1927 summer vacation and his meeting with Lawrence Grassi appeared in the 23 September 1927 issue of the *Jewish Post*, published in Winnipeg. Its title was "The Trail Maker," and it opened by distinguishing between those who are content to summarize and interpret the work of others and those, the pioneers and prophets, who "break with established customs and launch out on unknown seas. A prophet cannot stand – even in a strategic position – he must push forward – in advance of the crowd. That's his job!" Woodsworth then launched into an inspirational call for "trail makers," using Grassi as an apt illustration:

The world needs trail makers! This summer I spent a month in a little mining town in the mountains. For me, the most interesting individual in the community was an Italian miner, Lawrence Grassi. He came into public notice two years ago when at great personal risk he performed a feat of strength and skill in carrying an injured Alpine climber to safety. But years before he was recognized in the community as being different from those about him. In the course of a prolonged strike instead of loafing about the village he set off into the hills, axe on shoulder, to make trails to points of interest. It was a labour of love.[16]

72 Plaque honouring Lawrence Grassi, at Grassi Lakes. Courtesy of G. Scardellato, 2009.

73 Lookout point at the top of the Grassi Lakes trail, with an explanatory plaque describing some of Lawrence Grassi's trail building. Canmore is visible in the distance. Courtesy of G. Scardellato, 2009.

The description of Grassi's trail making to Twin Lakes was something that Woodsworth probably heard from Grassi himself, as he had indicated in the *Weekly News* of two months earlier.

He loved the mountains: he enjoyed having others share their beauties. So day by day he pushed through the bush discovering the best ways of approach, blazing the trail, cutting out the undergrowth, grubbing out stones and roots, bridging the little mountain streams, hollowing out a basin for a sulphur spring, erecting ladder stairs over a difficult cliff. Safeguarding a dangerous precipice, placing seats on jutting lookouts that commanded a view of valley and falls, building a rude out-of door fireplace at a delightful camping ground; even placing a serviceable raft on the little lake in the pass so that its clearness and wonderful colouring could be better appreciated; then cutting a zig zag path up and up through grassy slopes and among huge boulders and into the green timbers until it emerged on the pony trail on Whiteman's pass.

In the experience of walking Grassi's trail Woodsworth clearly found an ideal subject to convey an inspirational message worthy of a gospel parable. Its significance was brought home to him, and hence to his readers, by the impact it had on his own children:

> Again and again we climbed Grassi's trail – until Grassi became for us a symbol – and an inspiration. One day we left the boys to play at the lakes. When we returned, they had dammed up a little stream making a new tiny lake. This they had cleared of branches and floating debris. For hours they had worked, and as we approached one called gaily, "Grassi's in the making!" Grassi had done more than build a trail. He had given an effective lesson in a way of life!

How does one explain the serious misreading of the Woodsworth tribute to Lawrence Grassi in Wait's article? How could he, above all, misdate Woodsworth's account of his stay in Canmore and his encounter with Grassi by more than ten years? It is obvious, given the exact repetition of phrasing, that he read Woodsworth's 1927 column in the *Jewish Post*, so why did he cite a non-existent *Hansard* account and not Woodsworth as his source? The most likely explanation is that he was shown the article by Grassi himself, who had in all likelihood obtained a copy of it directly from Woodsworth. As he did with other newspaper articles that referred to his mountaineering exploits, Lawrence no doubt clipped this one *minus* either the title or date of publication and put it away.[17] Many years later, Wait, unaware of the circumstances surrounding the naming of Grassi Lakes, and relying on fragmentary information, may have made a number of wrong assumptions. It was perhaps natural to assume that Woodsworth, impressed by Lawrence's public spirit, had mentioned him in a parliamentary context, and equally natural to assume that being praised in parliament by a noteworthy member had contributed to the high regard in which Grassi was held locally. Having made these assumptions, he may have found it easy to make another, that the naming of the lakes was part of the same process. Regardless of how we explain it, however, Wait's view that the naming of Grassi Lakes was a result of Woodsworth's supposed parliamentary action took on a life of its own, re-emerging in a number of published accounts.[18]

Regardless of later embellishments of the story of trail building to Twin Lakes and Grassi's recognition for this accomplishment, his work was appreciated by both residents of and visitors to Canmore.

Margaret Fleming,[19] for example, an ACC member, described being picked up by car along with three friends from Banff by Lawrence, taken to his home in Canmore, and setting off from there on what she described as "his four mile trail" to Grassi Lakes:

> He has made the trail himself in odd moments and it is well planned and built. Came finally to a particularly fine waterfall and then by a series of steps to the top where almost surrounded by sheer walls are two almost round small green lakes – They were so unexpected and so extraordinarily beautiful that we could only gasp. He has tables and seats built and a sheltered fireplace made so we had our lunch in luxurious comfort. Rain started and we retired to an enormous cave and built a fire, however, [the rain] soon stopped and after a rest we returned and he drove us back to Banff for dinner in the evening. He is a most shy and retiring individual and has acquired a great deal of knowledge about mountains, birds, flowers and animals and is a most ardent climber.[20]

Fleming's diary entry ends with a perceptive insight into Grassi's character – extremely shy and introverted – that many of those who knew him remarked upon. Margaret Wylie also remarked on his accumulated knowledge of mountain fauna and flora, which he had obviously made a subject of study: perhaps Lawrence had a few books on the subject at his disposal. The steps in the trail to Grassi Lakes to which Fleming refers are still in place, a particularly prominent feature of the Grassi style of trail making, present in his subsequent work at Lake O'Hara. They are an expression of his concern for the average hiker, and for making the ascent – and the view at the end of the trail – accessible to all. To his concern for accessibility we must add his ability to achieve optimal exploitation of the terrain and to choose the most natural gradient, a sign of his thoughtfully planned ascent with the average hiker in mind. The hike, in other words, is made pleasant not only by the expectation of the view at the end of the trail, but also by the experience of the climb.

Sulphur Mountain, Banff

Work in the Canmore coal mine was never a full-time occupation, and Lawrence often found himself with extended periods of free time. Strikes, as noted earlier, provided the most extended and frequent breaks. The work on the trail to what became known as Grassi Lakes, over which he seems to have exercised continuous upkeep, did not therefore interfere with his mountain climbing. In the 1920s, after years of climbing either in solitude or with Pietro Cerutti or others, he became much sought after as a guide among the mountaineering community. Thanks in great part to Andrew Drinnan, Lawrence also gravitated towards the Alpine Club of Canada even though, as previously noted, he was never completely comfortable with the club's Anglo-Canadian middle-class ambience. Soon after its founding the ACC managed through debentures and loans from its members to build a very attractive club house in Banff, on the slope of Sulphur Mountain on a "superb" plot of land leased to the club by the government.[21] It was a sturdy stone building, whose main floor was taken up by a spacious lounge or assembly room with a large stone fireplace. On the second floor were the library and writing room. Members of the club slept in "tent houses scattered among the trees," many of which were built by Conrad Kain, and at first the dining room was also in a large tent. In 1926 a committee was formed to provide the members with more permanent and adequate sleeping and dining quarters. The supportive response allowed a transformation of the facilities: over the next few years a number of cabins were built to replace the tent houses, work made possible by donations from individual members or from groups, such as the members of the Mount Logan expedition, as well as from various sections of the ACC. It was while this work was going on that Lawrence decided to contribute his trail-making and landscaping skills to the club's efforts. It was characteristic of him, according to Nancy Lyall, then club house manager, to labour quietly on the margins:

> While the building was going on, Lawrence Grassi was busy making paths and steps to the new cabins and the fine stone walk and steps from the driveway into the Club House. He also built a trail up the slopes of Sulphur Mountain from the rear of the Club House, with rustic benches at convenient intervals to a lookout point from which a very spectacular view of the Bow Valley is obtained. A walk to Grassi's Lookout is a thrill for our non-mountaineering guests. All this and more had been Grassi's gift to the Club.[22]

The chairman of the ACC also formally recognized Grassi's contribution in his report to the members at the annual ACC camp held that year at Maligne Lake:

74 Lawrence Grassi Trail on Sulphur Mountain, leading to Grassi's Lookout.

Laurence [*sic*] Grassi of Canmore constructed an elaborate rock garden for us, with very substantial steps leading from the Club House to the main pathway, which latter we were very much in need of; this construction would have cost us quite a sum of money. In addition to this he recently built an easy trail up the slopes of Sulphur Mountain from the rear of the Club House, with rustic benches at convenient intervals, to a look-out point from which a very comprehensive and spectacular view of the Bow Valley and surrounding ranges is obtained.[23]

Grassi's Lookout became a favourite of visitors. Margaret Fleming's diary entry of 19 July 1931 contains a brief reference to it: "Hoofed and investigated 'Grassi's Lookout' from which one obtains an excellent view of Banff and its environments."[24] Jon Whyte's brief description of the trail and its destination, and in particular his comment on the happy "deviousness" of the calculated dramatic effect obtained by Grassi's studied exploitation of grade and terrain, are acute observations of what distinguishes Grassi's talent as a trail builder, a talent he would display even more skilfully years later, at Skoki Lodge and Lake O'Hara. As well, Whyte describes Lawrence's work at the ACC club house as a symbolic donning of the legendary "Conrad Kain's mantle." This is high praise indeed, but Whyte immediately appends a regretful afterthought: "The Clubhouse is gone now, and very few people explore or maintain that silent way in the woods so close to Banff."[25]

The ACC clubhouse and all the guest cabins were eliminated in 1974 as a result of Parks Canada's controversial decision to eliminate private leaseholds in Banff National Park.[26] Consequently nothing remains of Grassi's rock garden and landscaping work on the site. As for the trail, its closure to the public in order to prevent further degradation of the terrain has meant that nature has been allowed to take its course. The lucky few who occasionally walk it can still see along the way the remnants of the rustic benches Grassi made, now almost completely rotted away. For those privileged enough to walk the trail, the experience provides a revealing insight into Grassi's approach to trail making, which would be fully implemented thirty years later in his six seasons as assistant warden at Lake O'Hara.

One more piece of handiwork by Grassi, which in this case demonstrated his skill as a stonemason, is mentioned by Margaret Fleming, but it too, like his work at the ACC clubhouse, is gone. During the same 1931 camp at Prospectors Valley Margaret Fleming also spent a few days at the Fay Hut, in Kootenay National Park, which had been built in 1927 by the ACC, and was used as a base for climbing the surrounding peaks. On that occasion, Fleming and her friends "did" Mount Hungabee, and were guided by Edward Feuz, her "first" such climb on the rope of a Swiss guide.[27] In her 24 July entry she describes lighting a campfire in "Grassi's new fireplace in the evening," which Lawrence had built after his work at the club house. The original Fay Hut burned down in 2003 as a result of a major forest fire, one more example of the disappearance of Grassi's handiwork. A new cabin was built in 2005 to replace the original one but in 2009 it also burned down.

75 View from Grassi's Lookout, Sulphur Mountain, overlooking Banff, with Cascade Mountain in the distance.

Bragg Creek

In pursuit of information about the next project to which Lawrence turned his attention, we turn again to Jon Whyte's book *Tommy and Lawrence*, but once again with a caveat. Whyte was not a historian, but a journalist and poet, and as he makes clear in the book's subtitle, *The Ways and the Trails of Lake O'Hara*, his primary concern is the trails Dr George K.K. (Tommy) Link and Lawrence Grassi constructed at Lake O'Hara. As a trail builder, Link was exclusively interested in the trails in the Lake O'Hara area basin – some of which he either built or improved – as well as in mapping the trail system, on which he worked for many years.[28] These efforts and their ample documentation produced by Link and others provided Whyte with a rich collection of sources that allowed him to follow the work of both Link and Grassi in great detail. Whyte, however, is sometimes less reliable when discussing Grassi's trails beyond those in the Lake O'Hara area, and the Bragg Creek project is one such case. The plan was to build a trail to connect a string of Canadian Youth Hostel Association (CYHA) hostels sited between Bragg Creek, about thirty kilometres west of Calgary, and Banff National Park. The hostels were, for the most part, simple, canvass-covered wooden frames provided for the use of hikers venturing into the mountains. Lawrence apparently heard of a gap of "about six or eight" miles remaining in the trail east of Canmore, and "without anyone asking him, set out to make the trail."[29] This work, according to Whyte, took place five or six years after Lawrence began to work for the Canmore Coal Company, which would date it as 1921 or 1922. The evidence, however, shows that this trail was built more than ten years later. The misdating is understandable: by the time *Tommy and Lawrence* was published, in 1983, most of the trail had been destroyed by strip mining and the construction of the Trans-Canada Highway, and for the most part only memories remained to guide research. Whyte based his account on one of Sydney Vallance's tributes to Grassi,[30] in which Vallance wrote of a gap of "seven or eight" miles in the trail that Lawrence heard about, prompting him to "quietly" go out to make "a good walking trail through the forest over that whole distance." Vallance wrote this in 1960, but he did not provide dates for either the Grassi Lakes or Bragg Creek trail work, although he briefly describes them in chronological sequence.[31]

Much more pertinent to the work Grassi did on the CYHA Bragg Creek trail is a first-person account by Joe Clitheroe, a member of the CYHA. Writing in 1970 in support of awarding a life membership in the CYHA to Grassi, Clitheroe recalled how, at the opening of a youth hostel "in the large house owned by Mr. and Mrs. Smedley in Canmore, it was inevitable that we would meet Lawrence Grassi, for he had a large collection of photo slides of mountains, valleys, rivers, forests and flowers, and Hostellers were frequent visitors to his home to see them."[32] Clitheroe's account unfortunately lacks specific dates, but the earliest records of the CYHA, kept in the Glenbow Museum, begin in 1933, by which time, according to Clitheroe, Grassi's reputation as a mountain climber and guide was well known to hostellers. This seems to fit with what we know from other sources about Lawrence's growing esteem as climber and guide.

Clitheroe's account of the completion of the gap in the Bragg Creek trail, which must be considered a more reliable version of events than the one by Whyte and more detailed than what is presented by Vallance, describes not a solitary enterprise on Grassi's part, but a group effort.

76 Construction of hostel accommodation on the Bragg Creek Trail, 1934. Courtesy of Glenbow Archives, NA-2468-36.

Once the Canmore hostel was started, according to Clitheroe, there was a need to connect it with the Seebe hostel, "which consisted of two tee-pees belonging to Soapy Smith and which were situated on the banks of the Kananaskis River," a distance of about twenty-five kilometres. The decision to complete the trail was taken, the route was surveyed, and it was decided to "clear the trail on the south side of the Bow River." The work did not necessarily involve the building of a whole new trail, but rather took advantage as much as possible of pre-existing trails. Nonetheless, it was not an easy task, according to Clitheroe: "As the distance was too great to hike and clear bush over just a week-end, Grassi would drive his car down from Canmore to a spot where he would build a raft of logs big enough for two people. He would then ferry one person at a time across the fast flowing Bow River along with the axes and shovels, mattocks and, of course, lunches."

Those ferried across the river would then set to work on the trail, proceeding downstream. Joe Clitheroe travelled downstream on the raft to where another group – presumably working on the other end – were waiting. At the end of the day it was again Grassi's task to ferry the men back across the river to a waiting car, after which "he would drive back to Canmore, and we would come back to Calgary." There is no record of the time it took to complete the trail, but considering its length, and the complicated and labour-intensive nature of the work, it must have taken up most of one summer, and perhaps more. Time, and the construction of the Trans-Canada Highway, which has been widened to four paved lanes over the years, has all but erased any trace of the Bragg Creek Trail, but Don Gardner, who helped design the cross-country ski trails for the 1988 Calgary Winter Olympics in Canmore, and who is a leading authority on the subject of Rocky Mountains trails, remembers "a beautiful retaining wall on the trail towards Jumping Pound Creek" in the direction of the foothills, now also gone.[33]

Skoki Lodge and Lake Merlin

Almost a decade later Lawrence went to work to build another trail. Among his friends was Elizabeth (Lizzie) von Rummel, the "Baroness of the Rockies," who managed and then owned Sunburst Lake Camp at the foot of Mount Assiniboine in the 1930s. When Grassi retired as a miner, she had recently taken over the management of Skoki Lodge, a log chalet built in 1930–31 in a very attractive spot off the beaten track northeast of Lake Louise. One of the first commercial ski operations in the Rocky Mountains, it was managed by Peter and Catharine Whyte

77 Lawrence Grassi with one of the Swiss guide brothers, either Edward or Walter Feuz in the doorway, and ACC member Thomas B. Moffat at the Alpine Club of Canada's Fay Hut, c. 1927. Courtesy of Grassi fonds, Whyte Museum of the Canadian Rockies, v240-624(pd)464. This photograph also appears in the Moffat fonds, Glenbow Archives, file no. S-20-52, but without an attribution.

from 1931 to 1933, and was reached via an eleven-kilometre trail. Lawrence probably began to help with odd chores at the lodge, but he "worked on many trails in the Skoki area and added a new woodshed to the structures in the camp itself. The level trail across the scree slopes on the approach to Merlin Lake was one of his projects."[34] This trail began in front of Skoki Lodge, on a log bridge that Grassi built across Skoki Creek, and moved off towards Lake Merlin, a "little-known gem of the Rockies."[35] The lake is situated in a cirque nestled between the so-called Wall of Jericho, Merlin's Castle, and Mount Richardson and is reached "principally by a route up through the avalanche slopes that descend from Merlin Peak to Castilleja Lake,"[36] a distance of about two and a half kilometres. Lawrence felt that the lake deserved to be made more accessible than it was. The task involved "a great deal of movement of the rubble" on the avalanche slope, but the result was a more natural route to Lake Merlin along "a trail of the sort which O'Hara visitors will recognize at once as an exemplar of the Grassi style."[37] As Whyte correctly noted, Lawrence was unable to complete his work on the Skoki Trail; but he was wrong about where Grassi left off. Grassi's trail did not, as he assumed, include the route down to Castilleja followed by a climb back up from the lake for the reward of a view of Lake Merlin;[38] his efforts ended at a point on a prominence overlooking the steep decline to Castilleja Lake. From the statements of Walter Odenthal, a more recent hiker of the Skoki Trail and someone who contributed to its development long after Grassi's time, we can gain far greater insight into its history than was available to Jon Whyte.

The Miner and the Baroness of the Rockies

Lawrence Grassi was born in very humble circumstances, like countless other Italian immigrants before and after him who came from rural backgrounds, equipped with little formal education but, like him, with the determination to succeed in their individual goals that usually coincided well with the needs of an expanding North American economy. Railways, mines, lumber mills, and construction sites were powered by the toil, sweat, and often blood of such men. In this sense the story of Lorenzo (Lawrence) Grassi is typical. What is not typical of his story, of course, is the fame he would earn from expressing his passion for the Rockies.

Elizabeth von Rummel (1897–1980) was born on a very different rung of the social ladder, but her life also came to be shaped by the Rocky

Mountains. She was born the eldest of three sisters in Munich, Germany, the daughter of a German aristocrat from whom she inherited the title of baroness. Her mother came from a very wealthy publishing family. Eventually, with her third husband, an Italian painter named Roberto Basilici, she settled with her family in the foothills of the Canadian Rockies, near Priddis, Alberta, where she had bought a ranch.

Here World War I caught up with the Basilici-Rummels, preventing them from returning to Germany. More critically, the war cut them off from their funds, forcing them to adapt to a way of life for which they were completely unprepared. In response the cosmopolitan family settled into and ultimately embraced ranch life on the Canadian frontier.

Elizabeth, who like Lawrence never married, began another phase of her life after her two sisters did so. In 1938 she went to work, for three consecutive summers, as hostess-guide at a lodge near Mount Assiniboine. It is likely that this is where she and Lawrence became acquainted, as he was a frequent visitor to the area. He had been the first to make a solo ascent of Mount Assiniboine, and his many photographs of the mountain suggest that it was one of his favourite places.

In June 1943 Lizzie Rummel, as she had come to be known, became the manager-guide of Skoki Lodge, a very attractive year-round skiing and hiking spot in Banff National Park, reached by an eleven-kilometre trail from Lake Louise. Built in 1930, the lodge had passed through a series of owners, including Peter and Catharine Whyte. Lawrence spent some time at the lodge when Lizzie worked there, and this was when he began to shape the trail from the lodge to Lake Merlin, which he left unfinished, probably because of illness.

Elizabeth bought a small, abandoned log cabin at Sunburst Lake in 1950. It was located on the shore of the lake, not far from Assiniboine Lodge, with a clear view of Mount Assiniboine. She was determined to succeed with her Sunburst Camp, and she did so for more than twenty years. In 1953 she gave twenty-one-year-old Hans Gmoser, a recent arrival from Austria, his first job as a guide. He, along with two other young Austrians, Franz Dopf and Leo Grillmair, are credited with radically transforming the sport of mountaineering in the Canadian Rockies by introducing modern climbing techniques.

Until she retired in 1970, Lizzie lived at Sunburst Camp surrounded by the things she loved most. Of course she knew everybody in the tight-knit mountain community. Sydney Vallance, Lawrence's friend and climbing companion, was also her lawyer and life-long friend. Together, she and Vallance looked after Lawrence, including raising funds to pay for an operation. She gave up Sunburst in 1970 and moved to live in Canmore. Don Gardner remembers accompanying her to visit Lawrence Grassi, bringing him warm meals in his declining years, before he entered the retirement home where he died. She worked as an oral history interviewer for the Whyte Museum of the Canadian Rockies from 1966 to 1980, and in that capacity recorded (with Ken Jones) the interview with Lawrence Grassi now in the Grassi fonds. She was also active in various town affairs and conservation organizations in and around Canmore. Lizzie Rummel received the Order of Canada in 1980, just a few months before her death, for her contribution to the mountain community. (Lawrence Grassi died in February of the same year.) An elementary school and a street in Canmore, two lakes, and a creek are named in Lizzie Rummel's honour.

Walter Odenthal was introduced to Lawrence Grassi's trail at Skoki Lodge when, as a teenager, he was fortunate enough to fly over the area in the company of a Banff-area hiker and climber who was also a pilot. During the flight to Lake Merlin in the Merlin Valley the young Odenthal heard his first reference to "Grassi's Trail," which piqued his curiosity, partly out of amazement that a trail could be named to honour an individual. He returned to the lodge several years later, in the summer of 1995, to work for its proprietors, Blake O'Brian and Jennifer Lee.[39] Shortly after his arrival he hiked the trail and, like many others who have experienced Grassi's trails in the Rocky Mountains, he was enormously impressed by Grassi's handiwork. In particular he appreciated how the trail was thoughtfully and carefully placed in its landscape: "it wasn't just destination oriented ... it had a natural feel to it. I understood him [Grassi] a little bit ... playing with the landscape a little bit ... I sensed that's what he was about."[40] Others, notably Don Gardner and Chic Scott, would make the same insightful comments about the trails Lawrence built years later at Lake O'Hara .

In Walter's time the trail began in front of Skoki Lodge and continued along the scree slopes around the northern promontory of the Wall of Jericho as far as a prominence overlooking Castilleja Lake, a distance that Walter estimated as roughly 2.5 kilometres. Here, where Grassi's trail ended, hikers had devised a rough descent down the steep scree

78 Elizabeth (Lizzie) von Rummel in the Skoki Valley, c. 1944.
Courtesy of Rummel fonds, Whyte Museum of the Canadian
Rockies, M554-1029(pa).

slope to Castilleja Lake, from where they would climb again to the ridge overlooking Lake Merlin in the Merlin Valley to the south and west.[41] On his first hike Walter recognized that work on the trail was unfinished, and during his summer at the lodge, on his own time, he extended it to the destination that Lawrence likely had intended. For this extension Walter worked along the same contour (at an elevation of 2,200 metres) as that followed by Grassi's trail, ending at the ridge overlooking Lake Merlin, where stone steps were required to climb up through a chimney and over the top. He estimates that his extension of the trail is about a kilometre in length, and photographs suggest that his work is very much in keeping with Grassi's original vision.

We know that Lawrence's work on the Skoki Lodge–Lake Merlin trail was undertaken after he had retired from the Canmore Coal Company. Whyte claimed this work was undertaken in the summer of 1945,[42] assuming perhaps that he began it immediately following his retirement. There is, however, reason to question this date. As we have seen, the surviving Canmore Coal Company employee records state that Grassi retired in 1946, and other accounts, in particular the 1960 tribute produced by Sydney Vallance, also support 1946 as the year of Lawrence's retirement. Vallance wrote of Grassi: "he worked as a coal miner for *over thirty years* until illness brought on by years of working underground, often with water dripping on his shoulders, necessitated his retirement from that work" (our italics).[43] Since the Canmore Coal Company records list the beginning of Grassi's employment as precisely 12 September 1916, and given that Vallance was well informed about the details of his good friend's life, Grassi could not have retired earlier than September 1946.

Vallance also mentions "illness" rather than the more dramatic "injury" reported by Whyte as the reason for Lawrence's retirement. Vallance here refers to what we have discovered was a bout of ill health – in fact nearly fatal – that Grassi suffered at that time, which helps us to understand why he did not complete his Lake Merlin trail. In early 1948 Grassi was found "in his cottage in great pain and rushed to the hospital where an immediate operation was found to be necessary – tumour. At one point his life was despaired of, but he pulled through and is doing fine," Sydney Vallance wrote to Eric Brooks.[44] As well, in early February of that year a brief notice appeared in the *Calgary Herald* announcing Grassi's successful recovery from an operation.[45]

79 Portion of Lawrence Grassi's trail from Skoki Lodge to Lake Merlin. Courtesy of Walter Odenthal.

Sydney R. Vallance:

Lawyer, Mountaineer, and Friend

Among Lawrence Grassi's enduring friendships, that with Sidney Vallance is of particular significance. The photograph taken of the two of them atop of Castle Mountain (fig. 52) shows two men in the prime of their lives, probably in their early or mid-forties, and therefore taken, most likely with Vallance's camera, soon after they first met.

They met in 1932 when Vallance, who had just joined the ACC, took part in his first camp, at Mount Sir Donald, where he obtained his "graduation" badge, almost certainly "on the rope" of Lawrence Grassi, whose "very valuable expert knowledge" was singled out on that occasion by the honorary president of the club, Arthur Wheeler. It was the start of a friendship that lasted for the rest of their long lives. They were both talented photographers, whose work differed in one significant way: Lawrence's hundreds of photographs of the Rockies are invariably devoid of human presence, while Vallance derived pleasure in shooting images of the many ascents he made with his friends, some of which are now well-known photographs of Grassi himself.

Unlike Lawrence, all of whose photographs are in black and white, Vallance took particular interest in colour photography. Three of these colour photographs, taken with a second-hand Leica camera, appeared in the 1938 issue of the *Canadian Alpine Journal*, the first ever printed by the journal. They appeared in an article in which Vallance stated his intention to "take colour photography more seriously." Grassi and Vallance were almost exact contemporaries (Vallance's dates are reported differently in different published sources) and died a few months apart, Vallance in 1979 and Lawrence in 1980. Their lives were lived along parallel lines, with the Rocky Mountains as their constant, but not exclusive, common link. Vallance served as the president of the Calgary section of the ACC for many years and was also ACC national president from 1947 to 1950. In addition he became a very active member of the Skyline Trail Hikers of the Canadian Rockies, and in later years he joined the Lake O'Hara Trails Club, becoming its president just before Grassi was hired as assistant warden in 1956. By the time he met Lawrence, Vallance had built a successful law firm, which he started in 1929, with offices in Calgary and Banff. The practice was carried on by his son, and then his grandson, and is still active in Calgary to this day.

It might appear that the successful lawyer and the Italian coal miner had little in common except for the mountains, but a closer look reveals that their friendship was grounded on more substantial affinities. Sydney Vallance's admiration of and esteem for Grassi, as shown for example in his tribute to Grassi in the 1977 issue of the *Canadian Alpine Journal*, probably derived from his own background. He was born in England and emigrated to Canada in 1908. The ship manifest for the SS *Empress of Britain*, on which he sailed from Liverpool, listed him as an eighteen-year-old, single, male "clerk." His 1980 obituary in the *Canadian Alpine Journal* describes him as having had little formal education, and an obituary from a newspaper clipping from the Jon Whyte fonds of the Whyte Museum states that "he worked at many things until the outbreak of the First World War."[46] By that time he had gone back to England and married Doris Paush, who was listed as a twenty-four-year-old "housewife" on their return to Canada on the SS *Orduna* in March 1915. In July of that year Vallance joined the Canadian army; the record of his enrolment gives his "trade or calling" as "student at law." We do not know where he served in the war.

From these bare facts it appears that Sydney Vallance himself was not to the manor born, and his friendship and admiration for Grassi may have been rooted in part in his own working-class background. As Lawrence grew older, Vallance intervened when the need arose, collecting money to pay for medical emergencies, making sure that Lawrence received his old age pension, and mobilizing a support system around him. Vallance was able to rise beyond his working-class origins, but what we see exuding from the two friends in that early photograph at the summit of Castle Mountain is a friendship that went beyond class and privilege. The Sydney Vallance (Fryatt) Hut in Fryatt Valley, Jasper National Park – "a true gem of the Rockies" according to the Alpine Club of Canada – commemorates Vallance's contribution to and love for the Rocky Mountains.

After the tumour was removed, Lawrence spent thirty-three days in the hospital. The hospital bill was issued on 15 March 1948. The doctor in charge sent a copy of the bill to Elizabeth Rummel, who had apparently been close to Grassi during the emergency. The doctor advised her to "get the Alpine Club to assist him [to pay the bill]," and he also noted that "the bill is rather large, and although he desires to pay for it himself, he does not know what the bill amounts to."[47] Rummel contacted Sydney Vallance, then president of the ACC, asking him for an opinion on whether the club "would be willing to contribute something towards Lawrence's Hospital Bill."[48] Meanwhile, on his own initiative Vallance had already forwarded a cheque for thirty-five dollars to Grassi's doctor to put towards "your account against Lawrence Grassi."[49] At the end of his brief note to Rummel the doctor, J.B Fulton, provides an interesting clue about the manoeuvres that would be set in motion concerning the hospital bill: "I think it would be advisable to let Mr. Grassi pay say $75.00[,] otherwise, as you know, he will be very much annoyed. If you think the Alpine Club would assist with the balance, I am sure this would be very satisfactory to us." The fundraising campaign initiated by Sydney Vallance therefore occurred without Grassi's knowledge. In his reply to Rummel, Vallance informed her that he was going to "put the matter up to the Management Committee of the Club, and I am sure they will agree to whatever I suggest. And further I would contribute some-thing myself."[50] He had been in touch with a "Ken Betts," who appears to have had a connection with the Miners' Union in Canmore. The advice received from Betts was to "do nothing for the present" about fundrasing with the ACC, because Betts had spoken with the secretary of the Miners' Union in Canmore "who told him that Lawrence had a considerable sum due to him from the Union for sick pay or something like that, which he would never take, and the Union is thinking of using that money for him now to take on these bills." Any payment of hospital expenses through a union fund, however, was to be done "very Carefully, for you know how Lawrence feels about things of this kind." Nothing further is known about the union's contribution to Grassi's medical expenses. But the gingerly, secretive approach taken by friends continued. Vallance next formally approached the ACC in the person of H.E. Sampson (probably the head of the management committee he had mentioned in his 2 April letter to Rummel), asking if he was in favour of a club contribution.[51] Sampson, although sympathetic, was not in favour: "I do not like the idea of taking Club funds to pay Grassi's hospital bill. I realize what he has done for the Club in years gone by."[52] What he suggested, instead, was that the money be collected via a subscription from members, as he thought had been done "when we gave him a life membership."[53] On the same day he wrote to Sampson, Vallance also wrote to Eric Brooks, honorary secretary of the club, summarizing events: "Elizabeth Rummel (of Skoki Lodge) for whom Grassi worked *last summer* asked the Dr to send the bills to her, with the idea of seeing if she could raise the money to help Grassi without his knowledge, as he has been out of work so many years" (our italics). Once again, he stressed that Lawrence "would be very much annoyed" if he knew of the fundraising on his behalf.[54] Brooks wrote back with a very different reaction than Sampson's: "the Club can never repay Grassi in dollars and cents for his unselfish and very real assistance in so many ways," citing his "work at the Club House, guiding at camp, [and] packing in stoves to Fay Hut." He was absolutely in favour of the club shouldering "all debts not accounted for by private contribution."[55] A few days later Vallance acknowledged receipt of a "very generous" ten dollar contribution from Brooks.[56]

In the meantime Grassi, whether aware or not of his friends' efforts to pay his medical bills, did what he could to pay the doctor who had operated on him. Unfortunately, the correspondence is not clear about how much Grassi himself paid. Dr Fulton, after receipt of an unknown sum from Grassi, wrote to Liz Rummel to inform her that this "now completely protects him against any future bills. However, we have an original balance of $200.35. If Mr. Vallance does not wish to assume responsibility for this, we will drop the matter." Liz Rummel forwarded the letter to Vallance with a note on the reverse side in which she offered to "take the matter over, unless you or Ron Betts have already taken steps or would want to do it. I think I could speak to Lawrence about it."

There the matter stood in the summer of 1948. The story of Grassi's "near-death" experience in the days before Medicare shines some light on his financial situation. The bright side of the story, of course, is the way in which two close friends rallied to his side, not only arranging to relieve him of a financial obligation that he could not discharge on his own, but doing so in a way that protected his dignity and his pride. Of course, there were others who came forward, such as his doctor or Eric Brooks to name only two, whose willingness to act on Grassi's behalf shows a community spirit and solidarity that was characteristic of both the mining and alpine communities. Grassi's dogged self-reliance and determination not to accept "charity" – extended so far as what may seem his misguided refusal ever to take advantage of his union's sick pay entitlement – give us a sense of the man he was. But in a state of health that had become precarious he faced his old age – he was now fifty-eight – with few if any prospects for a dignified existence.

And Grassi's health problems were not over. At the beginning of January 1949, just as Sydney Vallance forwarded funds towards the bill for the previous year's operation, he learned from Grassi's doctor that his friend had "been in the hospital again and had his appendix out, on November 22, 1948."[57] Vallance relayed this information to Elizabeth Rummel, along with the observation that Grassi was "going along well" after his appendicitis,[58] and he intervened once again, writing to Fulton that the operation would be paid for with money "subscribed by a few friends and we shall appreciate it if you do not let him know anything about it."[59]

About two months later, in the spring of 1949, Vallance wrote to Grassi directly. He was concerned about the latter's health, but he also asked him not "to tie yourself up to anybody this summer, because you would be doing us a great favour if you will take [the construction of] the Bugaboo hut, and we can ... pay you – at a very different rate from what you received for your last year's work. I am sure we can give you a very good proposal."[60] As subsequent correspondence reveals,

80 Photograph by Lawrence Grassi of Lake O'Hara, looking east up the valley towards the plateau (middle distance) where Lake Oesa is nestled. Courtesy of Grassi fonds, Whyte Museum of the Canadian Rockies, v240-624(pd)73.

however, Lawrence was not employed by the ACC in the summer of 1949. According to Vallance, Lawrence paid him a visit in mid-May of that year "to tell me that he had been offered a surface job at the Mine which would have the effect of making him eligible for a pension, and he could not afford to pass it up, and so he will not be able to undertake the Bugaboo Hut for us."[61]

Lake O'Hara and Lake Oesa

After his retirement Lawrence continued to work at a variety of jobs, including at Skoki Lodge and for the ACC and in and around Banff, before he returned to the Canmore Coal Company as a surface worker. There are also local memories of Grassi being employed, probably as a handyman, in Banff itself.[62] His work as a trail maker, however, was far from complete. In fact, what is arguably his best work would not take place until he was well into his middle and late sixties, accomplished at what is commonly considered the "pearl" of the Rocky Mountains, Lake O'Hara in Yoho National Park. He first visited the area soon after arriving at the Great Divide. At the time the only way to reach O'Hara was by hiking or riding a horse up Cataract Brook Valley from Hector, near Wapta Lake in the area of the Kicking Horse Pass, where Lawrence was based when he worked as a navvy for the CPR. Lake O'Hara's proximity to the CPR's Hector Station made it a convenient and popular spot for the Alpine Club of Canada, which held many summer camps there, the first in 1909.[63] "Yoho" is a Cree Indian word meaning "wonder" or "astonishment," and the area's natural beauty made it a favourite of artists soon after it became accessible. Lake O'Hara itself, named after Robert O'Hara, a British Army colonel who visited the region several times beginning in 1892, is the centrepiece of an area criss-crossed by over eighty kilometres of scenic trails. Peoples of the First Nations had used some of them long before the arrival of Europeans, but starting in the 1920s park wardens and CPR personnel also built trails and contributed to their upkeep. The first European to visit the lake in 1892, shortly before Colonel O'Hara, was a surveyor for the Dominion of Canada, James Joseph McArthur, after whom Lake McArthur was named. This is what he wrote about his first impressions of the area:

> A beautiful piece of park-like country ... the view on all sides one of indescribable grandeur ... I counted sixteen Alpine lakes, one of which is more strikingly beautiful than any other I have ever seen ... a clear blue face ... dotted with miniature icebergs.[64]

Towering above the lake are Mounts Lefroy and Victoria, which on their reverse or eastern exposures provide the equally impressive setting for Lake Louise, accessible to the more courageous hiker through Abbot Pass and the "Death Trap." The latter, and the Abbot Pass Hut, are named in memory of Philip Abbot, who lost his life in an attempt to climb Lefroy in 1896, the first mountaineering fatality in the Canadian Rockies. Other peaks circle the area, most of them having Stoney First Nations names: Odaray (cone), Opabin (rocky), Oesa (ice), Hungabee (chieftain), Yukness (sharp) and Wiwaxy Peaks (windy). Wiwaxy is of particular significance because the formation includes a ridge running between two peaks that is known locally, if not officially, as Grassi Ridge, in memory of Lawrence's time in the warden's cabin at the lake, situated below it. These mountains and their environs attract climbers, hikers, and nature lovers fascinated by the rugged beauty of the place and its lakes and glaciers. Perhaps the most famous painting of Lake O'Hara is by the American painter J.S. Sargent, and now hangs in the Fogg Museum of Harvard University. Sargent painted it in 1916, soon after Grassi's first foray into the area.[65] Some renowned Canadian artists, notably Group of Seven members J.E.H. MacDonald, Lawren Harris, and A.Y. Jackson, also left impressive canvases of their stays at the lake. When Grassi first ventured into the area, probably as early as the summer of 1913, it was only shortly after the the Swiss guides hired by the CPR had constructed the first log cabin at the lake. What he experienced would have been very similar to what R.L. Glisan, writing in the 1908 *Canadian Alpine Journal*, saw and felt (and what most people still feel on first entering the area): "Not a trace of human presence, not a trace of any disturbing element, the whole scene was the personification of majestic peace."[66]

Beginning on 26 June 1956, forty-three years after his first exploration and probably his first climbs on the surrounding peaks, Grassi was appointed assistant warden at Lake O'Hara. He held this position for the next six summers. The opportunity, from what can be reconstructed from letters and documents, likely came about through the intercession of Glen Brook, who had arrived at Wapta (Hector) with his wife Irene first as district warden in 1955 and then as chief warden of Yoho Park from 1957 until 1962, after which he became postmaster in Field, where he resided until his death in 2003. He met Lawrence almost immediately and apparently saw something in the retired miner that qualified him for the recently created position of assistant warden at Lake O'Hara.[67] It is also possible that Lawrence's old climbing companion Sydney Vallance, who was president of the Alpine Club of Canada from 1947 to 1950 and had become involved with the Lake O'Hara

Trails Club, recommended his long-time friend for the job. The fact that Lawrence had passed the normal age of retirement was overlooked. A new cabin had been built on the very spot, still called Sargent's Point, from which Sargent had painted his view of the lake, and it became Lawrence's summer home for the next six years.

Glen Brook, chief warden of Yoho Park and the man who hired Lawrence, had given him the freedom to use his time as he saw fit. It is hard to say whether they had decided on anything approaching what Lawrence actually accomplished in the six brief summers available to him. It is quite likely that Brook trusted Grassi to do what Grassi did best, and not simply to make himself available as a caretaker. He no doubt expected that Grassi would do more than keep the trails clear, perhaps provide wood for the Elizabeth Parker Hut, and keep an eye on and give advice to campers and hikers. Lawrence did all of these things, but the position provided him with a golden opportunity to unleash once more the passion for trail making that he had displayed at Twin Lakes, on the Bragg Creek trail, and at the ACC clubhouse in Banff and the lodge in the Skoki Valley. And in this it was clear that he had Glen Brook's backing and encouragement. The results made Brook's hiring of the retired Canmore coal miner seem inspired.

Those results also drew the attention of a man who, like Lawrence, has left a deep imprint on the character and history of the lake and its trail system. Dr George K.K. (Tommy) Link, a botany professor at the University of Chicago, first visited Lake O'Hara in 1928 with his wife Adeline, who taught chemistry at the same university and was also Dean of Women. Jon Whyte describes how the couple laid out the trail for the Lake O'Hara circuit during the Second World War, collaborating with Swiss guide Walter Feuz and Carson Simpson, a Philadelphia lawyer.[68] Completed just three months before Adeline Link's death in 1943, the trail was officially named the Lake O'Hara Adeline Link Memorial Trail. His wife's death only strengthened Link's already strong attachment to Lake O'Hara, which manifested itself in the form of mystical experiences and visions of Adeline along the trails they had walked and worked on together. His attachment evolved into a thirty-year obsession with building more trails and producing a map of the Lake O'Hara basin. The map was completed with Simpson's help, but Link continued to revise the descriptive material intended to accompany it until shortly before he died in 1979.[69]

It is understandable, then, that when Lawrence Grassi came to Lake O'Hara and began not only repairing but also rerouting some of the existing trails, including ones Link had laid down, or began building

81 Lawrence Grassi and workmates excavating at Lake O'Hara. The heavy machinery visible in the background suggests that this work was undertaken on the grounds near the Lake O'Hara Lodge. Courtesy of Grassi fonds, Whyte Museum of the Canadian Rockies, v240-679.

new ones, he would come under the attentive gaze of the Chicago academic. That the paths of these two seemingly different men met, therefore, was true in much more than the metaphorical sense. Despite the social and cultural divide between them, however, there was no indication that Link resented Grassi. But neither does it appear that there was much direct interaction between them. Perhaps this was more the result of Lawrence's withdrawn nature and reticence than any fault of Tommy Link. But Link must have known of Grassi's work in Banff and elsewhere and, as noted above, of the Piedmontese talent with stone. Certainly, it did not take long for Lawrence to be acknowledged. At a 1956 meeting of the Lake O'Hara Trails Club, of which Link was the founder and chair for many years and eventually became honorary life president, he "spoke with pleasure of the appointment of Mr. Lawrence Grassi as Assistant Warden."[70] The next reference to Grassi in the minutes of the club is from three years later, 14 August 1959, which mention "the much improved trails Lawrence Grassi was making." At that same meeting Tommy Link also reported on "the new trails built by Lawrence Grassi to Lake Oesa and to Lake McArthur." The blandness of the reference does not do justice to what arguably is Lawrence's most notable accomplishment.

Tommy Link was also very gracious when he introduced Lawrence at a meeting of the Lake O'Hara Trails Club on 10 August 1961:

Dr Link then introduced Mr Laurence [*sic*] Grassi to the members, and mentioned that Mr Grassi's duties as warden did not require him to work on the trails, beyond keeping them clear of obstruction, and that the heavy work he did in the improvement of existing trails and bridges and the construction of new ones, was prompted by his innate love of the mountains and Lake O'Hara in particular, and it was in his nature to be always doing something for the enjoyment and comfort of others. His latest project is the building of an entirely new trail from the Meadow to Morning Glory Lake. Mr Grassi was warmly received and loudly applauded.[71]

Lawrence's work at Lake O'Hara would continue to draw Link's attention in the years to come. The latter's project of a definitive map of the area, which he called "part of my swan song to the Canadian Rockies, to all the Rockies,"[72] prompted him to write frequent and often long letters to park authorities or anyone connected with O'Hara. Glen Brook was on the receiving end of a number of these letters, some of which touched on the subject of Grassi's work at O'Hara. Link's concern – it would be more accurate to call it his fixation – was "accuracy," especially, he acknowledged, because Lawrence had rerouted and improved some of the trails Link himself had put in. For instance, in a letter dated 6 May 1961 that Link wrote to Brook, who had apparently failed to reply to a previous letter, he asked for answers "the sooner the better" to a series of questions concerning the work Lawrence had been doing at the lake. Not surprisingly, he was particularly interested in Lawrence's trails and how they connected to or affected the trails he had designed or built. He referred, for example, to the trail "from

82 Lawrence Grassi at Lake O'Hara, 1950s, probably at work on the stone staircase on the Lake Oesa trail. Courtesy of Grassi fonds, Whyte Museum of the Canadian Rockies, v191-accn.6035.

Schaffer Lake to Lake McArthur" that "supplants the path which I put in between those two points." He continued: "His lies slightly west of mine but does in some places make use of mine." He followed this with a generous recognition of Grassi's superior trail-making and engineering skills: "His is a better all-season path and has a uniform grade. That is to the good."[73]

It is an observation that goes to the heart of their contrasting styles, their different approaches and solutions to the problems posed by the natural lay of the land, their feeling for the most pleasing effect to be obtained along the way or at the end of the path. Don Gardner, a leading authority on Rocky Mountains trails, sees Lawrence's trails as the "antithesis" of Tommy Link's: "Tommy hated switchbacks, and went straight through bogs with not much care about grade and such. Some of his trails are not very friendly, and his [Lawrence's] are. Lawrence's

83 Lawrence Grassi and Dr K.K. (Tommy) Link. Courtesy of Grassi fonds, Whyte Museum of the Canadian Rockies, v240-686(pa)018.

grades were impeccable. The one above the Alpine Club House in Banff is beautiful for this reason. He worked puzzles out just beautifully ... he considered many factors."[74] Jon Whyte's admiration of Lawrence's "engineering" is expressed in a more hyperbolic way, and he reserves his most generous praise for the first job Lawrence set himself, the trail to Lake Oesa: "We may be in awe of the achievement of the pyramids; we should be in equal awe of Lawrence's accomplishment, for on the Nile's edge two or three hundred workers heaved a stone in a cool Egyptian winter, but Grassi worked alone."[75] Whyte correctly points out that Grassi originally placed the trail's starting point just west of the Seven Sisters Falls, as the Tommy Link map clearly showed. But in 1975 Parks Canada decided to discontinue this approach because the drainage flow from above, especially during spring run-off and in

84 Lawrence Grassi's high trail to Lake McArthur. Courtesy of
Chic Scott.

85 Lawrence Grassi's rock stairway on the Lake McArthur trail. Courtesy of Chic Scott.

rainy weather, caused some erosion problems.[76] The approach to the path was moved, therefore, to its present location, the northwest end of the lake, at what is now called the Outlet Bridge. This modern trail is quite controversial. Some consider it poorly planned and built: it frequently washes away in parts and is therefore difficult to maintain.[77] It is characterized by a series of switchbacks, which presents an unappealing sight from almost any high point in the valley, though it soon leads to a cliff offering a very nice view of Lake O'Hara. It then makes its way through boulder fields before rejoining Lawrence's trail. Then come the famous stone steps – a rock stairway really – that replaced the wooden ladder the Swiss guides had built to climb over this difficult passage. Few visitors to Lake O'Hara are left unmoved by this tangible evidence of a man's love for the mountains. It is here that the plaque honouring Grassi was placed in 1971.

Jon Whyte was wrong on one point, however: the trail to Lake Oesa was not Lawrence's first project. Glen Brook, who as Lawrence's boss must be considered a reliable source, summarized Lawrence's key contributions in a tribute on the occasion of the unveiling of the bronze plaque honouring the then octogenarian. The ceremony took place on 26 June 1971 at the Alpine Club of Canada Elizabeth Parker Hut in the meadows above Lake O'Hara, before the plaque's definitive placement on the trail to Lake Oesa.[78] The *Banff Crag and Canyon* described it as a "small, informal, but moving ceremony." In addition to Glen and Irene Brook, it was attended by Lillian Gest, Lizzie Rummel, and representatives of the ACC and Parks Canada, among others. In his tribute Brook outlined Lawrence's important work at the lake:

He first rebuilt the much used footpath circling Lake O'Hara.[79]

Next was the fabulous trail over extremely rough and rocky terrain to Lake Oesa. To accomplish this work he back-packed a wheelbarrow to wherever he wanted rocks moved.

The new footpath to Lake McArthur with its "rock stairway" made the hike to this lake much easier and exciting.

His new trail to Morning Glory Lake and Linda Lake bypassed the old "vertical" trail and gave the hiker a much easier grade for an easy walk to enter the Cathedral Basin.

His new trail from Lake O'Hara to Opabin Pass, via Mary Lake and West Opabin Cliff, is a most scenic and delightful hike for all.

Besides all the strenuous work of these projects he carried out continual maintenance, repairs and improvements on all other trails in the area.[80]

86 Lawrence Grassi's stone staircase at Seven Sisters (now Seven Veils) Falls, the beginning of his trail to Lake Oesa. Courtesy of E. Costa, 2010.

This list corresponds exactly to one Link sent to Austin Ford dated 23 March 1964. As Link continued to work on his map of Lake O'Hara into his retirement years, however, he peppered Glen Brook with questions about Grassi's "official duties." In one letter written in January or early February 1972, Link also asked, "Did [his duties] include trail or path rectification and construction of new ones?" The next question revealed a more personal concern: "Was [that work intended] ... to convert my foot-paths into graded trails for horses and humans?" Brook's answer is remarkable for its frank admission of the extraordinary creative freedom he had granted to Grassi, and also significant for its use of the honorific "Mr" in referring to Grassi. This may have been a subtle rebuke of Link for his slightly disrespectful use of simply "Grassi" in his letter, and might also indicate that Brook was irritated by Link's frequent and insistent missives.

One of the authors of this study met with Glen and Irene Brook in Field just a few years before the latter's death. Glen, though physically and mentally hale and hearty, had become totally deaf, and therefore it was left to Irene, who had a sharp memory, to reminisce about Lawrence. Her respect and admiration for him had no bounds; she lauded not only his mountain-climbing and trail-building achievements but especially his character: he was "a great man," she said, and would not entertain any reservations. Hanging in their house was a photograph of Grassi and the two young Brook boys by the side of what looks like Grassi Lakes. And among the Grassi papers in the Whyte Museum is another photo of the Brook boys in their pre-teens, a sign of a friendship that apparently lasted until Lawrence's death.

There is something in the tone of Brook's response to Link that may be more than marginally relevant. From a purely stylistic point of view, Brook's letter is a little work of diplomatic art – and perhaps very Canadian – in the way he draws a parallel between Grassi's activities and those of Link.

> It would be difficult to define Mr. Grassi's duties as they were as varied and unique as the area itself, and the people who frequented it. From my point of view the prime purpose of having him there was as a source of authentic, reliable information and advice to visitors, hikers and climbers in the area. Combined with this, his unique, sincere ability to exude marvelous public relations more than justified his being there. The outstanding trail work Lawrence accomplished was an added bonus to the area, far exceeding in quality and quantity that which could be expected of any one

87 Lawrence Grassi posing with his Alpine Club of Canada commemorative plaque at the Elizabeth Parker Hut on the day of its unveiling. Courtesy of Rummel fonds, Whyte Museum of the Canadian Rockies, v554-1764-ns.

person. The maintenance & improving of existing trails and paths were included in his itinerary of work, but the manner in which this was done, in my opinion, was not as a "duty" but rather, a "labour of love" very similar to that of another friend of mine, a Dr. Geo. K.K. Link.[81]

Brook's answer to Link's second question, concerning Grassi's work on Link's trails, was simple: "No, it was never intended to convert footpaths for horses. Some changes and re-routings were desirable, such as

Grassi's foot path from McArthur Pass to Lake McArthur, via the 'Golden Staircase,' and a less arduous route from the camp ground to Morning Glory." Was Link content with this response? Since we could find no further exchanges between them on this topic, we assume that the matter ended there.

There is little doubt that Lake O'Hara was a place Lawrence loved. The evidence lies in the trails and in the stones with which he paved them. One can imagine all manner of psychological explanations of this profound communion with nature; perhaps it was Lawrence's way of redirecting what surely was a profound human need to express love. But one must tread with caution in such matters; all we are left with to close such a meaningful phase of this man's life is the legacy he left for future generations. Few of the artists and writers who have left us their enduring and often moving impressions of Lake O'Hara have failed to express admiration for the work of the humble and unassuming Piedmontese miner. They often describe their experience of hiking the trail as profoundly significant. Journalist and author Ian Brown, for instance, wrote of his visits there: "I still long to go back. That's the only downside to a place as sublime, as memorable, as glorious, as important in one's life as Lake O'Hara is in mine." He concluded: "I don't want to imagine the day when I can't go there any more, when I will no longer be able to see its silvery, slivery light and lakes. That day will come, of course. But the place will still be there."[82] And it is thanks to Grassi that the experience is as accessible as it is.

An episode recounted by Jon Whyte makes apparent that the "old engineer"[83] Grassi was thinking of an enduring presence when he built his stairways in stone up the mountains:

> Major F. Longstaff,[84] a very old-time friend of O'Hara, met Grassi on one of his last visits to the lake about 1960. He said to Grassi, "I don't suppose I'll be coming up here again. I'm getting a bit past it now." To this Grassi replied, "Oh Major, hundreds of years from now, I'll be meeting you coming round these trails."[85]

He was right: it is not hard to imagine Lawrence coming towards us as we round a corner of one of his trails.

Epilogue: "A Symbol and a Legend of the Canadian Rockies"

Rising to a height of 2,685 metres, Mount Lawrence Grassi, the centre peak of a three-peak massif known as Ehagay Nakoda, stands as a powerful backdrop to the town of Canmore in the Bow River Valley.[1] In the pass between this massif and Mount Rundle to its north and west lies Grassi Lakes, at the end of the trail built by Lawrence Grassi in the 1920s and the beginning of the route that eventually leads through Whiteman's Pass between Ehagay Nakoda and Mount Rundle.[2] Looking towards the north and east, in the valley below the massif, in the city of Canmore itself, lies Lawrence Grassi Middle School. These commemorations of the life of a coal miner, mountain climber, and trail builder in the Rocky Mountains are a well-deserved tribute. They, as well as various plaques in and around Canmore and farther afield at Lake O'Hara, and other geographic place names like Grassi Ridge (whether official or popular), attest to the fact that Lawrence (Lorenzo) Grassi left an indelible imprint in the region, and indeed the country, that became his adopted home.

Lawrence Grassi was seventy-five when he left his position as assistant warden at Lake O'Hara. His work on the trails, much of it single-handed, was done when most men, especially after many years working in a coal mine, would long before have ceased to take on physically demanding tasks. As we saw in the previous chapter, Grassi's strong constitution was beginning to show signs of wear even before he became assistant warden. He would live for another fifteen years, during which he would face health problems and the natural effects of old age. As a result of a long life lived alone, he had developed careless and not very healthy eating habits, which also took their toll as he aged. His friends were aging, and over time there were fewer of them to visit and keep an eye on him. He and Bill Cherak devised a signal: Lawrence

88 Mount Lawrence Grassi is the middle peak of the three-peak massif Ehagay Nakoda. The northern peak is called Ha Ling, and the one to the south is Ship's Prow. Courtesy of G. Scardellato, 2010.

would open his kitchen blind in the morning to show Bill, who would drive by, that he was up and that everything was normal. His housekeeping practices gradually became minimal, and the cabin whose rock garden and profusion of flowers had once been shown with pride to visitors fell into disrepair. The once white picket fence around it fell into disrepair, as did the cabin itself. The interior, which had never been what one might call pristine, according to friends, increasingly became an unkempt, dark, and dingy hut, with a patina of coal dust covering all.

The passage of time after his years at Lake O'Hara dimmed but did not diminish the stature of his achievement. He continued to be remembered occasionally in local publications, and the 1971 dedication of the bronze plaque at Lake O'Hara, placed on the trail to Lake Oesa, became a permanent signpost and reminder of the lasting nature of Grassi's contributions to the mountains. Guidebooks and memoirs also began to recount the most familiar stories about him, but Lawrence's world shrank as he aged, and eventually he was unable to venture far from home, the result not only of physical deterioration but also of an

89 Lawrence Grassi Middle School, Canmore. Courtesy of G. Scardellato, 2010.

aggravated eye condition, probably an advanced cataracts problem that had necessitated an operation in October 1963.

He waited until the end of his season at Lake O'Hara to have the operation, and when he left he received a letter full of moving recollections from Nancy Lyall, who in the 1920s had managed the Alpine Club of Canada club house at Sulphur Mountain, where Lawrence had donated his services. Here is Lawrence's life as remembered by one who began with "My dear Lawrence," and who was able to recall

> pleasant memories of your doings at the Club House ... the many steps you built & the trails you made especially the one to Grassi's Lookout & its lovely view [and] the memorable walk I had with you & my nephew at the Grassi Lakes ... I sat at the fireplace while you & my nephew went on to see the Indian drawings ... Our walk to Consolation Lake when you gave me a bit of a scolding because I was not wearing the right footwear. I certainly deserved it!

She ended this fond letter by remembering the "many members you guided up Louis & gave them the thrill of a lifetime," referring to the thirty-two times he had done that climb, a fact in which he took pride.

IN APPRECIATION

OF

LAWRENCE GRASSI

1890 - 1980

MASTER TRAILMAKER

HE SOUGHT NEW PATHS, MADE ROUGH
PLACES SMOOTH, POINTED THE WAY
TO HIGHER LEVELS AND
LOFTIER ACHIEVEMENTS.

90 Commemorative plaque for "master trailmaker" Lawrence Grassi, placed at Grassi Lakes in 1980, the seventy-fifth anniversary of Alberta's entry into Confederation. Courtesy of G. Scardellato, 2010.

The emotional tone of the letter is smartly converted to humour by Lyall's reference to "the American man who asked if the Alpine Club had built the chimneys in the mountains."

Nancy Lyall was unable to visit Lawrence, since she herself was experiencing health problems and was forbidden by her doctors to travel. This underlined the inevitable widening gap between him and his friends brought on by old age. From time to time visitors who knew him or had heard of him would pay a visit, and with them he reminisced about the old days on the mountains and trails; he would happily bring out his photo albums or show his many slides. One such visit in 1969 resulted in an article published in the now defunct Canmore paper *The Hoodoos Highlander*. The article was reprinted, with an update, in 1979, a year before Lawrence's death.[3] The original article was a summary of previously published information about Grassi, with references to the well-known and oft-repeated "facts," such as that J.S. Woodsworth was behind the name change of Twin Lakes to Grassi Lakes. Other claims were better founded, like the story of the 1926 rescue of R.G. Williams and "many other rescues." The 1969 article refers to Lawrence as having reached the

> twilight of his years, still working his way up the mountain to cut dead trees for his fire wood in summer. He no longer takes long walks, confining himself to a mile or so. In the past he occupied himself in making baskets, crib boards and lamps but now he just "loafs around."

Lawrence is quoted as remarking that perhaps what he needed was a "wife who would chase him outside so that he would take those long walks." What he did appreciate, he confessed, was that "once in a while he does get a ride into the mountains." But what makes its way into this second story is the intrusion of a "new" Canmore into his life of an old man, in the form of "a boy in a motor bike [who] broke through the stillness of the twilight hours by roaring through Mr. Grassi's yard and on up the mountain path he so painstakingly blazed years before." Canmore was growing and changing fast, and many of the new residents "have not heard about this mountain man." Lawrence had become "that hermit" who was rarely seen in public. Yet the number of sites and structures named for him ensure that he remains "a symbol and a living legend of the Canadian Rockies." This status would take on both positive and negative aspects. Recently, for example, Lawrence Grassi's name and reputation were attached to a modern housing subdivision located at the foot of Mount Lawrence Grassi to the west and south of Canmore. The location rather than any honorific intent presumably prompted the name Peaks of Grassi for the subdivision, which includes a thoroughfare named Lawrence Grassi Ridge. A less commercial use of his name is associated with local wildlife and nature conservation efforts in the Bow River valley around Canmore: the Bow Corridor Eco Advisory Group has been active in evaluating and attempting to conserve wildlife movement corridors, including one known as the Grassi Secondary Wildlife Corridor, as well as the Grassi Lakes Local Habitat Patch.[4]

THIS PLAQUE IS A TRIBUTE TO
LAWRENCE GRASSI A.C.C.
"TRULY ONE OF NATURE'S GENTLEMEN"
WHO BUILT MANY TRAILS IN THE
BANFF-LAKE LOUISE AREA, INCLUDING
THIS TRAIL AND THESE STEPS, SO THAT
THOSE WHO FOLLOW MIGHT MORE
EASILY ENJOY THE MOUNTAINS HE LOVES.

ERECTED IN GRATITUDE BY
THE ALPINE CLUB OF CANADA
A.D. 1970

91 This Alpine Club of Canada tribute to Lawrence Grassi was created in 1970 and placed on his drystone staircase on the trail to Lake Oesa in 1971. Courtesy of E. Costa, 2010.

The 1979 article continues with an update on his life, by which time he had been a resident of the Bow River Retirement Lodge since 1976. His eyesight was reported to be "very poor," yet he could still vividly describe the best ascent routes to the mountain peaks he had climbed and guided, as others have confirmed. He could not be driven to "his" lakes, as had been possible until recently, because a barrier preventing car access had been placed across the road leading to them; and so he would not be up to see Grassi Lakes again.

One visitor who travelled to see him in his twilight years was a Falmentine acquaintance from the past. Tony Minoletti, Canadian-born but at one time a Falmenta chimney sweep, arrived at the Bow River lodge and began speaking to Lawrence in his native dialect.[5] In what

92 Bow River Retirement Lodge, Canmore, where Lawrence Grassi spent the last five years of his life. The Ehagay Nakoda massif with Mount Lawrence Grassi, its middle peak, is shown rising behind the retirement lodge. Courtesy of E. Costa, 2008.

must have been a sad moment for Lawrence, he was unable to respond in kind: he had lost the language of his parents.

It is not an easy task to pronounce on the definitive meaning of any one's life. It is even more difficult to do so in the case of Lawrence Grassi. He was not a very communicative person, as we have noted repeatedly, and the notion of a life's meaning was probably a philosophical concept at which he would have scoffed. Stoic to the last, he was quietly proud of his achievements and shared his love for the mountains until the end. Nowhere does one read about him boasting of the public recognition he had received in his lifetime, but he kept and framed the official certificates of his awards, such as the 1936 ACC Certificate of Life Membership, which was followed by life memberships in the Sky Line Trail Hikers of the Canadian Rockies and the Canadian Youth Hostels Association. In 1977 he received the Province of Alberta Achievement Award in recognition of his "Excellence in

ACHIEVEMENT AWARD

In recognition of

EXCELLENCE

in **Mountaineering and Trailmaking**

this award is presented to

Lawrence Grassi

with the best wishes and congratulations of the people and Government of the Province of Alberta.
Dated this 29th day of October, 1977

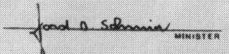

MINISTER

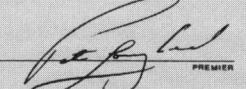

PREMIER

93 Lawrence Grassi received the Province of Alberta Achievement Award for Excellence in Mountaineering and Trailmaking in 1977. Courtesy of E. Costa, 2009.

Mountaineering and Trailmaking."[6] And there was, of course, the plaque on the trail to Lake Oesa, put in place in June 1971.

Lawrence also kept personal letters sent to him over the years, some of them expressing gratitude for the gift of his artefacts or for other treasures. One letter, written by the Rev. George W. Lang in 1942, referred to the "inspiring chat" with the "interesting man at the foot of the path in the little house" that became the theme for a sermon "preached to five different congregations." That he kept such letters over the years suggests he valued the private and personal recognition of others.

One other letter in particular is worth mentioning, because it was an expression of gratitude for a mission of mercy. The writer, H.E. Bulyea, thanks Lawrence for travelling to Lake O'Hara to retrieve the body of his son, who had perished some months earlier in a skiing accident.[7] Previous searchers, including the young man's father and his friends, had not been able to find the body. Grassi's familiarity with the topography of the area may have provided him with insight into the location of the body, insight unavailable to everyone else. Mr Bulyea wrote:

> It seems as if it was not for me to find him and although it was a great disappointment to have failed, I realize that it may have been for the best, that I could always remember him as I saw him last, when he shouldered his skis and started off looking so happy.
>
> Words fail me when I try to tell you how thankful I and my wife and family are for what you did for us. I can only say that I hope we shall be able in some way to show our appreciation, which I am sorry to say is already long overdue.

We do not know whether the Bulyea family ever had an opportunity to express their gratitude to Lawrence in addition to the sentiments Mr Bulyea so movingly expressed in his letter. There can be no doubt, however, that Lawrence kept the letter all those years because it meant a great deal to him. The incident seems also to powerfully give the measure of Grassi's generous nature, and in this regard is perhaps of greater significance than the much more famous rescue of Dr Williams.

The memory of Lawrence Grassi's life is alive and well both in his adopted town and in his native Falmenta, which is also keen to remember the young man who left over a century ago. In the Rocky Mountains he has become a symbol and a legend, but in his native Piedmont he is a reminder of the many thousands of men and women who left home and family "to put food on the table." The men who left for the rocky north shore of Lake Superior before Grassi's arrival, and who continued to arrive after him, were undertaking projects that followed a true and tried pattern: they sold their labour and their skills to be used for railway building and maintenance, for mining and shipping the coal to make the trains run, and for many other enterprises fundamental to the development of Canada's economic infrastructure. The earnings they received in return helped put their family on a more secure footing. Perhaps there was a piece of land to buy, aging parents to support, or a trousseau to provide for sisters who would otherwise not be able to make a good marriage. Once these family duties were discharged, the emigrant could turn his attention to his own future. If single, he could return home, get married, and then perhaps make his way back to his adopted land to begin the cycle again: home, work, family. The story of Lawrence Grassi deviates from this common narrative. Lawrence never returned to Falmenta; he never married or fathered children. In fact, in his subversion of the traditional path he may by choice or circumstance have contributed to the misery of his family, in particular by his failure to communicate with them. In addition, the earnings he sent to Falmenta might have done as much harm as good, for they elicited suspicion and sometimes jealousy in those who were aware of them: a mother who suspected her daughter's motives concerning her brother's savings, for example, or a brother-in-law who could only wonder why Grassi did not respond to advice about his substantial savings. Certainly the last letter from his niece and goddaughter Angiolina is a profoundly sad plea for a reconnection that would never occur either in writing or in person.

After his death, Lawrence's ashes were scattered at Grassi Lakes. In his will he had left a substantial sum of money to the Alpine Club of Canada for the construction of an alpine hut, additional funds for which were provided by Edmund Hayes Sr and his family.[8] After several years of preparation, the ACC decided to locate the large, prefabricated hut on wind-swept Cummins Ridge, next to the Clemenceau ice field. Mount Clemenceau itself, at 3,658 metres the fourth-highest peak in the Canadian Rockies, was located "an easy day's climb" to the north and east of the site chosen.[9] In 2006, however, the Lawrence Grassi Hut, as it was called, was inspected because of reports of deterioration. The inspectors' report noted that the "structure had deteriorated (rotted), that the mould contamination was such that the hut was uninhabitable, [and] should be decommissioned and that it was not possible to repair it ... The removal took place in September 2008."[10] This end strikes one as doubly a pity since the hut seemed, in one respect, the ideal means of celebrating the life of Lawrence Grassi: it is tempting, if limiting, to see in the remoteness of the hut – and its eventual removal – a metaphor for his life. But that story could not be written and cannot be understood as a narrative to which normal literary approaches apply: one has to walk his trails and look on his works to intuit the nature of the man, which then informs the written, factual text. Much about his personality still eludes us. Yet when we walk his trails, we can imagine his life unfolding before us, step by step, and we can only conclude that he was, and remains, in and of the mountains. We can image, to paraphrase his own words to a friend more than fifty years ago, that we'll be meeting him again coming round one of his trails.

Appendix: Letters from the Grassi Collection, in Translation*

The letters that follow were received by Lorenzo Grassi in Canada or, in four instances only, written by him to his family in Italy. The latter were retrieved from his kin in Falmenta; the others are part of the Lawrence Grassi fonds housed in the Whyte Museum of the Canadian Rockies, located in Banff, Alberta, donated between 1967 and 1984. The letters are arranged chronologically, which means letters from Lawrence to his family in Falmenta appear amongst the letters he received from home. The first letter, therefore, was written by Lawrence soon after his arrival in Jackfish, Ontario, in 1912. In it the young man demonstrates a quality that will remain with him throughout his life and that is evident throughout the letters: his reticence with words. At this early stage of immigration, however, he appears to be in touch with a number of individuals and to be making an effort to communicate with them, relaying messages to and from relatives. For instance, he sends his family greetings from "my cousin," probably G.A. Testori, the same cousin who four years later chides him for not keeping in touch.[1] Nonetheless, there is some communication, albeit desultory. A year later, already out west and in a letter postmarked Field, BC,[2] he acknowledges that he hasn't written in a long time. He has not written his father, who appears to be away from home, but he seems to be connected with family and possibly kin as well. In the next two letters from the 1920s, written from Canmore, where he moved in 1916, he limits himself to a terse few lines about his good health and best wishes to the family back home.

---

* All translations are by Elio Costa.

There are four main authors for the remaining letters in the collection, the first of which was written in 1922: Grassi's mother Caterina, his sister Virginia, his niece and goddaughter Angiolina, and his brother-in-law Enrico, whose family name is also Grassi. It is unfortunate that the letters sent to Lorenzo Grassi between 1912 and 1922 are lost. They would perhaps provide us with some details about his early years in Canada or make mention of other *paesani* or relatives who had also emigrated. This is to assume, of course, that Lorenzo provided his family in Italy with news about his life in Jackfish or his early period in British Columbia.

In all cases Caterina Grassi signs her letters with full given name and surname, but the surname varies between Testori and Grassi; she seems to prefer the latter towards the end of her life. She is the predominant voice in the correspondence, at least until her death on 3 February 1935, after which Virginia and her husband continue the mostly frustrating efforts to communicate with the distant and increasingly unresponsive Lorenzo. His silences, in fact, become longer and longer until letters from Grassi apparently stop altogether. One other voice, very poignant and pathos filled, is also present here: that of Angiolina, Virginia's oldest daughter. At first her voice is heard indirectly: Caterina conveys her granddaughter's request for a "pair of American shoes" in a letter.[3] Virginia also mentions her "little devil" of a daughter. Angiolina's own timid greetings appear from time to time in her mother's or grandmother's letters. Gradually, a distinct personality emerges in her letters, gentler and, one is tempted to say, more innocent and disinterested, anxious to make the acquaintance of her "American" uncle, but no less sensitive about the misery around her than the adults. In one letter she writes, "I am still young but I see that there is misery everywhere."[4] The last letter in the Grassi collection is from Angiolina, and the story it tells is one of sadness and even tragedy.[5] Her father and mother are dead and she has now left her sister Maria, her only remaining sibling, at home in Falmenta "with a cow and a goat" while she is working as a housemaid in a small town miles away. She does not say what has happened to Maria's twin sister Armandina, and one can only surmise that some tragedy has been visited upon the sisters after the death of their parents.[6] There is no evidence that there was any further communication between Lorenzo and his niece. Indeed, it seems unlikely that Lorenzo had further contact with any of his Italian kin.

From the very beginning the picture of conditions in Falmenta that emerges from the letters is one of unremitting hardship and misery.

The simple, unadorned language and faulty grammar, reflecting the basic literacy of the senders, seems a natural, effective, and affecting manner of articulating the substance and form of lives made up of daily struggles for survival. Three generations are present here in all the harsh reality resulting from a constant state of want, in particular from the late 1920s. Their state is made all the more poignant by the failed attempts to establish a modicum of dialogue with Lorenzo Grassi, the absent son, brother, uncle, and brother-in-law. There are, of course, requests for money: doctors and hospital to pay for Lorenzo's mother, shopkeepers to pay for food, the roof to repair to keep the rain from their heads, and similar needs. The requests for money, however, are muted and embarrassed. It is difficult to maintain one's dignity when bread is scarce, but Lorenzo rarely responds, sometimes even forwarding money with little or no accompanying communication. Until, finally, there is silence.

We have translated as literally as possible in order to retain as much as we could of the tone of the original. This was challenging, since the writing is often ungrammatical, words are misspelled, and accents and punctuation are often missing, which is not surprising: in rural Italian communities children usually were put to work at the age of nine or ten, and so achieved only a grade three education. In many cases sentences that in the original run on without regard for dependant clauses, making meaning difficult to grasp, have been reorganized to clarify meaning. Punctuation presented another challenge to readability. We adopted a non-interventionist policy: missing periods at the end of a sentence are indicated by "[.]", and if a sentence began with a lowercase letter we replaced it with an uppercase, but in most other cases we leave the text as it stands. A more assertive approach would have made the letters smoother and more "presentable," but would also have risked transforming language that is direct and down-to-earth – if at times rudimentary – into a falsely middle-class form of expression. Finally, the language in which the letters are written understandably reflects the spoken word, a characteristic that we tried to retain.

Some translation choices require clarification. The verb "credere" (to believe), for example, is often used, especially by Caterina Grassi, in the sense of "to hope": "credo che starai bene anche tu," which obviously means "I hope you are well too" rather than "I believe you are well too." There are other expressions throughout the letters that in some cases we decided to translate literally; for example, "vengo a dirti" we have translated as "I come to tell you" rather than the more grammatically correct "I would like to tell you" or "You should know."

In addition to the specifically linguistic aspects of the letters, it's worth noting the formulaic nature of their opening and closing sentences, as the Italian conventions of the time and place can seem unusual to English speakers. The initial salutation, with minor variants, almost always follows the same formula, "I come to you with these [two] lines to bring you news" or "I am well" or "We are well, and I hope the same of you," just as the final is a variant of "There is no other news, so I send you greetings" or "I don't know what else to tell you." The dateline for each letter from the Grassi fonds is preceded by its archival reference code.

jach Fish   3-12-1912[7]

Dearest mother father and sister
I come with these two lines to give you my news
I am well as I hope are all of you
I am informing you that I have received the salami and I thank you very much. I have sent 125 liras of which you will keep 100 liras for you and you will give 25 to my sister. You will let me know if my father has come home this year. I have written him two letters and I haven't received any answer I don't know if my letters have gone lost I haven't received anything. Two months ago I mailed a letter containing 25 liras but you don't say that you received it is a sign that it got lost on the way. It only remains for me to send the most heartfelt greetings and kisses to you and all the relatives on my behalf and my cousin's wishing you Merry Christmas and happy New Year.
Receive my most sincere greetings and kisses from your son and your brother
L Grassi
I return cordial greetings from Ignazio Tiboni
And you will give my regards to Bianconi Giacomo and his family for me.

Field, P.O. Box 161 B.C. Canada   10-11-1913

Dear mother and sister
With these two lines I bring you my news since I had not written to you in a long time. I enjoy very good health and I also hope that all of you are enjoying good health. I have received your letter but so far I have not written to my father. I hope you have received the Ł. 50 I sent in the month of June. It only remains for me to greet you and all relatives and friends.
And I am your son and brother
L. Grassi

M 45 1/1   Falmenta 16 July 1922

Dearest son

I come with these two lines to bring you news that I am well and I
hope the same of you. Dear son I inform you that your brother in law
has given me back the last thousand liras that I had given him and
I put it in the post office account. dear son I inform you that for the
interest I asked for some butter. Dear son I inform you that Virginia on
June 27 gave birth to two girls. And they are both in good health and
Virginia is well too I don't know what else to tell you except to greet
you from the heart and I am forever your mother Testori Caterina

Greetings from your sister and your goddaughter and brother in
law and all the relatives.

There are no news in the village, only that the road is finished the
weather here is quite rainy.

M 45 1/2   28 April 1923

Dear Brother in law and brother

It has been a long time without news and so I have decided to write
you two lines to give you news of us, that we are all well and we hope
the same of you, only your mother has an eye infection and I probably
have to take her to Novara to have an operation.

Dear brother in law I also want to tell you if you can do me another
favour to lend me a thousand liras for the family which I need because
I can't go out in the fields because I have these two little girls and your
sister is always a little sickly and therefore I can't leave her alone. The
girls are only ten months old. Dear brother in law therefore I need a
prompt answer either yes or no. I don't know what else to tell you
except to greet you most sincerely on my behalf your sister and your
goddaughter and I am your brother in law

Enrico Grassi

Dear son I am informing you that I have to go and have the eye operation and I don't have the means to pay for this expense. I have thought
therefore of going to the post office to withdraw what I need from
your account. Because I cannot wait for your answer because I need to
go now when there is not much to do because it will be much worse
later[.] And as security for this money I will make over to you the
monte in Baro[.][8] When I am in the hospital if I can I will let you know
how it went[.] Meanwhile I greet you wholeheartedly.
I [am] your mother

Testori Caterina

94 Caterina Grassi to Lorenzo Grassi, 16 July 1922. Courtesy of Grassi fonds, Whyte Museum of the Canadian Rockies, M 45 1/1.

M 45 1/3   Novara, 11 May, 1923

Dear son I give you this sad news that on 3 May I came to the Maggiore Hospital for the operation of a fistula in the right eye, I don't know when I will be able to go home as soon as I am well I will write you again I beg you dear son if you write home you will write to Rico[9] or Virginia and I hope that you are in good health. I beg to pray to God that I can go home soon

I have nothing more and receive many kisses from your dear mother
[No signature]

M 45 1/4   Falmenta, 25 June 1923

My dearest son
I come with this to inform you that I came home from the hospital and
I came out on June 2[.] Now as far as my eye is concerned I am quite
well[.] I was in for a month[.] Dear son I regret to tell you that I with-
drew two thousand liras because the cost was rather high[.] I don't
know what else except to thank you with my heart and I am your
mother Testori Caterina
    Enrico came to ask me for the money but I have not given it to him
yet. Greetings from Virginia's family

M 45 1/5   Falmenta, 5 July 1923

Dearest son I bring you my news[.] I have been sick for eight days in
bed[.] I have hired a woman to assist me in the house[.] Dear son on the
2nd the doctor examined me at home and he told me that my illness is
a bad case of arthritis in the knee which gives me excruciating pain and
he told me not to get out of bed and to sweat a lot[.] I have also received
the little note you sent along with Rico.[10] Many many thanks and the
Lord will reward you because if it were not for you I would have no one
else[.] I understand that Rico is looking for 1,000 liras from you I have
not given it to him yet[.] Dear son listen to me he has not given me any
receipt for the other 2,500 I have given him[.] I told him to give me IOUs
and he tells me that he doesn't want to write any IOU so that you don't
have to pay any government tax[.] Tell me right away what I should do
now you tell me what I should do because I have no intention of giving
him anything anymore if he doesn't give me some IOUs[.] You know
that I am old and I don't want to see you two afflicted by these things.
Virginia and her family I think are in good health. They are in the
mountains and I am at home.[11] Receive many fond greetings and kisses
from your dear mother Testori Caterina
    pardon me for the poor writing[.]
    Many regards

M 45 1/6   Falmenta, 1 December 1923

My dearest son
I come with these two lines to inform you about my health[.] Now
I am a little better[.] I am not bedridden but I am no longer able to
work. This little farm we have I am now forced to rent it out if I can
because the way I am now I am not capable to go out and work it.
    Dear son you will forgive me for the expense I caused you because
the illness was long. I was one month in the hospital and then the

trips[12] and then a bit of everything. I spent quite a lot[.] Then as if that wasn't enough I got arthritis in the legs and I could no longer stand up and I was forced to stay in bed for 46 days and I had to keep a woman in the house to look after me until I got out of bed[.] Even if Virginia wanted to look after me she could not because she has these two little girls and it was impossible for her to care for me and the same with him [Enrico] It was the summer season he could not because you know what the summer is like between working his farm and mine he had his hands full and for this reason I was obliged to hire a woman I had to get the doctor from Cannobio twice for the arthritis and since I did not get better I was taken to Craveggia[.] There I realized right away that I was doing better.

Dear son I want to tell you that if you intend coming [back to live] hereabouts uncle Sciurino wants to sell that little wooded piece of land under the rock[.] [Let me know] if I should get it for you or what[.] Therefore give me a yes or no answer about this. I don't know what else to tell you only to wish you a merry Christmas and a happy new year and I am your mother Testori Caterina

M 45 1/7   6 December 1923

Dearest brother and brother in law
We come with this letter of mine to bring you the news that we are well and my children are also in good health as we hope you are also mother is somewhat better now but she is no longer able to work[.] Dear brother I want to tell you that it is already close to three years that I haven't received any letters from you[.] I don't know what's the matter with you or if it's because the letters don't arrive. If you write don't forget the house password that is Giuvannun[.][13] I don't know what to say to you except to send you my best with my husband and your goddaughter and all the family[.]

Your sister Grassi Virginia
The little girls have been standing up for the past three months[.] Your goddaughter is going to school[.] The little girls' name is Maria for one and the other is Armandina

M 45 1/8   12 May 1924

Dearest son,
It has been a long time that I have not received any news from you and [I am writing] to bring you news of me[.] I am in fairly good health [and] I hope the same of you[.] I don't know what to think that you are sick or what else because you don't send money any more[.]

Are you sick or what[?] If you had money you could make money
with no sweat because there is always a possibility[.] If you are not
sick I tell you that I need it [so] send me something if you can[.] You
don't tell me anything anymore whether you want to come home or
whether you don't because I can't live in the house anymore because
of the water pouring through nowadays[.] I even had to [unclear:
"move"?] the bed because of the water coming down[.] If I have to fix
it up a bit or if you are planning [to] come home and put affairs in order then it's money thrown away[.] I also want to tell you that a little
while ago I gave Enrico the money he had asked to borrow from you
last year and he has given me an IOU for it[.] I also want to tell you
that the mayor and the secretary have sent me a document because
there is a tax owing in common[.] [Tell me] if you want to pay it to get
rid of it or what[.][14] The other [Lorenzo's sister] says that she wants
to pay [the tax] and you tell me either yes or no because the mayor
and the secretary want an answer[.] Mayor Grassi died last year and
Tiboni Emanuele died last year [and] now the mayor is Testori Daniele
and the secretary is Tiboni Federico and he says that he can force me
to pay and you will see that there is no way that I can pay[.] The sum
to pay is 50 liras and every year I have to pay 2.61 liras exactly[.] I
don't know what else to tell you except to leave you with my best regards and Virginia's and of all her family[.] They leave you with best
regards wishing you good health[.]

Signed your mother Grassi Caterina

M 45 1/9   1 December 1924

My dearest son
I come with this letter in order to give you news and also to ask for
yours[.] I am well in health of body but I suffer constantly from arthritis in the legs[.] I am almost completely unable to walk around[.] I hope
you at least are in good health[.] I tell you dear son that I have already
written you this summer in the month of May if you could send me
something and then also for that tax document but you did not even
answer me[.] If you want to send me something I really need it[.] I have
to pay the [grocery] store and I have called the doctor many times[.] I
have him to pay too[.] I don't know what else to tell you except to tell
you happy Christmas holidays and a happy new year wishing you
health I am affectionately your loving mother Grassi Caterina[.]

Virginia sends her affectionate greetings and a kiss from her daughter wishing you happy holidays from her and her husband[.]

Good bye

Canmore, 4 December 1924[15]

Dearest mother

Here I am with these two lines to bring you my news. With pleasure I can tell you that I am enjoying very good health and I hope that you also will be enjoying good health. At present I can't think of anything else except send you all my best wishes of a merry christmas happy new year's eve and and the best for the new year.

Your son

L. Grassi

M 45 1/10   Falmenta, 2 March 1925

My dear brother in law,

After a long time with no news from you today I write you a couple of lines to bring you the news that I am well. Everyone in my family is also well as is your mother. Your god-daughter was a bit sick with bronchitis but now she has recovered quite well. Dear brother in law I would also like to tell you that I would appreciate it if you came home this winter so that we could put our affairs in order because you see your mother's health is good as far as health goes, but she is not up to do any kind of work because of her age and her legs[.] She is almost infirm so you can see we need to find a solution. Now I have rented out the land belonging to your house starting last year since I was no longer able to work it myself because and also to set things straight between us. To keep things as they are is something that doesn't work. When I wrote to you two or three years [ago] to come home for a division of the property and you answered me to go ahead with the division and that you would be OK with it [and] that you had no intention of returning for another two or three years and I answered that in that case we will wait two or three years[.] Now the two or three years you talked about have passed [but] you don't bring it up therefore I am reminding you to have an answer on the matter. Because to go ahead with a division like you said is something that doesn't work because dividing like that you end up with half a farmhouse[,] half to one and half to the other [but] you can't sell or do anything with it because can you imagine who would want half a farmhouse [–] no one I think because neither one would be able to live in it.[16]

And another more important question is that as we have already mentioned before they [the dwellings] are all rundown[.][17] So what is to be done[?] You can't even fix it because if we are both in agreement then perhaps something can be done or either one or the other can withdraw[.] Then it can be repaired but this way what can you do it's impossible to do it[.] And the house is the same as it always was [and] would cost a lot to repair but it would be convenient to do it all at once, but not spend six or seven thousand lire this year and then perhaps tear everything down and having to redo it all over again in a few years. One more thing[:] my house is not big enough for the whole family and your parents' house can't be lived in because it's all rundown[.] Besides there isn't even room for the beds[18] and then I don't want to go and live in a rented house and leave all the other property go to ruin and then also rents are very expensive here too[.] To rent a house you have to pay from 300 to 400 liras a year[.][19] I hope you will understand me[?] I await your answer. I don't know what else to tell you except to take my leave on my and your sister's behalf and my family and your goddaughter and your mother and I am your brother-in-law Enrico Grassi

For a while now the exchange is about 23 or 24 liras per dollar therefore if you have some money it's a good chance and I expect that it will continue to go up, except one should be careful in case it goes up or goes down, again greetings[.]

M 45 1/11   13 October 1925

Dearest Son

Here I am with these two lines to bring you my news and also to have yours[.] At present I am so-so but I am no longer able to work and I hope you are well too. I come to tell you that on October 4 the *carabinieri*[20] came to see me to get your address and I could not refuse to give it to them. I also come to tell you that last year Enrico gave me back a thousand lire and now at the end of September he finished paying back the other two thousand five hundred[.] What he gave me back last year I deposited in the post office account and the latest sum I will deposit as soon as I am able but I will hold back because I am unable to earn anything[.] I repeat again that the *carabinieri* came to get your address[.] They told me that it is about the military service [–] to regularize your position[.][21] I tell you that your goddaughter Angiolina every time I write to you tells me to tell you to send her a pair of shoes from America[.] Her mother has now bought her a pair but she doesn't want to wear them[.] She keeps saying that she wants them from America. I don't know what else to tell you only to send a fond goodbye and leave you with a kiss from the heart

your beloved mother

I beseech you my dear son I beseech you to write more often to your poor old mother not only once a year[.][22]

Fond greetings from your sister and her family[.]

M 45 1/12   Falmenta, 8 December 1925

My dearest son
I come with this to bring you my news[.] At present I am fairly well as I hope you are[.] I also tell you that I wrote to you some two months ago but you haven't even answered me[.] At least tell me something about what I told you[.] Here the weather is so cold that no one remembers it ever being so cold[.] I don't know what else to tell you other than leave you wishing you merry Christmas and a happy new year[.] Cordial greetings from your mother Caterina Grassi

Receive the most heartfelt greetings and best wishes and happy holidays from Virginia with all her family

M 45 1/13   Falmenta, 7 December 1926

My dearest son
Here I am with this to bring you my news[.] I am well and I hope you are also in good health as is your sister and her family[.] Your brother in law returned too from Switzerland two days ago[.][23] There are no news in town except that Grassi Aurelio too has returned from America[.] I don't know what else to say only that I have a great desire for more frequent letters from you for my consolation[.] I don't know what else to tell you except greet you fondly and I am your mother Testori Caterina

I also send you greetings from your sister and your goddaughter and your brother in law and wish you happy Christmas holidays and happy new year and I am your mother Testori Caterina

I hope you will not delay coming home so that we can see each other again before I die because I am old and one can't live beyond old[.] Good bye a kiss[.] I also send you greetings from the Baraggia woman[.] I enclose here this photo which I think you will recognize[.] Your brother in law is in it too[.] I think you will recognize but to make sure I place a mark over his head[.]

M 45 1/14   Falmenta, 23 October 1926[24]

My dearest brother
I have not had any fond news from you[.] Today I decided to send you this letter to give you news of me[,] of mother and of all my family[.]

95 Caterina Grassi to Lorenzo Grassi, 20 September 1927. Courtesy of Grassi fonds, Whyte Museum of the Canadian Rockies, M 45 1/15.

We are well[.] My husband wanted to write you from Switzerland too but there would not be enough time to receive your answer[.] He tells me to write to you [and] to send you his regards[.]

I also tell you that we must repair the [G]inesco farmhouse to either repair or else it will come down[.] Grassi has warned me that if we cause him any damage we have to pay[.] It's a pity to let it fall down and one feels shame[.] The Remigio [farmhouse] just above there came down all by itself[.][25] Everything was ruined [so] we said we either buy it ourselves or you buy it after we have it appraised because it is going to fall to the ground at any time[.][26] I ask you dear brother to give me an answer on this matter as to what your intentions are[.] I also want to inform you that the chestnuts here [are] ripe[.] Raise your hand if you want some roasted ones[.][27] Nothing more occurs to me[.] A fond hello from mother and from all of us[.] I am your sister Grassi Virginia[.]

Whenever you write to me address it to our family's house because where I'm staying everybody enters from the same door and for this reason I have the mail delivered to our house[.][28] Write to Grassi Virginia c.o. Testori Caterina also known as Minoggi [?] Greetings

M 45/1 15   Falmenta, 20 September 1927

Dear son,
with the present letter I bring you news of us [.] We are well I your mother and Virginia and family. I don't know why you don't write me anymore[.] After such a long time we await your news to no avail. I hope you are well and that you are working[.] Can you then not remember your mother and send a letter as a greeting? It would be so dear to me[.] Remember that I am your mother who was so good to you who always loved you that I always think of you. Dear son write to me send me your news who you are with and what you do and would like to see you home soon. I have now passed my 70th year and therefore I would be very happy to see you come home soon. I inform you that you have been requested to pay a tax because you are not married, like all the others have had to do who are not married.[29] You will have learned that the government makes it compulsory and I had to answer for you and I will still have to pay for you I don't know how much yet I will tell you later. I have also learned that you have been awarded a gold medal because you have done a good deed[.][30] I have learned from the newspaper that you have endangered your life to save someone else[.] You have done a very admirable deed, though

I regret it if you have put your life in danger too, I saw your portrait in the newspaper, and this deed and you did not think of writing to me. Dear son I beg you write to me[.] Do this favour for me.

That newspaper article was sent by a woman from Falmenta who has been in America for about 30 years[.][31] I was happy to get it to have your news[.] I thank that good woman who wanted to know who that young man Grassi Lorenzo [was] and her relatives told her that you are my son. Now I hope that you too will write and tell me many nice things, therefore I wait. I add nothing more except our good byes keep well Good bye my son. Your mother

M 45 1/16   Falmenta, 6 December 1927
My Dear Brother
… we are all well except for myself[.] I have a foot that is always sore [and] that will probably have to be operated[.] I haven't had any news from you for a long time[.] I hope you at least are in good health[.] My husband is still in Switzerland he will be home about December 20[.] Mother is well but is in tears[.] She says you forget that you have a mother and as far as that is concerned she is right because you could find ten minutes either for her or for me[.] I am not saying often but … My little girls are always saying that they have an uncle in America but he never comes home[.] Your goddaughter is already in the fourth grade[.] She will be 11 years old on March 30[.] She has a fine head on her shoulders but she is a very naughty girl[.] She is a devil.
I leave you wishing you merry Christmas a happy new year cordial greetings from my husband[.] I leave you with the pen never with my heart so long
your affectionate sister Grassi Virginia
    Dearest godfather,
    After a long silence I bring you my news[.] I am well as I hope you are. I write to you once in a while but you never answer me. I would be very happy to receive a greeting. Merry Christmas A kiss from me and my little sisters. I am your goddaughter Grassi Angiolina of Enrico

M 45/1 17   Falmenta, 6 December 1927
My Dearest Son
I come to bring you my news that I am in good health as I hope the same of you[.] I tell you that I wrote to you in the month of September but I have not received any answer. It always rains in these parts

I don't know what else to tell you except to send a fond greeting
Wishing you merry Christmas happy new year a big kiss from your
affectionate mother Testori Caterina widow Grassi[.][32]

Canmore, 5 December 1928[33]

Dear sister and brother in law
Here I am after a long time with the present letter to bring you my
news. I enjoy good health I hope you too enjoy very good health. There
is nothing else new I don't know what to tell you except greet you and
all the family. Also christmas greetings happy new year's eve and an
even better new year to you all.
    Your brother

L. Grassi

M 45 1/18   10 December 1928

My dearest son
    I come to you with this letter to tell you of my health[.] I have been
bedridden for some days although not so seriously. Dear son I also
want to tell you to write a little more frequently because being old it
would be a consolation for me to read one of your letters. [I] have a
great desire to see you but I don't know what you are thinking you
never come home[.] [Y]ou have been away for umpteen years and
could easily take a quick trip home to see me since I am so anxious to
see you[.] And you could also come and take care of your affairs[.] I
don't know what else to tell you except to greet you fondly
    your mother Testori Caterina
    I wish you Merry Christmas and Happy New Year from me your
mother and your sister Caterina [sic] and Virginia and your little
nieces Angiolina Maria Ermendina and your brother in law. The girls
continue to ask when my [sic] uncle Lorenzo is coming home. Good
bye again your mother T.C.

M 45 1/19   Falmenta, 22 April 1929
... at present I am well at least I am no longer confined to my bed
and I have begun to walk about[.] Your sister and family are also well
at present [.] I am also informing you have had the good fortune of
a premium of 1,000 lire in your post office savings account. Dear son
I am also telling you that Virginia has bought the marshal's house
and they said that they want to move out of ours and of the Ginesco
farm.[34] When they told me this I accepted their decision because things

could not continue as before either to live in or to sell[.] But they asked that for the payment on the house they bought they are short six thousand liras so if you want to give it to them let me know yes or no as soon as possible.[35] You will let me know regarding the house and the Ginesco property whether you want to purchase it yourself. And you will also let me know if you want to have an assessment done or whether you want to come home yourself some time soon[.][36] You will therefore give me an answer on this[.] The opinion I can give you is to pick it up yourself because two families would not work because it's small and the farmhouse too[.] It's a little extension of the house [good for] storage or for a few chickens or something[.] I don't know what else to tell you only greet you fondly along with your sister and all her family[.] Your brother in law is leaving today for Lucerne[,] Switzerland. I also want to inform you that aunt Giacomina has died in Solduno in February.[37] Again greetings I hope you are well

I am your mother Testori Caterina

M 45 1/20   Falmenta, 11 December 1929

Dearest son

I come to bring you news of me[.] I am enjoying good health and I hope the same of you. I am informing you that Virginia had asked for a loan[.] You never answered me[.] I gave it to them to finish paying for the house[.] I hope I will not be reproached[.] If you don't do good for each other I don't know who you can rely on. Virginia and her husband will write you soon. I don't know what else to write to you except to wish you a Merry Christmas and a Happy New Year greetings[.] Receive many greetings and kisses from your mother goodbye and I am forever your dear mother Testori Caterina

Greetings from your sister and all her family[.]

M 45 1/21   Falmenta, 12 December 1929

Dear son

After a long silence today I thought I would write you a couple of lines to bring you my news. As far as health goes I am well and I hope the same of you. I haven't told you anything else about the house and now I tell you that I have had it assessed by Agostino del Maolo and by Carlo Mansueto and they have estimated its value at 50.20 liras[38] and they assessed that bit of land above the house at 70 liras[.] The Ginesco property's estimate was 1,600 liras but now I can't have the documents drawn up because by law it's no longer possible to buy for

a third party and therefore the buyer must be present[.][39] A little later I
will write more[.] Nothing else occurs at the moment only to greet you
and kiss you and wish you Merry Christmas and happy New Year[.]
Loving kisses from your mother Testori Caterina

I forgot to tell you that on June 9 I went to deposit 50,000 liras at the
bank in a different account because Lorenzo who works at the post
office kept telling me that by doing this you get more interest[.] Before
you earned 3% and now you get more[.] Nothing else occurs to me[.]
Greetings

M 45 1/22   Falmenta, 6 December 1930

Dear brother,
After a long silence I come to bring you my news[.] At present I am
well as I hope the same with you[.] I enjoy excellent health with my
whole family. I leave you and I kiss you with your god-daughter and I
am your sister Grassi Virginia[.]

Under here your dear goddaughter will write
Dear godfather and uncle
After a long time that you don't write to me today I thought of writing you this letter to bring you my news[.][40] At present I am well as I
hope you are[.] You have been away from Italy a long time[.] In fact
you never saw me when I was born and yet you are my godfather[.]
Now I am grown up if you saw me you would say that I am a young
woman but I am very tall for my age. I don't know what else to tell
you. It remains for me to greet you and kiss you dearly[.] I am ever
your dear goddaughter Angiolina Grassi[.]

M 45 2/19   Falmenta, 6 August 1931[41]

Dear son I haven't had news from you in a long time[.] Today I
am thinking of you[.] The health is not bad and I hope the same of
you[.] Dear son I inform you that I have had your news from Emilia
[Cerutti] Zanni and I am very happy that I have learned about you
and she has told me that you injured a leg[.][42] Let me know if you
have healed well and I would really like you to let me know right
away and dear son here at home I have a pair of corduroy pants and
here they are going to waste and I would like to send them to you
if you like or if I should give them to Enrico because he is at home
without a job[.] He went to Switzerland [?] to look for work but he
hasn't found it so write to me what I should do[.] And here there
is a lot of hardship[43] and they are also coming home from America

because it's bad over there too[.] Angelo Minoletti has come back
and Pietro Minoletti but others too are on their way back[.] There is
nothing new in Falmenta[.] I only tell you that on St. Lawrence day[44]
we will inaugurate a new bell on our church tower and also that
Sabino Minoletti has donated an elegant clock to the church tower
and if you could see Falmenta it has almost turned into a city and
the town of Falmenta was grateful to its benefactor[.] When the day
of the inauguration came they gave him a gold medal and he was
very happy with Falmenta and they also had a dinner celebration[.]
I won't go on but I send you my sincerest greetings from me and
from Virginia her husband and family[.] Sincere greetings from your
mother Caterina write soon

The pants which I mended [?] for you are those that belonged to
your poor father and I have always kept them for you because I always lived in the hope of seeing you come home[.] Your goddaughter
Angiolina always tells me that you never send her a gift but when you
write to me tell me if I should give her something[.]

M45 1/23   Falmenta, 7 December 1931
Dearest brother and brother in law
We come to you with these two lines to let you know about our
health[.] We are well and so is the whole family but mother has been
ill for quite a while[.] Always her usual arthritic problems as well as a
bad eye but now I think she is doing fairly well[.] She manages to get
out of bed on her own. Nothing else occurs to me except to leave you
with all our greetings for a merry Christmas and a happy new year
wishing you happiness[.]

I am your sister and brother in law

Grassi Virginia Enrico[45]

Falmenta, 7 December 1931[46]
Dear godfather and uncle
A long time without hearing from you it occurred to me to write this
short letter to bring you some news[.] I am in good health and I hope
the same of you[.] My mother at present is in good health as are all the
members of the family[.] Grandmother unfortunately has been ill for
more than a month although she seems to be a little better now.

Dear godfather you have been in America for almost nineteen
years and it never occurs to you to come for a little trip to Italy[.] We
would be very happy if we could embrace you and grandmother
would be happy too if she could see you one more time[.] And even

this summer when Emilia Cerutti came home she told us that you are very well and that you are quite fat and we were very happy to have your news.[47] Many people from Falmenta came home from America for lack of work and because of the great hardship[.] My father also stayed home[.][48] There is great misery in Italy and we hear that it's like this everywhere. It only remains for me to leave you and greet you most affectionately and kiss you. Greetings from my little sisters and from my family[.] Grandmother sends kisses[.] I am your goddaughter Grassi Angiolina a warm kiss a thousand kisses[.] We wish you a happy new year and a merry Christmas Ciao

M 45 1/24   Falmenta, 1 December 1931

Dearest son
I come with this to bring you news[.] My health is very poor[.][49] I hope you are in good health[.] Dear son in addition I have an eye condition as I did in the past[.] It's likely that I will have to go to the hospital again to have an operation[.] Meanwhile I am trying to wash it with a water that the doctor has prescribed for me to try and cure it that way[.] Otherwise I have to go to the hospital[.] There are no news except that there is a great deal of hardship and lack of jobs[.] Almost everybody is unemployed[.] I don't know what else to tell you except to send you my fondest wishes for a merry Christmas and a happy new year[.] I am your mother Testori Caterina
    Greetings from your sister and brother in law and nieces

M 45 2/1   Falmenta, 12 January 1932

Dear godfather
Today I thought of writing a little letter to you to give you some news of myself[.] My family and I are well and I hope the same of you[.] We spent the Christmas holidays and new year's fairly well in the company of *nonna* [grandmother]. I also want to thank you because *nonna* bought me a gift in your name because she received your letter and I thank you but I can't repay you in any way because we are too far away[.] I can't do more than thank you with all my heart. I am still young but I see that there is hardship[50] everywhere and I understand that there is hardship there too because there probably is no work. There is nothing new. It's cold we have not had snow until today but only a little. *Nonna* got better without having to go to the hospital because we followed the cure prescribed by the doctor. We received your letter on the 27th and we saw that you are well. I have nothing more to tell you. Only kiss you dearly. Receive a kiss from me and the

whole family and from *nonna*. Affectionate greetings and kisses your
loving Angiolina Grassi
    A thousand kisses, ciao, and a thousand thanks
    Goodbye fond kisses

M 45 2/2   Falmenta, 4 April 1932
Dearest son
I bring you my news at present I am well and I hope the same with
you. Dear son I thought I would have to go to the hospital again for
my eyes but thank god I healed without going to the hospital. Agostino
Grassi came home he told me that last year he came to your house
and I was very happy to hear that he came to visit. When Agostino left
again I gave him a salami and I trust he sent it and that you received
it. At present there is no news except it's always very cold and there is
great hardship. I have nothing else to say except to greet you fondly[.]
Virginia's whole family also greets you fondly[.] Your granddaughter
also [unclear][.] Many greetings and heartfelt I am your mother Testori
Caterina[.]
    A thousand kisses and a handshake Ciao.

M 45 2/3   Falmenta, 8 August 1932
Dear Godfather and uncle,
After a long silence I come to you with these two lines to bring you
our news[.] We are all well as we have heard in your letter that you
are also very well and that you have received the package that we
sent you through Agostino Grassi and with the greetings I enclose this
photograph although we came out badly because the sun was bright.
I would appreciate it if you sent me your photo too I would be very
pleased to see you because I have not seen you yet[.][51] I have nothing
else to tell you there is nothing only *miseria* [hardship] and unemployment[.] I greet you and kiss you fondly with all my greetings of the
grandmother[52] a kiss goodbye ciau
                    I am your affectionate goddaughter Grassi Angiolina

M 45 2/4   Falmenta, 9 December 1932
Dearest son
I come to you with this letter to bring you my news[.] I am well and I
hope you also enjoy good health. Dear son I also inform you that the
credit you have in your savings books is 66,462.95 and I converted
the others into postal vouchers two years ago[53] and they yield a little

[Handwritten letter in Italian]

Falmenta li 9 — 12, 82

Carissimo figlio —
Eccomi a te con questa mia per farti sapere
le mie notizie che io sto bene e così ne spero di
te che godrai buona salute

Caro figlio ti faccio pure sapere che il credito
che ai sui libretti il credito che ai sui libretti e
66, 462, 95 e gli altri e 2 anni che li ho convertiti
in buoni postali i quali rendono un po di più.
La somma che ti ho convertito in buoni postali e cinquanta
mila lire i quali quando e sei anni che sono giù in
deposito prendi il 6 per cento d'interesse
insomma al presente in tutto tra capitale e interessi
ai un credito di ~~121,88~~ — di 121, 832.
altro non so che dire solo che salutarti caramente
da parte mia e della Virginia con tutta la sua
famiglia e sono tua madre Testori Caterina
di novità non c'è niente solo che c'e un mucchio di
miseria dato la disoccupazione di nuovo saluti
                                        tua madre
Vengo pure augurandoti buon Natale e buon fine
d'anno e buon principio e spero che tanto alla lunga
non starai più in quei paesi addio tua madre

96 Caterina Grassi to Lorenzo Grassi, 9 December 1932. Courtesy of Grassi fonds, Whyte Museum of the Canadian Rockies, M 45 2/4.

more. The sum I converted in postal vouchers is fifty thousand lire which after six years from deposit yield 6 percent interest. In short at present in total your capital and interest credit is 121,832. I don't know what else to say except to send a fond greeting from me, from Virginia and her whole family, I am your mother Testori Caterina[.]

There is nothing new except a whole lot of *miseria* because of the unemployment[.] Again goodbye your mother[.]

I also want to wish you a merry Christmas and happy new year and I hope that in the long run you won't stay much longer in that part of the world[.]

Goodbye your mother

M 45 2/5 [no date on orginal]

Dearest brother

I come to you with this to bring you news that I am well and my family are all in good health and mother too at present is well and I hope that you too are in good health[.] Dear brother there are no news except they have extended part of the main road[54] and they have reached the house of the Brusetta in town just so as to give a little work to the un-employed because there is great *miseria*[.] There isn't even a chance for a day's work and emigration has been restricted[.][55] My husband could not obtain the permits [to do so][.] He had to stay home and for the whole year he worked 10 days and even then had to work at a reduced salary that is at half the hourly rate which is normally 2.3 Lire instead they had to work at 1.25 per hour[.] There is nothing else except the weather is very bad[.] It has snowed since All Saints almost every day in short the sun rarely shines. I don't know what to say except to greet you fondly on my part and all of us and wishing you happy Christmas and happy new year[.] I am your sister Virginia Grassi

M 45 2/6   [no date on original]

My dear son,

I come to bring you my news[.] At present despite my age I am still rather well and I hope that you will also be in good health[.] There are no news in town except there is great *miseria*[.] Almost all the men are home unemployed[.] I hope you can still put in some days' work[.] If it continues like this who knows where we'll end up but let's hope it will change. I don't know what else to tell you except to greet you dearly on my part and all of us and I am your mother Testori Caterina[.]

I also wish you merry Christmas holidays and happy new year and I am your mother Testori Caterina

M 45 2/7   Falmenta, 15 May 1934

My dearest brother
I come to you with these two lines to inform you that I am in good
health and my family is well too and I hope the same with you. I also
tell you that mother has been bedridden for two months and 20 days
and there is no improvement from day one to today[.] If my husband
weren't here there is no way I could move her[.] Jobs are very scarce
but if someone offered one to him he would not be able to take it
because she is too heavy[,] something like 80 kilos[.] There is great
miseria here and there are no jobs and it's almost impossible to emigrate either abroad or from one town to another[.] As well[,] if you
wanted to buy things on credit they wouldn't serve you anymore[.]
It's either cash or you are out the door[.] The worst that can happen is
to die of hunger[.] I hope out there it is not as bad as it is here. It only
remains for me to say goodbye from me and my husband and family
and sincere greetings from mother[.] I am your devoted sister Grassi
Virginia   Also called Giuvannun[56]

M 45 2/8   Falmenta, 9 September 1934

My dearest brother
I come with this to inform you of our health[.] My husband and I
and daughters are well but I must tell you that our dear mother has
gotten much worse[.] She has been sick for about seven months as
I told you last spring when I last wrote that it had been 2 months
and twenty days but you were not up to write not ever even for a
word of comfort because she is your mother too and that I believe
[you could find] the time to write a couple of lines day or night[.]
Put yourself in my place: it's been seven months with all my family
in anguish[.] Before it was always the legs that were very swollen
from the water in her system and with the chronic heart problem[.]
Now on the contrary her pain is all in her belly and stomach[.] She is
literally like a barrel full of water[.] In the last 15 days she has gotten
much worse[.] They gave her the last rites[.] While the water is stable
goodbye[.] If the water passes out above she will never get up[.][57] I
will write you again shortly it's unlikely that mother will get through
this[.] Even Enrico has almost never been able to work in order to
attend to her because I have not been strong enough to put her to
bed and get her up[.] Imagine our situation[.] I don't need to tell you
more my dear brother[.] It only remains for me and my husband
and all our family to greet you fondly[.] I just asked her now what I
should say to Lorenzo as I am writing to him[.] With great difficulty

she said tell him this[,] that I greet him very very fondly from the bottom of my heart and that [barring a miracle][58] this is the last time that I greet him and she tells me to tell you don't ever forget Virginia who [has] nobody.[59] Fond greetings from all of us[.] Courage[.] She has been sick before but she has never suffered as much as in the last seven months. Enough now[.] I am your loving sister Grassi Virginia called Giovannun[.]

M 45 2/9   Falmenta, 15 October 1934

My dearest brother

I come to you with these two lines to inform you as I was telling you [in the previous letter] that I wanted to write you again[.] We are all well in the family but mother who for many days and nights seemed to be on the verge of dying from one moment to the next improved somewhat[.] For a few days we were even able to take her out into the yard[60] for a spell[.] Now however she is *sicutera in principio*[.][61] One has to be there day and night to fan her because of her difficulty in breathing[.] The doctor also says that she could be gone today just as she could last God knows how long[.] It has already been 8 or 9 months that we have been living this way[.] It does not seem like much to say it but it's a lot of [unclear] I don't know what else to tell you except I leave you with the sincerest greetings from us all and from mother[.] I am your most affectionate sister Grassi Virginia called Giuvannun

M45 2/14[62]   Falmenta, 10 December 1934

Dear brother and brother in law

I write to bring you news of us and of mother. We are all in good health and we hope you are as well. Mother is always in the same con- dition[.] One day she seems to be a little so-so tomorrow it seems like she is dying from one moment to the next. She has been like this since August! She also turns very mean and at times she even soils the bed. She doesn't want to be left alone even for the moment it takes to go to the toilet. We even have to help her sit up in bed[.] In a few words she is completely infirm. You can easily imagine that we no longer know how to please her[.] It's enough to drive one crazy. There are no news here except that there is a great crisis in short a serious lack of jobs[.] The men are all without work[.] We hope that where you are it's not really this bad[.] There must be a little more work. My husband too is always without work – it's been two years. There is nothing else to say except to wish you a merry Christmas and a happy new year. The most heartfelt greetings from my family and my husband. Mother says hello. Ciao

I am your sister Virginia and brother-in-law Enrico

M45 2/10   Falmenta, 21 January 1935

Dear brother

I come to you again[.] We are in good health and we hope the same of you[.] Mother is still the same if not worse! She will not be able to get out of bed anymore she is totally infirm[.] One has to be there by her bedside day and night[.] She is not really grave but certain days she does not even bother to [get up] for her physical needs[.] She just lets herself go. A few days ago I received the twenty dollars you sent me[.] I thank you with all my heart! In the other letter you tell me we have money here that we could use. But ten of the 5,000 lire accounts are only in your name. Then you have four or five accounts also in your name[.] Then there four more or five account books with 1,000 lire in one 2,000 lire in the other in both your names [i.e., in Caterina's as well]. She only [uses them] to buy her stuff. Should she close her eyes tomorrow no one can claim a thing not even for the [funeral] expenses. I am telling you this because perhaps when she dies you will also have to pay the inheritance tax since the two of you are joint holders [of the accounts]. She wanted to read the letter you sent me herself. She even put on her glasses and read it twice then she said that they are fine words but that she cannot in good conscience go and get your money[.][63] She is not at all afraid to withdraw from your accounts for her things but we have to take care of everything else ourselves[.] Despite all that I do she always tells me that I would love to live off someone else[.] She can't even move anymore but there is nothing wrong with her tongue. If you yourself don't tell her directly she will not come up with as much as a cent[.] Just to give you an idea when you gave that 3,000 lire a few years ago I had to go down to city hall to get the clerk's authority to give them to me.[64] She told me she would not give it to me if I did not go either before a post office official or the town clerk. Even though she had your order to give it to me. I will not dwell[.] You figure out what kind of person she is. The house is still the way it was when father was still alive[.] She says she is in charge of everything [and] she keeps everything under lock and key[.] The keys she keeps under her pillow[.] I don't tell you this because I want anything but it's only so that you get the idea. I won't dwell[.] A heartfelt greeting from my family and me. Greetings from mother[.]

Your sister Virginia

Kisses from your goddaughter Angiolina   Ciao

M 45 2/11   Falmenta, 6 February 1935

Dear brother in law and brother

We come with these two lines to bring you the news that we are all well as we hope you are also in good health[.] But we are saddened to bring you the unhappy news of our dear mother who after a year of pain and suffering died on the third day of February and we gave her a funeral on the fifth[.] She was beside herself in almost constant terrible pain for about three weeks. On the first night of the crisis she kept mentioning your name and continued speaking as if you were standing next to her bed[.] Try to give yourself courage as we are doing[.] I will say goodbye for now and I will write you a little later and bring you up to date on everything after we have had time to put things in order a little[.] I send you greetings and a kiss from your nieces[.] We are your brother in law and sister Virginia Grassi

M45 2/12   Falmenta, 10 April 1935

Dear brother and brother in law

Here I am with this[.] I was expecting your answer but so far I have received nothing[.] Perhaps your letter got lost or whatever[.] It's already two months since I sent you the letter announcing the death of our poor mother but so far I haven't received a reply and for this reason [I write to you] again.[65] We had a funeral as is usually done for other household heads and we ordered a little wreath and we spent over 500 liras including funeral and casket expenses[.] Afterwards I went to declare the inheritance[.][66] Of her own she had *monte Baro*[67] and she had the usufruct of the other property that is our father's property[.][68]There too I had to pay about 150 lire[.][69] I hope I have explained myself[.]

Now I will tell you again about your interests here that you have a large sum in savings accounts and folders[.][70] If you want to know how much you have you will let me know. Now I have to get it all registered that is have the interest added[.] I will not fail to have them registered but be careful in case they have to liquidate the folders we can't do anything because both types of accounts are in your name only and for this reason I am warning you in time just in case something happens because if they should liquidate something after a prescribed period if nobody comes to claim them the government takes possession[.] I think you too will realize this[.] Now I hope I have explained more or less everything. I also want to inform you that your bed linen is here at home[.] She made you sixteen sheets and two pillowcases. And then there is still some old and almost worn out [literally, "rotten"] material because you will understand she was bedridden for a year losing her urine and in the end I don't know how to put it she was not aware of anything[.] I won't say anymore only to send you a fond goodbye. I am your sister Virginia Grassi[.]

I also inform you that on April 11 the wife of Giovanni Zanni the *pecorino* is leaving again[.][71] I don't know what to send you [through her][.] I thought I would send you a little salami if she can get it through customs[.] There is no news only misery there is no work and the cost of things is rising again[.] A fond goodbye from me and my husband and daughters I am your sister Virginia Grassi

M 45 2/13   [no date in original][72]
After a long time with no news from you I don't know what to think[.] Today I decided to write a couple of lines to try and have some news from you and also to convey mine and my family's. I don't know what to think[.] I have had no news of you since mother's death[.] I don't know if it's because you haven't received [my] letters or what but in any case if this is not the reason I believe I haven't done anything bad to offend you. I have been sick for the past year and a half not so sick that I have to stay in bed but I'm no longer able to work[.] I also have nephritis as well as a heart condition[.] I have to go to the doctor often and you will understand one needs money for everything[.] I hope that at least you will be in good health[.]

Dear brother I also want to ask you a favour if you can send me at least one hundred dollars because I am in real need of it and even if you can a little more because here everything is expensive[.] Bread is two liras and twenty cents a kilogram flour is 1.30 a kilo[.] There are few jobs more time spent doing nothing than the time spent working[.] I also have a cow that I thought would give birth to a calf instead she is empty and I get nothing if I sell it as it is therefore I wanted to wait and get it pregnant to get some money[.] I hope you can send it as soon as you can. In the meantime I greet you fondly with my husband and daughters   I am your sister Virginia Grassi

Dear brother I would also like to tell you that I would be very happy if you could take a little trip back home because I am very anxious to see you[.] Look even Aurelio Bianconi it had been twenty years that he was away and this year he came back[.] Yesterday he left because he has all his family there in America[.] And then Amedeo Cantoni Gaba's brother he had been away more than forty years he's been home for six months already[.] So you too could come and I would be so pleased[.] Again I greet you fondly and a heartfelt kiss from your sister Virginia Grassi[.] I hope you will give me an answer on what I asked[.]

M 45 2/15   Falmenta, 13 November 1935

My dear brother in law

I come to you with this letter to bring you my news[.] I am well and so is my family they are well at present as we hope you are[.] I also come to tell you that a ceiling joist in the house broke and I am forced to repair at least a quarter of the roof[.] I never told you anything when there were minor repairs to be done but now there is quite a job to be done [since] the rain comes through [and] there is a lack of a bit of everything[.] In short I am asking for your advice if I should repair only as I told you or if perhaps you have different ideas[.] I hope I explained myself. I would ask you to write me a couple of lines on this matter. Dear brother in law I would also like to refer with respect to the interests that you have here at home and as my wife that is your sister has already written to you making it known that you incur a serious loss that is costing you at least 1,760 liras annually because by leaving it in the savings accounts the interest is no more than 2.50 percent[.] By converting to government bonds it's 5 percent but they must be locked in for twenty years though they are also redeemable and convertible[.] By converting them into post office bonds like the other fifty thousand you can get up to 6 or more percent if you leave them for at least six years[.] However they can be withdrawn at any time if the request is made at least three months before[.] So I hope I have explained clearly so that you can figure out what you want to do because in my opinion it's a pain having to work and then see 1,760 liras go down the drain[.] As for the other amount it took a big effort to convince your mother to agree to put it into post office bonds but these 66,460 are in your name and she could not convert them into post office bonds and for this reason they are still deposited this way to this day[.] So therefore you think about it and I will await your answer[.] In my opinion if you don't want to depend on me if you

don't trust me you can take a trip home if afterwards you don't want
to stay you can always go back[.] But in my opinion with the interests
on your capital you could stay home if you feel like it because what
you have saved in bonds you make 3,000 in interest and the other
66 thousand now you only earn 1,560, but by depositing in another
type of account you could earn at least 3,320, so I think that with 5 or
six thousand lire a year you could stay home and live on the interest
alone[.] So I leave you with my greetings and greetings from Virginia
Angiolina Maria Ermendina[.] At least for the house give me an answer to my request soon[.] Again fond regards Your brother-in-law
Enrico Grassi

M 45 2/16   Falmenta, 4 January 1938

My dearest brother
Here I am to inform you that I have received the money order and I
have received it on December 31 and I got 1887[.][73] Let's agree for now
that when I can I will try and pay you back. I also want to thank you
for the favour you did to me[.] I was really in great need of it because I
still had doctor's bills to pay[.] Now I seem to be a little better but I'm
under strict medical care [and] I can no longer work[.] If I work for a
few days I'm back where I started from so as far as this is concerned
I have to resign myself to do little or nothing[.] I also want to inform
you that next year my daughter Angiolina your goddaughter will
probably get married.[74] We are well at present and the holidays just
past went well and we hope that you too will have spent your holidays well[.] The weather is nice but it is very cold in fact it goes down
to 12 degrees below zero cold that rarely occurs in our part of the
world[.] I don't know what else to tell you except for a fond goodbye
from me and all of us[.] I am your sister Virginia Grassi

I have received the money order but no letter[.] I haven't a note
from you in three years I don't know what to say[.]

M 45 2/16   Falmenta, 4 January 1938

My dear godfather and uncle
I add a brief note to my mother's letter; we are all well except my
mother who is always a little sick and can no longer work. We hope
you are well too, we haven't had any news from you which would be
greatly appreciated.

Last year I sent you my photo but I don't know whether you received it or not. I enclose again here also my photo and my fiancé's

Talmenta li 25 x 2 x 1939

Carissimo fratello
Io vengo con questa lettera per darti le mie
notizie e anche quelle di mia famiglia
che noi al presente stiamo tutti bene e così
ne spero di te che sarai in buona salute
Caro fratello vengo pure per dirti che ti avevo
chiesto se potevi mandarmi qualche cosa in denari
ma non ho ricevuto ancor niente non so se non
ai potuto ma ad ogni modo io adesso mi son
rangiata indifferente cioe ho venduto l'una vacca
e solo per farti avviso se alle volte se li ai mandati
e che si andato smarrito il vaglia affinche ti
possi riclamare in merito.
Caro fratello ti porto a conoscenza anche riguardo
i soldi che ai qui sono andata a riscotere i libretti
che li avevo mandati via per registrare gli affitti e
mio a detto l'ufficiale della posta se siamo matti o
e se non siamo buoni di fare i nostri conti o lascia
un capitale così con una così misera rendita.
io ci ho risposto ma io vedo pur troppo ma senza una
autorizzazione da parte tua non posso far niente
e lei mi a risposto che ti faccia avvisato di mandargli
una lettera registrata in ufficio che ugualmente mi
autorizzi me di fare tutto quello che occorre

97 Extract from Virginia Grassi's last letter to Lorenzo Grassi, 25 February 1939.
Courtesy of Grassi fonds, Whyte Museum of the Canadian Rockies, M 45 2/20.

which I hope will please you[.][75] It's likely that next year I will get married we were planning it for this year, but since mother has been sick we decided to wait until next year. I now end and hope this letter will find you in good health and will also please you.

I send you a hundred fond kisses. Greetings from my fiancé. Your goddaughter Angiolina   ciao...

M 45 2/17   Falmenta, 30 November 1938

Dearest brother in law brother and uncle

We come with these two lines to bring you our news[.] At present we are quite well thank God[.] Virginia too is rather well compared to last year. We are hopeful that you too are well[.] Here there are no news except that everything is going up especially the cost of food[.] Imagine bread is 2.10 [liras] a kilo when mixed with corn flour[.] The other kind made with wheat is 3.10 a kilo[.] Corn flour is 1.40 a kilo pasta is 3.30 and rice is 2.30 a kilo[.] In short everything is expensive jobs are scarce and even then salaries are miserably low compared to the high cost of living[.] The hourly rate goes from 1.90 to 2.60 an hour but working for more than forty hours a week is not allowed[.] But if only there were this kind of work but it's only available for maybe a month or two and then you don't find work for another month and then in going around looking for work you have to fritter away the little you have earned[.] At the end of it all it's almost impossible to cope if you have a family[.] I hope it's not quite so bad over there as it is here because they are countries with a little more resources and not like here where you can't find a place to hit a nail[.] I don't know what else to tell you except goodbye from me and all my family and wish you a merry Christmas and a happy New year[.] Your brother in law Grassi Enrico

Greetings and kisses from everyone in the family

Dear brother in law I want to ask you a favour if you could lend me something at least as much as you gave me last year if you can.[76] You will surely tell me that I am constantly annoying you but please believe me that if you were in my situation you could not help yourself either therefore if you can[,] give it to me if you can't I will have to turn to someone else. So whether you intend giving it to me or not let me know soon because you see we are at the end of the year there are taxes there is the store in short things are coming to a head. In short one has to try and keep the lid on things. I thank you in advance and I am your brother in law

Grassi Enrico

M 45 2/18   Falmenta, 15 March 1938

Dearest brother

I come with this to bring you my and my family's news at present we are well only I am always a little sick[.] We hope you too are in good health. I am also informing you in case you don't know Cousin Giovanni [Testori] called *buan* died in Fort William on February 17[.] He was hit with pneumonia and in 10 days he died[.] I am also informing you that my husband was injured at work behind a wire carrying lumber[.] He was struck by a load and he injured his head and shoulder but now he is getting better he was on worker compensation for almost two months[.] There are no other news only it has been a very cold winter but very little snow really almost none[.] Lately the weather has been beautiful there is a drought[.] It only remains for me to send you my greetings and my family's and wish you a happy Easter. I am your sister Grassi Virginia

M 45 2/20   Falmenta, 25 February 1939

Dearest brother

I come with this letter to give you news of me and also of my family[.] We are well at present and I hope you are well. Dear brother I also come to tell you that I had asked you if you could send me some money but I haven't received anything yet[.] I don't know if you couldn't, but at any rate I have now made other arrangements that is I sold a cow. I say it only to warn you in case you sent it and the money order went astray so that you can reclaim it. Dear brother I also want to make you aware of the money you have here[.] I went to pick up the account books that had the interest on them registered and the post office clerk asked me whether we are crazy or whether we can't add two and two by leaving such an amount to collect such a measly interest. I answered that I can see but that without an authorization from you there is nothing I can do and she answered me to instruct you to send her a registered letter to the office that would authorize me to do whatever is needed[.] Therefore she assured me that sending a registered letter is sufficient even without a power of attorney[.] Lorenzo is now dead but one of Brocca's daughters is now working in the post office that is Grassi Giovanni postal officer Ponte di Falmenta[.][77] I hope therefore that I have explained myself if you trust me I am only trying to protect your interests and nothing else because you will understand that by leaving [accounts as they are] is not to your advantage because the small sum that has been put in post office bonds yield 6 percent, and the rest yield barely 2 percent or so[.] Therefore you decide how you want to do things you're the boss[.] I don't know what else to say to you except to send you a fond greeting from me and all of us[.] I am your sister Virginia Grassi

M 45 2/21[78] Cunardo, 1 May 1956[79]

Dear uncle Lorenzo

After many letters sent to you some of which were returned because of a wrong address and others that went unanswered, I hope that at least this one will reach you! Now I will only repeat the most important news contained in the others[;] it will mean that if this letter reaches its destination in the ones that follow[80] I will give you more detailed news. With great sorrow I inform you that on March 5, 1946 mother died and on April 5, 1954 father died too. So Maria and I are the only ones left. For the past 4 years I have been working as a maid with a family in a town near Varese and Maria is living in Falmenta and she is making do with a cow and a few goats. Life is certainly not very easy but patience, as long as there is health which by the way at present is excellent as we hope so is yours. We have always had a desire to hear from you especially now that we no longer have our parents or any other close relatives except you. I will not make this too long since I fear that this too will be returned to sender[.] It means that if it reaches you I would be very happy to write you again[.]

I am anxious to receive a letter from you after so many years of silence and hoping to find you in good health I extend very affectionate greetings also on behalf of my sister Maria. Your niece Angela Grassi and Maria

This is my exact address[:] Angela Grassi c/o Montecucco Giuseppe Family Cunardo Prov. Varese

98 Angela's last letter to her uncle and godfather, 1 May 1956. Courtesy of Grassi fonds, Whyte Museum of the Canadian Rockies, M 45 2/21.

non avendo più nessun parente stretto,
all'infuori di voi

Chan mi prolungo in quanto temo che
anche questo mi ritorni indietro vuol
dire che se questa vi giunge mi sarei
molto lieta di scrivere di più

Con ansia di ricevere una vostra lettera
dopo tanti anni di silenzio e di trovarvi
in buona salute vi porgo i miei più
affettuosi saluti a nome di mia sorella
Maria pure

                 Vostra nipote
                 Angela Grassi e Maria

Questo e' il mio indirizzo preciso
Angela Grassi fu mio familia
Montenero Giuseppe Cunardo
prov. Varese

Notes

Introduction

1 He was baptized Andrea Lorenzo Grassi but, like most of his contemporaries in Falmenta, he never used his baptismal name. Rather, he was known as Lorenzo Grassi to his family and in his village of origin. This continued after his emigration to Canada at least until September 1916, when he began his employment with the Canmore Coal Company, at which point he signed himself as "Lawrence Grassi." His family and other Falmentine acquaintances, however, continued to refer to him as Lorenzo. In what follows we have generally used the name he would have used at the point in his life under discussion.

Chapter 1

1 See Whyte Museum of the Canadian Rockies, Archives and Library, Grassi fonds (henceforth simply "Grassi fonds"), M 45 1/10, Enrico Grassi to Lorenzo Grassi, 2 March 1925, for a discussion of the division of the property of Giuseppe Grassi between his son Lorenzo and his daughter Virginia.
2 Grassi fonds, M 45 1/1, Caterina Grassi to Lorenzo Grassi, 16 July 1922.
3 Grassi fonds, M 45 1/5, Caterina Grassi to Lorenzo Grassi, 5 July 1923; authors' conversations with Armanda and Marisa Grassi, Giuseppe Zanni, and others, Falmenta, June 2010, confirmed the importance of transhumance in the agricultural life of the valley. See also Grassi fonds, M 45 1/14, Virginia Grassi to Lorenzo Grassi, 23 October 1926, and Grassi fonds, M 45 1/19, Caterina Grassi to Lorenzo Grassi, 22 April 1929, for the references to the Ginesco *cascina*, the family's dwelling place in the alpine meadows, used when they moved to higher elevations in the summer.

4 Bergamaschi, *Conoscere la Valle Cannobina*, pp. 185–91, reproduces in full a journalist's account, published in March 1906 in the Milanese magazine *Il Secolo XX* (The Twentieth Century), of the recruitment of chimney sweeps from the Cannobino Valley.

5 Tony Minoletti's life was described Nancy Wolfer in conversations with the authors in 2010.

6 The records for this tragic litany of births and deaths are found in the archives of the municipality of Falmenta and those of its parish church of San Lorenzo.

7 For a sense of the isolation of the various valley settlements, see the 1906 account by a journalist of a visit to friends in the valley reproduced in Bergamaschi, *Conoscere la Valle Cannobina*, pp. 185–6.

8 On the use of the term "transshipment point" see Pozzetta, "The Mulberry District," p. 7.

9 On the exploitation practiced in locations like Como and Chiasso by steamship companies and their agents, often acting on behalf of padrones in North America, see Harney, "A Case Study of Padronism," p. 146; Harney, "The Commerce of Migration," pp. 19–36. There is no information to suggest that their often nefarious practices reached into the Cannobino Valley.

10 A receipt made out to "Grassi Giuseppe Antonio fu Cipriano," Lorenzo's father, dated 28 January 1913, for return travel by steamer on Lake Maggiore, indicates the importance of the lake for travellers to and from the region. Giuseppe's ticket was issued to him on the basis of his passport, further suggesting sojourning outside of Italy, in nearby France or Switzerland. The receipt is part of the Grassi family papers in Falmenta.

11 A date for the passport would help to determine whether it had been issued to a young Lorenzo when he travelled with his father or whether he obtained it immediately prior to his departure for New York, as he appears to have done with his birth certificate. Bill Cherak, Grassi's long-time friend, and executor of his will, was responsible for the disposition of Grassi's personal papers. Unfortunately, we were only able to retrieve, in photocopy form, the first two pages of the original passport discussed here. All of the other travel documents discussed in these pages are from the private collection of Bill Cherak and are reprinted with his permission.

12 N.A. Wait, "Grassi of Canmore," pp. 24–5.

13 See the discussion below of the life and travels of Stefano Zanni, named by Grassi in 1912 as his cousin and contact in Fort William.

14 It is not clear from this French Line ticket whether the manifest page and line number were recorded before or after Grassi boarded the SS *La*

Provence. See figs. 28 and 29 for reproductions of relevant pages from the manifest for the 2 March 1912 voyage by the SS *La Provence*.

15 "L'émigration des colons allemands et italiens vers l'Amérique a pris un tel développement que la Compagnie Générale Transatlantique a dû créer, de concert avec les Compagnies de chemins de fer, des trains spéciaux qui vont à Bâle et à Modane chercher les émigrants qui s'embarquent chaque semaine au Havre sur ses grands paquebots de la ligne de New-York." (The emigration of German and Italian colonists to America became so significant that the Compagnie Générale Transatlantique had to provide, in concert with railway companies, special trains to travel to Basel and Modane to provide transportation for emigrants who travel weekly to embark at Le Havre on the company's great liners for the voyage to New York.) P. Lefèvre, *Le chemin de fer* (1889), downloaded from the Modane, France, website, January 2014. We have been unable to locate the original volume by P. Lefèvre.

16 An advertisement by Compagnie Générale Transatlantique booking agent Jorio Desire runs as follows: "I passaggeri proseguono direttamente per New York senza soggiornare nè a Modano nè all'Havre" (reproduced in Dante Presotto, *Luigi Angelo Manias: "Laborer"* [self-published, 2010], p. 59.

17 The late arrival of the SS *La Provence* is confirmed by consulting shipping reports in the *New-York Tribune* available online at http://chroniclingamerica .loc.gov, which appear within that newspaper's daily column titled "Marine Intelligence." The following "Marine Intelligence" columns were consulted to track the departure and arrival of Grassi's ship: 3 March 1912, p. 14; 7 March 1912, p. 14; and 8 March 1912, p. 14. The ship's manifest for this voyage also records its arrival on 9 March.

18 Information about the SS *La Provence*, conditions in steerage, and similar information is available at http://www.gjenvick.com and also at the Ellis Island Port of New York passenger records site, http://www.libertyellis foundation.org.

19 Several weeks after Grassi's crossing a much more famous voyage was cut short by conditions in the North Atlantic when RMS *Titanic* struck an iceberg and sank, with the loss of fifteen hundred lives. One of the ships known to have sent a message of warning to the *Titanic* about the presence of sea ice in the North Atlantic shipping lanes was the SS *La Touraine*, part of the Compagnie Générale Transatlantique fleet.

20 See the advertisement by Compagnie Générale Transatlantique booking agent Jorio Desire reproduced in Presotto, *Luigi Angelo Manias*, p. 59.

21   The health inspection at the Ellis Island hospital facilities conducted by the Public Heath and Marine Hospital Service is discussed in Conway, *Forgotten Ellis Island*.

22   A tally of all the Falmentines who emigrated between the 1880s and the mid-1920s reveals that more than 80 per cent travelled onboard ships owned and operated by the CGT. Either by choice or by coincidence, three CGT ships – the SS *La Touraine*, SS *La Lorraine*, and SS *La Provence* – carried more than 65 per cent of all Falmentine passengers bound for New York, with SS *La Provence*, the ship on which Lorenzo Grassi travelled, the clear "favourite" of the three.

23   SS *La Provence*, arrived 9 March 1912 at New York, p. 59, line 22 for Andrea Grassi, lines 24 and 26 for Edoardo Grassi and Francesco Milani, respectively. Giovanni, Agostino, Vittorio, and Giovanni Zanni were recorded on p. 61, lines 2, 3, 4, and 5.

24   Henceforth we use "paesan" rather than "villager." "Paesan," sometimes used in English-language studies of Italian immigration, translates as "countryman." The term "villager" doesn't convey the same sense as the Italian, which signifies someone from the *same* village, town, city, province, or country.

25   It is likely that this is the same Agostino Zanni who was later named as the contact resident at 505 McPherson Street by Stefano Zanni on his return voyage to Fort William in 1913.

26   This earlier Lorenzo Grassi was also single and twenty-one years old, but declared his next of kin to be his mother Lucia, and his final destination was "Quebec Montreal," where his contact was his friend "Anselmo Andrea." Anselmo's address, however, was reported as "Box 101 Fort William Ont." The two Lorenzos were wrongly conflated in Silvano Dresti's account of Grassi's life in "Emigrazione," p. 259.

27   Quoted in Marty, *Switchbacks*, p. 52, apparently drawn from a personal conversation with Grassi when he was assistant park warden at Lake O'Hara. Much in Marty's account of his encounters with Grassi and his contemporaries appears to be romanticized as masculine creative non-fiction and should be read with caution.

28   Grassi family collection, Falmenta, Italy: "Foglio di Congedo Illimitato," issued to "Grassi Andrea," dated 7 November 1911; "Libretto Personale di Grassi Andrea"; and "Libretto di Tiro di Grassi Andrea" (Andrea Grassi's target practice booklet).

29   Grassi fonds, v240 / 889(PA), G.A. (Giovanni Antonio) Testori to Lorenzo Grassi, Ripple [Ontario] 14 August 1916.

30 Grassi fonds, M45 1/11, Caterina Grassi to Lorenzo Grassi, 13 October 1925.

31 With these three sums alone he had remitted more than the cost of his trans-Atlantic ticket.

32 Wait, "Grassi of Canmore," pp. 24–5.

33 Grassi fonds, v240/887(PA), Edoardo Grassi to Lorenzo Grassi, Mobert, Ontario, 26 July 1914. The Falmentines in Jackfish, Ontario, are discussed below.

34 Forestell, "Bachelors, Boarding-Houses, and Blind Pigs," p. 267; see also Sandilands, "Where the Mountain Men Meet the Lesbian Rangers," pp. 142–62. The possibility of same-sex relationships in this homosocial cultural environment was suggested in a decidedly homophobic way by R.F. Harney: "often the eyes of the village followed the migrant into the remotest setting. If a man became a drunkard, consorted with the rare prostitutes to be found in the North, *dabbled in perversion* or just seemed to go crazy, word might get back to family and town" ("Men without Women," p. 88, emphasis added).

35 Lawrence is quoted as saying this in a newspaper account of his life, written by an unknown author and published in 1969 in *The Hoodoos Highlander.*

36 The sheets and pillowcases added to the trousseau by Lorenzo's mother are described in a letter by Virginia to her brother (Grassi fonds, M45 2/12, 10 April 1935). The embroidery was discussed by Armanda Grassi and other Grassi family descendants in conversations with the authors, Falmenta, June 2010.

Chapter 2

1 Copies of these letters and other documents were obtained from descendants of Lorenzo Grassi in Falmenta in 2008. Comments in the family letters in the Grassi fonds also indicate that Grassi sent his family a number of letters that have not survived.

2 Biographical data for Virginia Grassi and her family was obtained from the registers of the parish Church of San Lorenzo, Falmenta. One of Virginia's twins was baptized Luigia Maria but was known as Maria, while her sister was baptized as Ermendina Pierina and was later known as Armandina or Armanda.

3 In the registration of Virginia and Enrico's marriage in February 1914 at the parish church of Falmenta, Virginia was recorded as the daughter of the "living" Giuseppe Antonio Grassi, son of the deceased Cipriano

(Grassi). The power-of-attorney document was drawn up by a notary in Cannobio on 28 August 1916 and is now part of the Grassi family papers in Falmenta.

4 The pay slips were deposited in the Canmore Museum and Geoscience Centre by Bill Cherak, Lawrence Grassi's executor.

5 Margaret Fleming noted in 1954 that she and other guests at the Alpine Club of Canada club house in Banff "saw Grassi who came … and showed us lovely but endless slides" (Reichwein and Fox, *Mountain Diaries*, p. 76). Grassi's use of slides and photographs might have been his way of "communicating" with an audience using a type of language (i.e., images) that could speak for him. At least in the early period of his emigration, apparently, he was concerned with written and spoken language, as is suggested by a copy of the handbook *Grammatica Accelerata* (1912) preserved with his memorabilia, which promised to teach "the Italian in America" how "to write, speak and understand the English language in a brief period of time and without need of an instructor."

6 From their arrival in Canada in 1911 Elizabet and her sisters Johanne and Eugenie adopted or were given a variety of nicknames. In time the three sisters anglicized their names, and Elizabet became Elizabeth. Later in life she was simply called Lizzie, often shortened to Liz (Oltmann, *Lizzie Rummel*, p. 15).

7 In a letter dated September 1927, Caterina reported that she had passed her seventieth year (she was born in April 1856, so she was in fact seventy-one). She expressed a strong desire for her son's return to Falmenta, a desire perhaps made stronger by her advancing years and the arrival of news from "America" about his rescue of an injured climber, Dr Williams, from near the summit of Mount Bastion (see chapter 3) (Grassi fonds, M45 1/15, Caterina Grassi to Lorenzo Grassi, 20 September 1927).

8 Grassi fonds, M45 2/10, Virginia Grassi to Lorenzo, 21 January 1935.

9 Grassi fonds, M45 2/12, Virginia and Enrico Grassi to Lorenzo Grassi, 10 April 1935.

10 This quotation is drawn from documents in the possession of Armanda Grassi, Lorenzo Grassi's great niece. Photocopies of these documents are held by the authors.

11 Grassi fonds, M45 1/8, Caterina Grassi to Lorenzo Grassi, 12 May 1924, emphasis added.

12 Grassi fonds, M45 1/9, Caterina Grassi to Lorenzo Grassi, 1 December 1924.

13 Riva, *Survival in Paradise*, p. 59.

14 It is worth noting that this account is limited, here, to the available correspondence in the Grassi fonds. For the period October 1925 to April 1929 a

total of six letters from Caterina to Lorenzo survive, and none of these mention finances. It is not clear whether the loans repaid by Enrico Grassi were those that Caterina had granted him in 1925.

15 Grassi fonds, M45 1/19, Caterina Grassi to Lorenzo Grassi, 22 April 1929. The "premium" on Lorenzo's savings in Falmenta might have been a form of interest earned on his postal savings account.

16 Enrico and Virginia appear to have moved in with Caterina some time after the birth of their twins in 1922. According to municipal records they had resided at house number 94 in Falmenta, and Caterina's residence was listed as number 133. They lived with her until 1926, when Virginia informed Lorenzo that they had moved out of the house.

17 Grassi fonds, M45 1/20, Caterina Grassi to Lorenzo Grassi, 6 December 1930.

18 Grassi fonds, M45 1/21, Caterina Grassi to Lorenzo Grassi, 12 December 1929. Caterina wrote that the Grassi house was valued at "50.20" liras; we can only assume that she omitted a zero in reporting this sum to Lorenzo. Her daughter's and son-in-law's purchase of a house was part of a discussion that had begun some years before and that included a desired division of family property between Virginia and her brother, discussed below.

19 Grassi fonds, M45 2/4, Caterina Grassi to Lorenzo Grassi, 9 December 1932. Photocopies of some of the postal vouchers (singular, *buono postale*) were provided by Lorenzo's descendants in Falmenta and are in the authors' possession.

20 Grassi fonds, M45 2/2, Caterina Grassi to Lorenzo Grassi, 6 August 1931. In the same letter, perhaps as further enticement, she asked what she should do with a pair of her deceased husband's corduroy trousers that she had mended and kept for him.

21 Caterina Grassi reported *miseria* or hardship in Falmenta in a letter to Lorenzo dated 6 August 1931. In the same letter she noted the return of emigrants from "America" (Grassi fonds, M45 2/19). The reference to "great hardship" is derived from a letter she wrote on 4 April 1932 (Grassi fonds, M45 2/2). The term "*miseria*" was used in the previously cited letter of 9 December 1932 and repeated in her last letter to him, c. December 1933 [?], with the observation that almost "all the men are home unemployed" (Grassi fonds, M45 2/6). The Christmas greetings in this note suggest the December date in 1933, after a similar seasonal letter sent the year before (Grassi fonds, M45 2/4, 9 December 1932).

22 Grassi fonds, M45 1/9, Caterina Grassi to Lorenzo Grassi, 1 December 1924. This letter appears to have crossed in transit one written by Lorenzo to his mother on 4 December 1924.

23 Grassi fonds, M45 1/11, Caterina Grassi to Lorenzo Grassi, 13 October 1925. It is difficult to determine whether Lorenzo was, in fact, writing "once a year." The desperation in his mother's letters suggests otherwise.

24 Grassi fonds, M45 1/12, Caterina Grassi to Lorenzo Grassi, 8 December 1925.

25 Grassi fonds, M45 1/13, Caterina Grassi to Lorenzo Grassi, 7 December 1926. For discussion of Aurelio Grassi and other Falmentines in western Canada, and Alberta in particular, see chapter 3.

26 Grassi fonds, M45 1/15, Caterina Grassi to Lorenzo Grassi, 20 September 1927.

27 Grassi fonds, M45 1/15, Caterina Grassi to Lorenzo Grassi, 20 September 1927. The rescue is discussed in chapter 3.

28 Grassi fonds, M45 1/18, Caterina Grassi to Lorenzo Grassi, 10 December 1928.

29 Grassi fonds, M45 2/19, Caterina Grassi to Lorenzo Grassi, 6 August 1931. This letter is incorrectly recorded in the fonds listing as having been written in 1938: Caterina Grassi died in February 1935. Lorenzo's mother declared herself to be happy to have news about her son from Emilia (Cerutti) Zanni despite the fact that it included news about a leg injury Lorenzo had suffered; see also note 40.

30 Grassi fonds, M45 2/2, Caterina Grassi to Lorenzo Grassi, 4 April 1932. In this letter Caterina discusses the return to Falmenta of Agostino Grassi and the fact that she has entrusted him with a salami for her son on Agostino's return to Canada.

31 Grassi fonds, v240-878(pa)022. The name of Lorenzo's proxy as godfather was found in the record of her christening in the register of births and baptisms of the parish of San Lorenzo, Falmenta. The pin in the shape of a maple leaf on the knot of Zanni's tie is visible when the photograph is magnified. There are several Falmentines with the name Giovanni Zanni who were emigrants to Canada. See note 40 for discussion of Giovanni Zanni, husband of Emilia Cerutti, who had connections to the Grassi family.

32 Grassi fonds, M45 1/145, Virginia Grassi to Lorenzo Grassi, 23 October 1926. Chestnuts were a mainstay of the peasant economy and diet in the Cannobino Valley, and Virginia also may have been joking about them. She knew how tiresome they were likely to become over the following months, a memory no doubt shared by her brother.

33 Grassi fonds, M45 1/16, Virginia Grassi to Lorenzo Grassi, 6 December 1927.

34 Grassi fonds, M45 1/23, Virginia, Enrico and Angiolina Grassi to Lorenzo Grassi, 7 December 1931; for the contents of Angiolina's portion of this letter see below.

35 Grassi fonds, M45 2/9, Virginia Grassi to Lorenzo Grassi, 9 September 1934.
36 Grassi fonds, M45 2/10, Virginia Grassi to Lorenzo Grassi, 21 January 1935.
37 Grassi fonds, M45 2/10, Virginia Grassi to Lorenzo Grassi, 21 January 1935.
38 Grassi fonds, M45 2/11, Virginia Grassi to Lorenzo Grassi, 6 February 1935. Caterina Grassi died on 3 February 1935.
39 Grassi fonds, M45 2/12, Virginia Grassi to Lorenzo Grassi, 10 April 1935.
40 *Pecorino*, Giovanni Zanni's nickname, means "little sheep." Emilia Zanni, the *pecorino*'s wife mentioned by Virginia, and her three children boarded the *SS Montcalm* at Cherboug three days after the date of Virginia's letter, and arrived at Quebec City on 23 April 1935. According to the ship's manifest "Amelia" [Emilia] Zanni and her fourteen-year-old son "Peter" had been in Canada before, from 1922 to 1931. They were both listed as "British," so they had been naturalized before their departure. Emilia's daughters Nelli and and Mary, respectively nine and four years old, were listed as Canadians, born in Banff. This was the return voyage to Canada of Emilia (Cerutti) Zanni and her children whose visit to Falmenta had been reported to Lorenzo in 1931 by his mother and, as we will see, by his goddaughter Angiolina. The Zanni family's connections to Lorenzo were close, and included Emilia's brother Pietro Cerutti, who climbed with Lorenzo in the Rockies in the late 1920s, after he emigrated with his sister in 1922. Pietro Cerutti is discussed in chap. 3. It is not clear whether Emilia was married to the Giovanni Zanni who was Lorenzo's proxy godfather for his niece Angiolina (see note 31).
41 Grassi fonds, M45 2/16, Virginia Grassi to Lorenzo Grassi, 4 January 1938. Three years without a note from her brother would place his last known communication with her in December 1934 or January 1935; in her 21 January 1935 letter to him she acknowledged having received twenty dollars and his advice about using his money in Falmenta; see Grassi fonds, M45 2/10, Virginia Grassi to Lorenzo Grassi, 21 April 1935.
42 Grassi fonds, M45 2/10, Virginia Grassi to Lorenzo Grassi, 21 January 1935. Virginia reports her mother's suspicions about Virginia's desire to have access to her brother's funds.
43 Grassi fonds, M45 2/20, Virginia Grassi to Lorenzo Grassi, 25 February 1939. There is no information to suggest that Lorenzo provided Virginia with a registered letter to grant her power of attorney: if he did so, it is possible that a response was disrupted because of the outbreak of war in September 1939. The receipt, now preserved in the Grassi family papers in

Falmenta, for Virginia's letter to Lorenzo names him as the recipient at "Canmore Canada."

44 In the municipal record of the birth of his daughter, Angiolina, his occupation was reported as *muratore* or mason, while birth records of his other daughters described him as *contadino* or peasant.

45 Grassi fonds, M45 2/10, Virginia (and Enrico) Grassi to Lorenzo Grassi, 21 January 1935. It is not clear from this letter whether Enrico and his family continued to live in what was legally still Virginia's and Lorenzo's house (fig. 21).

46 Grassi fonds, M45 2/17, Enrico Grassi to Lorenzo Grassi, 30 November 1938.

47 An anecdote involving Angiolina as negligent babysitter of her twin sisters while the family was in the alpine meadows gathering hay is recounted in Petrosina, ed., *Chilò: Falmenta si racconta*, p. 96.

48 Grassi fonds, M45 1/16, Virginia (and Angiolina) Grassi to Lorenzo Grassi, 6 December 1927.

49 Grassi fonds, M45 1/23, Angiolina Grassi to Lorenzo Grassi, 7 December 1931, enclosure included with a letter by her mother, Virginia.

50 Grassi fonds, M45 1/23, Angiolina Grassi to Lorenzo Grassi, 7 December 1931, enclosure included with a letter by her mother, Virginia.

51 Grassi fonds, M45 2/1, Angiolina Grassi to Lorenzo Grassi, 12 January 1932. The gift Lorenzo gave his niece may have been in response to a letter from his mother in which she relayed a complaint from Angiolina "that you never send her a gift"; Caterina Grassi to Lorenzo Grassi, 6 August 1931.

52 Grassi fonds, M45 2/3, Angiolina Grassi to Lorenzo Grassi, 8 August 1932. Angiolina's complaint that she has never seen her uncle could be understood to mean she had never met him in person, or that he had not sent a photograph of himself to his family.

53 Grassi fonds, M45 2/16, Angiolina Grassi to Lorenzo Grassi, 4 January 1938. In this letter Angiolina refers to a photograph of herself she had sent to her uncle but that he had not acknowledged receiving, and wondered if it had gone astray. No photograph of Angiolina alone as a young adult survives in the Grassi fonds.

54 Grassi fonds, M45 2/21, Angela Grassi to Lorenzo Grassi, 1 May 1956.

55 Information about the death of Maria's twin sister Armandina ("Ermendina" according to her baptismal record) was obtained in conversations with her descendants in Piedmont, who have asked that her wartime death be treated with respectful silence.

56 The date and location of Angiolina's death were noted in the margin of her municipal record of birth, in the civil register of births for the municipality of Falmenta.

57 Lawrence Grassi's will and documents recording the attempt to find his
relatives in Italy are now in the possession of Bill Cherak, who shared
them with us during a meeting in 2009 in Canmore, Alberta. A copy of the
will is also included in the ACC fonds, Whyte Museum of the Canadian
Rockies, M200/AC 421/591, Series I.A.2.e/.

58 The manifest of the SS *Duca D'Aosta* (arr. New York 28 December 1914) for
Carlo Piazza of Falmenta, seventy-four years old, contains the declaration
that he had been in Canada for the period 1873–1914. He was travelling to
his son Vittorio in Winnipeg, but also had "3 nephews in Wiinnipeg 1 son
in Montreal." He was reported in this record as "Canadian." His is the
earliest presence from the Cannobino Valley we have found in Canada.
The second earliest is that of Giovanni Cantoni (1848–1876) whose death
"A Montreal (America)" (in Montreal [America]') is recorded on a Cantoni
family tombstone in Crealla, a hamlet of Falmenta. We thank Marilena
Milani for making a photograph of the memorial available to us.

59 See, for example, Potestio, *Italians of Thunder Bay*; Piovesana, *Italians of Fort
William's East End*; Pucci, "Thunder Bay's Italian Community," pp. 79–102.

60 Potestio, *Italians of Thunder Bay*, p. 35, notes that 107 Italian nationals were
listed in the 1901 census, so Falmentines were then almost one-third of the
total Italian-national group.

61 According to Potestio, *Italians of Thunder Bay*, p. 35, the Tiboni family was
one of the two largest Italian-national families in Fort William.

62 Evidence for other emigrants from the Cannobino Valley, and from the
settlement of Gurro in particular, is not included in this overview, but it is
important to note that in the 1911 census many of those with Gurro surnames often shared accommodation with Falmentines.

63 Potestio, *Italians of Thunder Bay*, p. 37, reports an Italian-national population
of 710 from the 1911 census.

64 Dresti, "Emigrazione," p. 259, discusses the knowledge in Falmenta of "via
di Falmint" in Fort William. On 20 September 1904 a weekly published in
the Cannobino Valley, *La Vedetta*, printed an article, "Orribile disgrazia"
(Horrible misfortune), describing the death of a Falmentine, Antonio Zanni,
in an area of Fort William so densely populated by Falmentines as to be
known there as "Borgo Italiano dei Cannobini," or the "Italian neighbourhood of residents from the Cannobino Valley."

65 Potestio, *Italians of Thunder Bay*, p. 50, and abundantly documented in
Piovesana, *Italians of Fort William's East End*, pp. 22–31.

66 Potestio, *Italians of Thunder Bay*, p. 64.

67 This photograph is also reproduced in Potestio, *Italians of Thunder Bay*, p. 278,
but no further details about the club's history are available in his study,
and we do not know whether it was related to the Principe di Piemonte.

68 Ship's manifest, SS *La Gascogne*, arr. Ellis Island, 27 April 1903. This can plausibly be taken to refer to the Paolo or Paul Tiboni described above. There were also four emigrants from Gurro listed on this manifest page, three of whom were headed for Heron Bay, Ontario, on the north shore.

69 The record of Stefano Zanni's 1920 marriage was obtained from Archives of Ontario, *Registrations of Marriages, 1869–1926*, MS932, Reels 1–793 (from ancestry.ca). The marriage license shows that Zanni married twenty-eight-year-old Lucia Milani and that they were married by a Presbyterian minister.

70 The facts in this paragraph are in tension, but it seems unlikely that Stefano and Rosalia completed another trip between 1911 (after the census enumeration) and 1913 for which no record has survived.

71 Agostino Zanni was named, about two years after his arrival, as contact by Steve and Rosalia Zanni on their return to Fort William after their 1913 trip to Italy. This suggests that Agostino lived in his brother-in-law's boarding house after his arrival in Fort William. The term *la tracca* was used by Edoardo Grassi, who travelled with Lorenzo, in a postcard he sent in 1914 after Lorenzo had left the north shore.

72 Ramirez, "Brief Encounters," p. 20.

73 His union membership card is now in the Grassi fonds, Whyte Museum of the Canadian Rockies, M45/8; the membership cards were issued for 1913 and 1914.

74 The letter, dated at Solduno, Switzerland, on 23 January 1913, is part of the Grassi family papers in Falmenta. The Giovanni mentioned here may be Caterina Testori's nephew, Giovanni Antonio Testori, who in other correspondence was said to be known as *"il buan"* ('the good one' or 'the sweet guy'). As well, in 1929 Caterina Grassi wrote to Lorenzo that "aunt Giacomina" had died in Solduno (Grassi fonds, M45 1/19, Caterina Grassi to Lorenzo Grassi, Falmenta, 22 April 1929). This was her sister and, possibly, Domenico's mother.

75 Giovanni Testori to Virginia Grassi, Jackfish, 6 October 1913, letter from the Grassi family papers, Falmenta. Testori addressed Virginia as both his cousin and as *comare*, or godmother, and he signed himself as cousin and godfather, forms of address that suggest the two of them had served together as godparents or that Virginia was godmother to one of Testori's children. In closing his letter Testori asked that Virginia greet his young children for him. He would later write to Lorenzo, after Lorenzo left the north shore. Virginia reported Testori's death in Fort William in 1938 to her brother in a letter dated 4 January 1938 (Grassi fonds, M45 2/16).

76 The letter is shown in fig. 13. The way in which he wrote "Jackfish" in this letter shows Grassi's unfamiliarity with the letters *j* and *k*, which are absent from the Italian alphabet.

77 In this manifest entry Giacomo Bianconi also reported a previous stay in Canada for the period 1894–97, which fits with the 1894 journey discussed above.

78 Ship's manifest, SS *La Lorraine*, dep. Le Havre 29 April 1910, pp. 5–6. The dates 1906–10 cited for a previous sojourn in Canada do not match the date of Giacomo's previous voyage, which occurred in 1907. In other words, the previous stay probably lasted from 1907 to 1910.

79 Census of Canada, 1911, according to which he had immigrated in 1907.

80 Ship's manifest, SS *La Bretagne*, arr. 27 April 1891, p. 5. The remaining seven travellers were travelling to Missouri.

81 Ship's manifest, SS *La Torraine*, arr. New York, 11 April 1903, p. 5, lines 29 and 30; Falmenta municipal register of marriages, 1903, where the twenty-two-year-old bride signed herself as "Matilda Minoletti."

82 The birth of the Bianconi's daughter was registered in Ontario, Canada Births, 1869–1911, District of Thunder Bay. For Matilde Bianconi's death see Province of Ontario, Deaths, 1869–1936, District of Thunder Bay, Division of Fort William, p. 12. She died on 13 March 1906, according to this register one of many Fort William residents who succumbed to typhoid fever in that year.

83 The voyage before the one in 1925 was by means of the SS *Empress of Ireland*, December 1913, to Halifax, NS, when Salvatore travelled with his brother, Aurelio Bianconi, and Aurelio's family.

84 There are some interesting differences between the information recorded in the Ellis Island manifest record for this voyage and that recorded by Canadian authorities on his entry into Canada. The former, for example, reports that he was a "worker," resident at "Canada Penensula [Peninsula]" and that his next of kin was his daughter, "Helena Danconi" in "Canobio Italy."

85 Grassi fonds, M45 2/10, Virginia Grassi to Lorenzo Grassi, 21 January1935. Virginia was writing, in part, to urge her brother Lorenzo also to return: by the date of this letter he had been away even longer than Aurelio Bianconi. Her ability to date the travels of Bianconi (and others) to and from Falmenta with some accuracy suggests that families followed the lives of Falmentine emigrants with interest and concern. In the same letter Virginia Grassi mentioned the return of another emigrant, Amedeo Cantoni, who had been away for "forty years"; see SS *La Champagne* manifest, 18 June 1904, for Cantoni's departure.

86 Ship's manifest, SS *La Bretagne*, arr. New York, 29 April 1900, p. 21, lines 18–19, 21. The kinship is confirmed in the birth and baptism registers of the parish church of San Lorenzo in Falmenta. Giovanna Assunta Bianconi was born on 26 June 1873. A marginal note beside this record reported her marriage to Francesco Cerutti on 10 February 1900.

87 For Marco Bianconi see card number 12998 and for Aurelio Bianconi see card number 12854 in National Archives and Records Administration (NARA), Washington, DC; *Manifests of Alien Arrivals at Buffalo, Lewiston, Niagara Falls, and Rochester, New York, 1902–1954*; Record Group 85, *Records of the Immigration and Naturalization Service*, microfilm M1480, roll 13.

88 Ship's manifest, SS *Empress of Ireland*, arr. Halifax 7 December 1913, p. 4. This chance discovery, because of the 1919 border crossing card, of the journey of a number of Falmentines aboard the SS *Empress of Ireland* is a useful reminder that emigration from Falmenta to Canada is probably under-recorded. The same voyage included two other Falmentines: Gaetano Milani and Lucia Minoletti, both headed for Jackfish, the latter travelling to join her husband there. The manifest listings are ordered alphabetically, so these two passengers are listed separately from the Bianconi family, but no doubt they travelled together. The ill-fated *Empress of Ireland* sank in the St Lawrence River in May 1914, after a collision with a Norwegian collier.

89 Ship's manifest, SS *La Bretagne*, arr. New York 14 May 1894, p. 7, lines 296 ("Cerutti Francesco") and 297 ("Cerutti Virginia"), both travelling to "Ontario." Francesco and Virginia were married on 18 January 1888 as recorded in the Falmenta municipal register for marriages. This marriage record and that for Aurelio Bianconi and Lucia Milani show that Lucia and Virginia were sisters.

90 "Giovaninna" may have been a diminutive, with "Giovanna" her given name.

91 At least one of the Cerutti Canadian-born children returned to northern Ontario, perhaps as a sojourner. In 1924 John (Giovanni) William Cerutti travelled on the SS *Antonia* with a final destination of Heron Bay, Ontario. In the same year, his father Francesco, resident in Heron Bay, swore a declaration for the birth of his son "John (Giovani [sic]) William Cherutti" at Fort William on 2 November 1902 (Canada, Ocean Arrivals [Form 30A], 1919–1924 and Ontario, Canada Births, 1869–1913, Thunder Bay, 1902.

92 See, for example, the record of the baptism of Aurelio and Lucia's son on 13 September 1902 at which "Franciscus Cherutti" stood as godfather (Ontario, Canada, Catholic Church Records [Drouin Collection], 1747–1967, P, Port Arthur, 1872–1904, f. 72). Similarly, in 1931 Aurelio Bianconi swore a declaration that he had been present at the birth of Aurelio Cherutti, his nephew (Ontario, Canada Births, 1869–1913, Thunder Bay, 1896).

93 It is possible that a fifth Bianconi brother was part of the Falmentine migration network to Ontario. The first reference to Aurelio Bianconi as a contact in Canada was made by Giuseppe Bianconi, forty-three years old, on a voyage in 1905; he declared Fort William as his destination and Aurelio as his brother. He may have begun his travels to Canada as early as 1893; see manifests of SS *New York*, dep. Southampton 29 April 1905, page K, line 9755, and SS *La Champagne*, arr. 17 April 1893, line 246.

94 SS *La Lorraine*, arr. 29 April 1910, pages 11–12, line 6. Line 13 on the same double page lists Pietro Zanni, travelling to meet his brother Francesco Zanni, also at Jackfish. Tiboni's wife was Virginia Bianconi but he did not name Aurelio Bianconi as his brother-in-law.

95 Both photographs are preserved in the Grassi fonds, v240-886; v240-885b. The postcard photograph was franked at Jackfish on 9 May 1914.

96 Catherine (Whincup) McKinnon, personal correspondence with authors, November 2008. Ms McKinnon's mother, Pauline Minoletti, spent part of her childhood in Jackfish, and Ms McKinnon notes that the added room "contained a wood-burning stove that was used for cooking in the heat of the summer (rather than heat up the main house) and used for doing laundry year-round."

97 Grassi fonds, v240-885. Unfortunately the original photograph was somewhat blurred and attempts to enlarge it, beyond allowing identification of Aurelio Bianconi, were not very successful. We can speculate, however, that some of those shown were Aurelio's brothers. No source has provided a reason for the party hats.

98 See manifest, SS *La Lorraine*, 1908, for the voyage of Geromina di Giuseppe Minoletti with her daughters Caterina and Elisa. The 1911 census information concerning the ages of mother and daughters and their date of immigration concurs with that in the ship's manifest. Emilio Minoletti was reported as thirty-eight in 1911 and his immigration date was listed as 1896, but on a voyage in 1899 he had reported a previous stay in Canada from 1892–97. His death certificate, witnessed by his son Joe Minoletti in 1932, stated that he had been resident at his place of death for forty years, confirmation of his arrival on the north shore in the early 1890s.

99 For information on Tony Minoletti see text box, p. 14. Information about the family of Emilio and Geromina Minoletti, and photographs, were provided to the authors by Nancy Wolfer, granddaughter of Tony and Elisetta Minoletta, and by Catherine (Whincup) McKinnon, grandaughter of Amedeo and Caterina Minoletti.

100 Grassi fonds, v240-881(pa)025. The membership cards shown in the photograph are corroborated by those now in the Grassi fonds that Lorenzo kept amongst his possessions.

101 The authors are grateful to David Falzetta for taking them on a tour of the remains of the village in fall 2009. Mr Falzetta is the grandson of Giuseppe Falzetta, a long-time resident of Jackfish who arrived in 1903 and whose obituary is reproduced in Marcella, *A History of Jackfish*, p. 19.

102 Marcella, *A History of Jackfish*, p. 5. The Roman Catholic Church in Jackfish was served by Jesuit missionaries from their Immaculate Conception Mission on the Fort William Reserve and their home base of St Andrew's Parish in Port Arthur. Information from the Thunder Bay archdiocesan archives was provided by Roy Piovesana.

103 Only five of the fourteen residents in the Rossport-Gravel-Pays Plat 1911 enumeration bore Falmentine surnames; the rest, judging from their surnames, were from the Cannobino Valley settlement of Gurro. For Peninsula-Marathon only one of the six listed appears to have been an emigrant from Gurro.

104 Grassi fonds, v240/887(PA). Edoardo Grassi's greetings are addressed to both Lorenzo and to *"tutti i compagni,"* literally "all of the companions/comrades."

105 SS *La Provence*, arr. New York, 10 Mar. 1912; see figs. 28 and 29 for a reproduction of the manifest double page. Edoardo's name was listed at line 24, two below the entry for Andrea (Lorenzo) Grassi.

Chapter 3

1 Wait, "Grassi of Canmore," pp. 24–5.

2 Wait, "Grassi of Canmore," p. 24.

3 Appleby, *Canmore*, pp. 100–4. To her credit, Appleby in her account of Grassi's life generously thanked Wait: "We are indebted to the late Mr. Norman Waite [*sic*], a former Canmore resident, for his sympathetic portrayal of Lawrence Grassi, edited in *The Canadian Golden West* magazine" (p. 104).

4 Appleby, *Canmore*, p. 102.

5 Whyte, *Tommy and Lawrence*, pp. 48–62. Val Poschiavo is mentioned on p. 49, and is even more puzzling because Whyte had access to Wait's 1969 article as well a tribute to Grassi written by Sydney Vallance (see note 7).

6 Reisenhofer, "Yamnuska's Secret," pp. 90–2. Reisenhofer, probably drawing from Whyte, places Falmenta near the Swiss border, "a stone's throw [away from] ... the Dolomites," and speculates that Grassi had learned to climb with legendary Italian climbers of the Dolomites.

7 Vallance, "Lawrence Grassi," pp. 41–2. The same date of Grassi's move is in the original version of Vallance's tribute, written in 1960.

8 Lorenzo Grassi to Caterina Grassi and Virginia Grassi, Falmenta,
   10 November 1913:
   Cara madre e sorella
   Con queste due righe vi fo sapere di mie notizie che da lungo tempo
   non vi avevo scritto. Io godo buonissima salute e spero pure che voi
   pure godrete buona salute. O ricevuto la vostra lettera ma finora non
   o ancora scritto a mio padre. Io credo che avrete ricevuto L 50 che
   o spedito il mese di giugno. Altro non mi occorre che salutarvi tutti
   parenti e et amici.
   E mi firmo vostro figlio e fratello L. Grassi
   A copy of the original letter was provided by the Grassi family, Falmenta.
   The lira symbol before "50" is probably an error: it was most likely meant
   to be the dollar sign. This is one of only four letters written by Lorenzo to
   his family in Falmenta that have been preserved. In it, as discussed above,
   Grassi is uncertain whether his father has returned to Falmenta. Another
   letter, dated 3 December 1912, is discussed in chapter 2 in the context of
   the network of Falmentine sojourners and settlers that included Lorenzo
   Grassi during his stay on the north shore.
9 Grassi fonds, Ignazio Tiboni to Lorenzo Grassi, 9 May 1914, v240/886(pa).
10 Grassi fonds, G[iovanni] A[ntonio] Testori to Lorenzo Grassi, 14 August
   1916, v240/889(PA). Testori used the English spelling of the calendar
   month in dating his postcard.
11 The reference is to the Tyrol region – present day Trentino-Alto Adige
   – where the Italian and Austrian armies faced each other in protracted
   trench warfare in World War I. Poles, and other nationalities from the
   Austro-Hungarian Empire, were fighting on the Austrian side.
12 The expression used is *sulla tracca* (on the track), an interesting example of
   "italiese," linguistically an ethnolect or hybrid of English and Italian, a
   typical immigrant linguistic adaptation still very much used by Italian
   Canadians. Testori's use of "August" at the head of the letter is another
   example of linguistic blending.
13 See chap. 2, note 75, for discussion of Giovanni Testori, whose death in
   Fort William, Ontario, Lorenzo Grassi learned of in a letter from his sister
   Virginia dated 15 March 1938. In a 1923 record of a voyage to Canada on
   the SS *Conte Rosso*, Giovanni Testori declared that he had previously lived
   in "Jachfish Ontario." For his 1923 return he named his "brother in law
   Zanni Stefano 706 Pacific Str. Fort William" as his contact.
14 See Heron, *Booze: A Distilled History*, pp. 179–80 for a detailed account of
   the introduction of prohibition in various Canadian jurisdictions during
   World War I. Ontario began to adopt prohibition in the spring of 1916.

15 Whymper (1840-1911) was a famous climber and explorer as well as an illustrator, who is best known for the first ascent of the Matterhorn. (On the descent four members of his party fell to their death.) In the early 1900s he accepted an invitation from the CPR to promote the Canadian Rocky Mountains. He made the first ascent of Mount Whymper and Stanley Peak in the Vermillion Pass area of the Rockies.

16 "Ken Liddell's Corner," a column in the *Banff Crag and Canyon* (no date, but the description of Grassi as "in his seventies" suggests a publication date in the 1960s) mentions "three bookcases ... [with] two shelves of which one [was] occupied with [books] of a correspondence course in civil engineering." J.S. Woodsworth also mentioned seeing books and book-cases in Grassi's cottage ("Study Groups and Holidays," n.p.), as did Wait ("Grassi of Canmore," p. 25).

17 Louis Trono (1909–2004) eventually became a columnist for the *Banff Crag and Canyon* newspaper for which he wrote, for a number of years, an occasional column titled "Sentimental Journey." The Tronos were from Baio Dora, near Ivrea in the province of Turin, some distance to the south and west of the Cannobino Valley. In one of his columns Trono reminisced about Lawrence Grassi's life, among other things recalling that Lawrence and his father Mario conversed in Piedmontese when they met.

18 Listing of Falmentines in "West Calgary," a subdistrict of the enumeration district "Calgary West," in the 1916 Canada *Census of Manitoba, Saskatchewan, and Alberta*, p. 8.

19 The Massole family is briefly discussed in Appleby, *Canmore*, pp. 66, in a photograph caption showing the family on the front porch of their home in Canmore. Information about Ludovico's naturalization is taken from the 1916 census.

20 Information about the Riva family is gathered from the arrival record of the SS *Pittsburg* at Halifax on 6 March 1925. In that record they were listed as returning Canadians and gave their destination as Canmore, Alberta. In this record both Giovanni (but John in the 1916 census) and Francesca were said to have first arrived in Canada in 1890. The 1916 census reports them as having arrived in 1900 and 1901 respectively, and reports that John was naturalized in 1910.

21 Adolfo and Edirge Besso arrived at New York in April 1915 on the SS *Duca Degli Abruzzi*, with Canmore, Alberta, as their destination. They were on the same voyage as two Falmentines, both of whom were destined for Port Arthur, Ontario.

22 See SS *La Lorraine*, arr. 14 March 1914, pp. 1059–60, line 22 for Aurelio Grassi, said to be headed to Calgary, Alberta. Giovanni Grassi was listed on the same page at line 27, with the same destination declared.

23 On the back of this photograph postcard, unfortunately undated but sent from Calgary, Alberta, to "Signor Lorenzo Grassi, Field," Aurelio Grassi wrote, "I send again my greetings I am enjoying perfect health and I hope the same for you and the companions[.] Here all of the 'paesani' are well and it remains only for me to greet you truly from my heart and I sign myself as your friend always Aurelio Grassi." In 1917 a border crossing was registered at Eastport, Idaho, USA, for Aurelio Grassi, who was travelling to Spokane, Washington. He married in Falmenta in June 1932, after his return there as reported by Caterina to Grassi. Peter and Angiolina Zanni of Calgary were reported on the same border crossing manifest as Aurelio and were also headed for Spokane.

24 The 1914 journey by Agostino and his family was recorded in the manifest for SS *France*, arr. New York 20 June 1914.

25 By 1915 some Falmentines in or near Stalwart, Saskatchewan, were in communication with paesans in Falmenta, according to postcards received there and since displayed as part of an exhibition in the village on emigration from the valley. The authors were provided copies of these cards courtesy of Marilena Milani, Falmenta.

26 See the record for a voyage by Agostino Grassi on the SS *Melita* that arrived at Liverpool from St John, NB, on 24 January 1932. He was reported as "British [i.e., a Canadian citizen] Through Booked" for Turin and destined for "Ponte del Falmenta." Perhaps because of this return trip, Lawrence thought it best to precede him with a letter, whose receipt was reported by his goddaughter (Grassi fonds, M 45 2/1, Angiolina Grassi to Lorenzo Grassi, Falmenta, 12 January 1932).

27 Grassi fonds, M 45/2, Falmenta, 8 August 1932, Angiolina Grassi to Lorenzo Grassi.

28 Cruise and Griffiths, *Lords of the Line*, p. 378.

29 Lavallée, *Van Horne's Road*, p. 194.

30 For a complete historical and illustrated survey of the topic, see Pole, *The Spiral Tunnels*.

31 Buchik and MacDonald, *Field Town Site*, p. 10.

32 Buchik and MacDonald, *Field Town Site*, p. 188.

33 The register is housed at the Canmore Museum and Geoscience Centre.

34 He was listed as a "miner" in the 1921 Canada census, five years after he signed on with the Canmore Coal Company.

35 The dialect of Falmenta, now used by a dwindling number of older people because of the growing influence of standard Italian, belongs to the Alpine-Lombard group of languages, with gallo-celtic elements. Certain of its aspects made it distinct from even some of the neighbouring villages of

the Cannobino Valley, according to the *Atlante toponomastico del Piemonte montano: Falmenta*, p. 30.

36 Pole, *The Spiral Tunnels*, p. 112.

37 Alexander, *The History of Canmore*, p. 70.

38 Bercuson, *Alberta's Coal Industry*, p. ix; see also Gadd, *Bankhead*, pp. 11–29, for a brief overview of mining methods.

39 Riva, *Survival in Paradise*, p. 51.

40 Bercuson, *Alberta's Coal Industry*, p. xiv.

41 Riva, *Survival in Paradise*, pp. 59–60.

42 Riva, *Survival in Paradise*, pp. 59–60.

43 Wait, "Grassi of Canmore," p. 25, and Appleby, *Canmore*, p. 102, reproducing Wait's words exactly, named the Vassos as the family with whom Grassi lived for his first two years in Canmore. We have not been able to locate a Vasso family in Canmore or elsewhere in the region.The closest name we have found is that of Adolfo and Edvige Besso: he is from Lessolo in Piedmont and first travelled to Canmore in 1904. On a 1915 voyage (aboard SS *Duca degli Abruzzi*) he was listed as a Canadian citizen and miner. He was accompanied by his wife Edvige from Prazzo, also in Piedmont. The Italian family with whom Grassi lodged may have been the Bessos and not the Vassos as reported by Appleby.

44 The documentation for the purchase of the house is now in the possession of Steve Cherak's son Bill.

45 The nationality is clear despite the clerk's misspelling of "Itallian" or "Itattian," possibly further evidence for the mistaken place name "Staven" for "Stephen" caused by Grassi's difficult pronunciation.

46 Whyte, *Tommy and Lawrence*, p. 55

47 These and other items were donated to the museum by Bill Cherak after Lawrence's death.

48 Whyte, *Tommy and Lawrence*, p. 50. The quotation about water dripping on shoulders is taken from Vallance's tribute to Lawrence Grassi, Jon Whyte fonds, Whyte Museum of the Canadian Rockies, M88 18.

49 Elizabeth (Lizzie) Rummel and Ken Jones, interviewers,Whyte Museum of the Canadian Rockies, Whyte Museum Oral History Programme, Lawrence Grassi interview, S1 /3, November 1971.

50 "Report of Upper Yoho (1914)," *Canadian Alpine Journal*, 6 (1914–15): 182.

51 Sandford, *High Ideals*, p. 20. The English Alpine Club, founded in 1857, did not grant membership to women until 1974, but it did establish a Ladies Alpine Club in 1912 (Robinson, "The Golden Years of Canadian Mountaineering," p. 17; La Force, "Modernization," p. 79 n1).

52 MacCarthy, "The First Ascent of Mt. Louis," p. 79; see also Kain, *Where the Clouds Can Go*, p. 425.

53 Sandford, *High Ideals*, pp. 20–1.
54 La Force, "Modernization," p. 74.
55 Parker, "The Alpine Club of Canada," p. 13.
56 Fox and Reichwein, "Margaret Fleming and the Alpine Club of Canada," pp. 35–6.
57 Henshaw, "Mountain Wildflowers," p. 137.
58 Parker, "Report of the Secretary," p. 126.
59 These points are for the most part taken from Gina La Force, "Modernization," pp. 69–79.
60 Scott, *Pushing the Limits*, p. 107.
61 Robinson, "The Golden Years of Canadian Mountaineering," p. 3.
62 Patillo, *Lake Louise at Its Best*. Patillo acknowledges Lawrence Grassi in his dedication and writes that he met him in 1958 at Lake O'Hara. He manages to insert a substantial number of errors, however, in what he writes about Grassi, including place of birth and time spent in Ontario (supposedly one year), after which "he journeyed to Hector ... became a section-man for the CPR," and similar discrepancies. In this account Patillo writes that well-known personalities in the Kicking Horse Pass area staged the arrival of Santa Claus for the children of its various settlements (Field, Hector, Silver City, Lake Louise, and Banff) and that Lawrence Grassi, while based at Field, took part in the Christmas entertainment, but we have been unable to find any confirming documentation of this story, this despite the claim that it was photographed for and written up in the local newspaper, the *Banff Crag and Canyon*.
63 Roger Patillo, quoted in Reisenhofer, "Yamnuska's Secret," p. 90 and note 5. After quoting Patillo, Reisenhofer indulges in considerable speculation that Grassi learned to climb with legendary mountaineers in the Dolomites.
64 Chic Scott, in conversation with the authors, 12 August 2010.
65 He was born in Bankhead but after that town was closed in 1922 by the company that built it, he lived the rest of his life in Banff, becoming a well-known musical entertainer who performed regularly at the Chateau Lake Louise and the Banff Springs Hotel.
66 The review of Meade's book appeared in the *Canadian Alpine Journal*, 27, no. 1 (1939): 110–12. The journal was running late in its publication schedule, as that issue, according to its preliminary pages, was in fact published in July 1940.
67 We are grateful to Chic Scott for bringing a copy of this letter to our attention after he came across it in the Whyte Museum. The writer, James R. Webb of Victoria, BC, realized his mistake on this matter in a telephone conversation with the authors, 15 November 2010, leaving the record, confusing as it is, as we set it out here. The "redoubtable Scot" to whom

he refers, Bill Smith of Vancouver, in a telephone conversation of the same date reported that he had indeed climbed "most of the mountains" around Banff with Grassi, but he denied any memory of first ascents with him.

68 Reisenhofer, "Yamnuska's Secret," p. 90 (quoting Perry and Josephson, *Bow Valley Rock*, p. 304).

69 Ricker and Morton, "How Many Routes on 'The Finger'?" all quotations p. 87. The Finger was made famous in the poem "David" by the poet Earl Birney, written in 1941 in remembrance of a close friend of his youth, David Cunningham Warden, who in 1927 died from a fall in the Coast Mountains north of Vancouver. The poem is a fictitious recounting of the event, which Birney imagines as taking place on the peak that Grassi had named and climbed by his challenging route for the first time. For further information about Birney, who grew up in Banff, and his poem "David," see http:www.peakfinder.com.

70 Trono, *Banff Crag and Canyon*, n.d., taken from a clipping file in Grassi fonds, Whyte Museum of the Canadian Rockies, M45/15-3.

71 Reichwein and Fox, *Mountain Diaries*, p. 2.

72 Whyte, *Tommy and Lawrence*, p. 51.

73 See ship's manifest, SS *Dante Aleghieri*, voyage of 29 April 1922, p. 3, lines 9–11, for Emilia Cerutti Zanni, her son Pierino, and brother Pietro Cerutti. Other Falmentines were resident in the province as CPR employees, among them Agostino Grassi. On the same voyage were a number of other paesans, including two – Giovanni Grassi and Luigi Zanni – who were travelling to Jackfish, Ontario, to meet their "cousin" Aurelio Bianconi.

74 A portrait of Pietro Cerutti and genealogical information about him and the family of Giovanni and Emilia Zanni were provided by Nancy Wolfer. Pietro Cerutti died in 1946 near Hedley, BC. The date of death is confirmed in the BC Register of Deaths, and was recorded at Princeton, BC. It was reported to the municipal offices in Falmenta, where it was entered into the local register of deaths.

75 See chap. 2, note 39, for an account of Emilia (Cerutti) Zanni's visit to Falmenta.

76 A year later Drinnan corrected herself, substituting the name of Ernest Ward for that of T.B. Moffat, in "Corrigendum."

77 N. Drinnan, "Lawrence Grassi: 1891[*sic*]–1980," p. 44.

78 Reisenhofer, "Yamnuska's Secret," p. 91. For the recollections of Tim Auger, see Beers, *The Wonders of Yoho*, p. 201.

79 Grassi fonds, undated and untitled newspaper clipping, but possibly "Lawrence Grassi, Canmore Guide, to Join Climb," *Calgary Daily Herald*, 16 June 1936, p. 9.

80 Kain, "The First Ascent of Mt. Robson," p. 27.

81 Fynn, "First Ascents of Mt. Barbican, p. 61.

82 A.W. Drinnan, "Turret Mountain," p. 51.

83 A.W. Drinnan, "Turret Mountain," p. 53.

84 The clippings discussed are part of the Grassi fonds. The otherwise anonymous clipping from the *Calgary Daily Herald* was located by means of the
website www.ourfutureourpast.ca/newspapr.

85 The clipping from the *Albertan* is from the Grassi fonds, M45/15-3.
Unfortunately, the relevant issue of the original newspaper is not available
online.

86 "Dr. R.G. Williams," p. 128.

87 Malcolm Geddes was not mentioned in the description of this climb written by Drinnan for the *CAJ*, and nothing in his account provides any clue
to explain Geddes' absence. Certainly Geddes was present at both the 1926
and 1927 camps where, in his capacity as honorary treasurer of the ACC, he
presented financial reports on the planned construction of what became the
Fay Hut, a project on which he worked with T.B. Moffat. The 1926–27 issue
of the *CAJ*, however, also contains his obituary, written by Moffat, with a
full-page photo. No cause or date of death is provided in the obituary, but
in the photo Geddes appears to be a man considerably beyond middle age.
A few pages later another article provides some details about "the death
of one of the most devoted and highly esteemed members of our Club,
M.D. Geddes [and his] untimely end on Mt. Lefroy last summer" (Moffat,
"Malcolm D. Geddes," p. 191; Hickson, "Alpine Accidents," p. 175).

88 "Notable Climbs at Alpine Meet," *Calgary Daily Herald*, 9 August 1926,
p. 13.

89 See Hickson, "Alpine Accidents 1927," pp. 175–6.

90 Hickson, Alpine Accidents," p. 175, for the deaths of the climbers Slark
and Lauser.

91 Information about Thomas B. Moffat is taken from the Glenbow Museum
online catalogue description of the Moffat fonds found at http://www
.glenbow.org (M855, NA-4681, S-20). The photograph of Moffat with
Grassi in front of the Fay Hut is in fig. 77.

92 "Thomas Black Moffat, 1870–1939," *Canadian Alpine Journal*, 27, no. 1
(1939): 103.

93 "Laurence [*sic*] Grassi," p. 191.

94 Appleby, *Canmore*, p. 103, claims that people had to resort to subterfuge in
order to show their appreciation for Grassi's generosity. She reported one
instance in which an anonymous admirer gave Grassi an automobile. The
claim is problematic: there is a 24 September 1928 receipt in the Grassi

fonds, Canmore Museum and Geoscience Centre, for the purchase by
Grassi of a "Chrysler Coupe (65)." Since Appleby provides no date or
further information, we are left to wonder whether this purchase by a coal
miner was sufficiently unusual as to provoke assumptions about gifts.

95 The report, incidentally, mentions Drinnan both as a climbing partner and
as an admirer of Grassi's skills, so it might have been Drinnan or another
member of the Calgary ACC, Thomas B. Moffat (discussed below), who
provided the information to the newspaper.

96 For more information about Sydney Vallance see the text box outlining
his life in chapter 4.

97 "Mt. Inglismaldie (9725)," p. 195.

98 Margaret ("Peggy") Wylie (1894–1984), like Sydney Vallance, was an
active member of the Calgary section of the ACC. She is listed as "chairman" of the section in the 1933 edition of the *Canadian Alpine Journal*. Her
photograph appears in the 1977 tribute to Grassi written by Vallance and
published in the journal. The obituary appeared in *Canadian Alpine Journal*
(1981): 45.

99 "Mt. Ishbel," p. 197.

100 Wait, "Grassi of Canmore," p. 25.

101 This claim is based on a telephone conversation with Bill Cherak, 20
August 2010; see also the logbook text box in this chapter.

102 Beers, *The Wonders of Yoho*, p. 201.

103 The version provided by Don Beers, related to him by Bill Cherak, is
different: "[He] hiked from Canmore to Mt. Assiniboine, climbed the
mountain, walked to Banff via Citadel Pass, and back to Canmore via
Goat Creek. It took him four days to make the climb and to backpack 135
km (84 miles!)" (*The Wonders of Yoho*, p. 201).

104 The original, unidentified newspaper clipping is in the Grassi fonds. The
wording of the newspaper report is essentially self-contradictory: Grassi's
alleged failure to reach the summit is described as a "spectacular
achievement."

105 Vallance, "Lawrence Grassi," p. 41

106 This mountain was named for Donald A. Smith, a Scottish immigrant
who had an extraordinarily successful career, first with the Hudson Bay
Company and then with the CPR. He drove "the last spike," signalling the
completion of the CPR on 7 November 1885, at Craigellachie, less than one
hundred kilometres from Rogers Pass and the mountain bearing his name.
He was named Lord Strathcona and Mount Royal and appointed chancel-
lor of McGill University and Canadian High Commissioner in London.

107 Conant's role as education reformer and political ideologue is well summarized in Menard, "Diversity."
108 Grassi fonds, Nancy Lyall to Lawrence Grassi, 29 October 1963, M45 ?/4 (reference number is partially illegible).
109 Sampson, "President's Address," p. 206.
110 "Club Proceedings and Club News," p. 202.
111 Wheeler, "Honourary President's Address," p. 211.
112 See Scott, *Pushing the Limits*, pp. 108–16, for a full account of their exploits and the eventual conquest of Mount Waddington.
113 Scott, *Pushing the Limits*, p. 109.
114 Leonard, "Can Mt. Waddington Be Climbed?" pp. 31–6.
115 The newspaper in question was probably the *Vancouver Province*. The article, like all articles cited here in connection with the Mount Waddington expedition, is in the Grassi fonds. All except one were clipped from newspapers, unfortunately almost all without any clear indication of date or source. See Grassi fonds, M45/15-7, M45/15-9, M45/15-12,
116 Scott, *Pushing the Limits*, p. 114.
117 Beers, *The Wonders of Yoho*, p. 201.
118 Grassi fonds, Nancy Lyall to Lawrence Grassi, 29 October 1963, M45 ?/4 (reference number is partially illegible).
119 Don Gardner, telephone conversation with author, 12 August 2010.

Chapter 4

1 The authors thank one of the University of Toronto Press's anonymous readers for this observation.
2 See *Banff Crag and Canyon*, 30 June 1971, p. 5. Attached to a copy of this article in the Rummel fonds in the Whyte Museum is the handwritten text of Glen Brooks's tribute to Lawrence delivered at the unveiling. The unveiling is discussed below. Preparation for the creation of the commemorative plaque was underway long before the Rummel-Jones interview, and the interviewers should have been aware of the recognition to be awarded to their interviewee.
3 Whyte, *Tommy and Lawrence*, p. 9.
4 Whyte, *Tommy and Lawrence*, p. 62.
5 For a useful and informative study of Falmenta's place names, see *Falmenta: Atlante Toponomastico del Piemonte Montano*.
6 Appleby, *Canmore*, p. 102; Beers, *The Wonders of Yoho*, p. 202.
7 Grassi fonds, M45/3-2, 21 May 1925, R.S. Stronach to Lawrence Grassi.

8 In addition to the CYHA, the Alpine Club of Canada, the Skyline Hikers of the Canadian Rockies, and the Rocky Mountain Ramblers Association were involved in this request to bring official nomenclature in line with general usage: the name people used was already "Grassi Lakes." The agency they petitioned was then known as the Canadian Board on Geographic Names, although in their 1960 letters the CYHA and other organizations addressed themselves to the "Canadian Board of Geographical Names" or the "Geographical Names Branch." In 1961 the name of the agency was changed to Canadian Permanent Committee on Geographical Names.

9 This passage is quoted almost entirely, with minor deviations, in Whyte, *Tommy and Lawrence*, p. 53, but with no attribution.

10 On Woodsworth's life and politics, see McNaught, *A Prophet in Politics*; Mills, *Fool for Christ*.

11 Whyte, *Tommy and Lawrence*, pp. 53–4.

12 Alexander, *The History of Canmore*, p. 109, describes the Memorial Hall as "a large three-and-a-half storey building on the site of the Oskaloosa Hotel … The Y, as it was known, opened on January 14, 1921 … For the most part, Memorial Hall served as a community centre." These details confirm Appleby's description of the Woodsworth family's time in Canmore, in that she also describes them as having stayed "as guests at the 'Y'" (p. 100).

13 A slight error: Lawrence was twenty-one when he arrived.

14 Riva, *Survival in Paradise*, p. 59.

15 Sydney Vallance, "Lawrence Grassi," p. 68.

16 Woodsworth, "The Trail Maker." Woodsworth's dating is somewhat skewed in this account – Lawrence rescued Dr Williams in 1926, a year before Woodsworth's stay in Canmore. The words "years before … [i]n the course of a prolonged strike" probably refer to the labour unrest of 1924–25. Copies of both of Woodsworth's accounts of Grassi were accessed in Library and Archives Canada, microfilm C13,077, J.S. Woodsworth Papers, MG 27III C7 Scrapbook, vol. 32, p. 80. Neither clipping in this scrapbook preserves the page numbers of the original newspapers.

17 There is no clipping of Woodsworth's article in the Grassi fonds; perhaps Grassi loaned it to someone who never returned it. In chapter 3 we speculate about other items that Grassi might have loaned out, including a logbook of his mountain ascents.

18 A relatively recent one is Beers, *The Wonders of Yoho*. Although the author refers to Grassi as "the finest trail builder the Canadian Rockies has seen" (p. 200), we also read that "in 1938, Dr. J.S. Woodsworth proposed naming Grassi Lakes (near Canmore) in his honor. As recorded in *Hansard*, his speech

ends, 'The world needs Grassis ... men who will seek new paths; make the rough places smooth; bridge the chasms that now prevent human progress; point the way to higher levels and loftier achievements.'" The quotation seems to be taken directly from Whyte, *Tommy and Lawrence*, p. 53. See also Sandford, *Yoho*, p. 112, where the statement that "the world needs Grassis" is attributed to a House of Commons speech; Sandford adds a further error, claiming that Twin Lakes was named for Lawrence *after* his death in 1980.

19 Fleming was a Winnipeg school teacher who joined the Alpine Club of Canada at the invitation of the club's co-founder, Elizabeth Parker, and who later became a regular visitor and avid climber. In her diary she wrote vividly of her first visit to the Rockies and her first climb when she was guided by Lawrence Grassi during the Rogers Pass camp in 1929: "Charlotte B. and myself were practically hauled up by Grassi the last 100 feet. Except for him we had never reached the top" (Reichwein and Fox, *Mountain Diaries*, p. 2). She went on to serve as secretary-treasurer of the Winnipeg ACC section, and eventually became the first female editor of the *Canadian Alpine Journal*, from 1942 to 1952.

20 Reichwein and Fox, *Mountain Diaries*, pp. 10–11.

21 Wilson, "The Club House," p. 112.

22 Wilson, "The Club House," p. 114.

23 H.W. Allan, "Chairman's Report re: Club House," 156.

24 Fleming, *History of Lake O'Hara*, p. 16.

25 Whyte, *Tommy and Lawrence*, p. 55.

26 Reichwein, "Mountaineers and Mountain Parks." Reichwein is critical of this and other Parks Canada decisions, including the neglected condition of Claremont House, the summer home of ACC co-founder Arthur Wheeler, referring to them as "the loss of cultural heritage due to inconsistent public policies" in the context of "the prevalence of capitalist development influence in the national parks."

27 Reichwein and Fox, *Mountain Diaries*, p. 19.

28 Various versions of the Link map were distributed by the Lake O'Hara Trails Club over the years. Contributions to it were made by A.C. Simpson, G. Rutherford, and Tim Auger. The last two were park wardens between 1968 and 1973. Only a few copies of the map remain; we thank Alison Millar, director of the LOHTC, for providing us with one.

29 Whyte, *Tommy and Lawrence*, p. 52.

30 Vallance, "Lawrence Grassi: A Tribute," 10 March 1960; a copy was included in the files Whyte compiled while he was writing *Tommy and Lawrence* (Jon Whyte fonds, Whyte Museum of the Canadian Rockies, M88 II.C./18).

31 Whyte relied on a copy of Vallance's "Lawrence Grassi: A Tribute," dated
    10 March 1960 (Jon Whyte fonds, Whyte Museum of the Canadian
    Rockies, M88 II.C./18).
32 Glenbow Museum, Calgary, Canadian Hostelling Association fonds,
    M-2169-16. The hundreds of photos taken by Lawrence over the years,
    kept in the Whyte Museum, are not for the most part datable. Clitheroe
    himself made some effort to organize Lawrence's mountain photographs
    in this collection according to the mountains depicted. He attributes
    Lawrence's naturalist inclinations, corroborated by other accounts, to his
    roots: "In his youth, he had helped his father in the woods in his native
    Italy, and so he knew the names of trees and flowers, rocks and the miner-
    als. It was natural for hostellers to hike with him."
33 Don Gardner, telephone conversation with authors, 14 August 2011.
34 Manry, *Skoki*, p. 84.
35 Patton and Robinson, *The Canadian Rockies Trail Guide*, p. 87. Jon Whyte
    evidently was familiar with the area, as Catharine Whyte was his aunt.
    Although Whyte refers to "Merlin Lake," the name on official maps, and
    used here, is Lake Merlin.
36 Whyte, *Tommy and Lawrence*, p. 56.
37 Whyte, *Tommy and Lawrence*, p. 56.
38 Whyte, *Tommy and Lawrence*, p. 56.
39 Blake O'Brian and Jennifer Lee have run Skoki Lodge since 1988 (Manry,
    Skoki, p. 92).
40 Walter Odenthal, conversation with authors, 23 February 2012.
41 Whyte's description of this portion of the trail – down to Castilleja Lake and
    back up the steep slope to the ridge overlooking Lake Merlin – clearly con-
    fuses Grassi's work with that of less thoughtful hikers who came after him.
42 Whyte, *Tommy and Lawrence*, p. 55.
43 Sydney Vallance "Lawrence Grassi: A Tribute," Whyte Museum of the
    Canadian Rockies, Jon Whyte fonds, M88/18, dated 10 March 1960.
    Another version was written in 1976 when Grassi was eighty-six years old,
    in support of Liz Rummel's effort to have Grassi awarded a Province of
    Alberta Achievement Award, which he received in 1977 (Whyte Museum
    of the Canadian Rockies, Rummel fonds, M28/46).
44 Whyte Museum of the Canadian Rockies, ACC fonds, M200/AC 90/20B,
    Vallance to Brooks, 7 May 1948.
45 The notice stated: "Lawrence Grassi, local alpinist, who was brought to
    hospital in a serious condition, a week ago, is improving" (*Calgary Herald*,
    14 February 1948, p. 21).

46 The clipping carries no indication of the name of the newspaper.
47 ACC fonds, M200/AC90/20A. The bill was itemized as follows: doctor's fee $75.00; hospitalization (thirty-three days at five dollars/day) 165.00; OR charges 12.00; lab. 2.00; drugs 21.35; for a total of $275.35.
48 ACC fonds, M200/AC 90/20A, Elizabeth Rummel to Sydney Vallance, 29 March, 1948.
49 ACC fonds, M200/AC90/22B. On the evidence of the correspondence between Vallance and others in the course of the fundraising campaign, this contribution was not mentioned.
50 ACC fonds, M200/AC90/20A, Sydney Vallance to Elizabeth Rummel, 2 April 1948. Valance did not therefore inform her that he had already made one contribution.
51 ACC fonds, M200/AC 90/20B, Sydney Vallance to Herbert Sampson, 7 May 1948.
52 ACC fonds, M200/AC 90/20B, letter from Herbert E. Sampson to Sydney Vallance, 11 May 1948.
53 This last comment, although not phrased as fact, is the only extant description of the circumstances behind the 1936 award of Grassi's life membership in the ACC.
54 ACC fonds, M200/AC 90/20B, Sydney Vallance to Eric C. Brooks, 7 May 1948.
55 ACC fonds, M200/AC 90/20/B, handwritten, Eric [Brooks] to Sydney Vallance, n.d.
56 ACC fonds, M200/AC 90/20B, Sydney Vallance to E.C. Brooks, 18 May 1948. In the same letter Vallance informed his friend that "we have sold our house [in Calgary] and hope to move [to Vancouver] by the 1st June."
57 ACC fonds, M200/AC 90/23A, Sydney Vallance to J.B. Fulton, MD, 5 January 1949.
58 ACC fonds, M200/AC 90/23, Sydney Vallance to Elizabeth Rummel, 17 January 1949.
59 ACC fonds, M200/AC 90/22B, Sydney Vallance to J. Blair Fulton, 4 January 1948; but this is clearly a dating error in the letter itself because both Fulton's acknowledgement of receipt of payment and the receipt, both from ACC fonds, M200/AC 90/23/A, are dated 5 January 1949.
60 ACC fonds, M200/AC 90/23B, Sydney Vallance to Lawrence Grassi, 24 March 1949.
61 ACC fonds, M200/AC 90/23B, Sydney Vallance to John F. Brett, 27 May 1949.
62 Binni Robinson (née Albina Del Col), conversation with the authors, Banff, 24 February 2012.

63 According to Fleming, *History of Lake O'Hara*, p. 34, the total was thirteen camps. Fleming, an American from a privileged Philadelphia family, was a well-known regular in the Rockies and at Lake O'Hara, beginning in the 1920s and continuing well into the 1980s. Her short book provides a useful, well-written overview of the topic.

64 McArthur, "Topographical Survey of the Rocky Mountains, 1892," quoted in Christensen, *A Hiker's Guide*, p. 67.

65 Other notable artists have tried their hand at depicting the Lake O'Hara scenery, including two members of the Group of Seven, J.E.H. MacDonald and Lawren Harris, as well as Walter Phillips and Peter and Catharine Whyte.

66 Glisan, "Expedition to Lake O'Hara," 20.

67 Lawrence was not the first person to be named assistant warden at Lake O'Hara. Frank Colonna, who lived in Field and is buried in its cemetery, occupied the position for one summer in 1955 (Whyte Museum of the Canadian Rockies, Sydney Vallance fonds, Glen Brook to Tommy Link, 11 January 1972).

68 Whyte, *Tommy and Lawrence*, pp. 25–31.

69 Whyte, *Tommy and Lawrence*, p. 47.

70 Lake O'Hara Trails Club minutes, 9 August 1956, Whyte Museum of the Canadian Rockies, Sydney Vallance fonds.

71 Minutes of the Twelfth Annual Meeting of Lake O'Hara Trails Club, held at Lake O'Hara Lodge on Thursday 10 August 1961, Whyte Museum of the Canadian Rockies, Sydney Vallance fonds, p. 2. At this meeting Vallance was selected as president, with Lillian Gest continuing as secretary and Major F.W. Longstaff elected club historian/treasurer.

72 Whyte Museum of the Canadian Rockies, Sydney Vallance fonds, Link to Austin Ford, 23 March 1964, p. 2.

73 Whyte Museum of the Canadian Rockies, Sydney Vallance fonds, Link to Glen Brook, 6 May 1961, p. 1.

74 Don Gardner, telephone conversation with authors, August 2010.

75 Whyte, *Tommy and Lawrence*, p. 59.

76 We thank Tim Wake for providing this information. Mr Wake began working at Lake O'Hara Lodge in 1969 and in 1975 was in charge of maintenance. Eventually he became, until 1994, a partner in the business. In 1976 he revived the Lake O'Hara Trails Club, which had been dormant for a few years, and became its president.

77 It is useful to remind ourselves that all trails in the area, including Grassi's, require constant upkeep and repairs. At times wear and tear, often in combination with weather damage, necessitates a complete reconstruction of

parts of a path. This work is frequently done by volunteers, sometimes by park wardens, and the Lake O'Hara Trails Club has contributed significantly to this important maintenance.

78 The plaque is dated 1970, but the ceremony described in the *Banff Crag and Canyon* took place on 26 June 1971.

79 This is the trail Link built in 1943 with A.C. Simpson and Walter Feuz, known officially as the Adeline Link Memorial Trail.

80 Brook's typewritten tribute is in Whyte Museum of the Canadian Rockies, Grassi fonds, on a sheet of paper that also contains the Grassi obituary from the *Banff Crag and Canyon* (with the date simply recorded as "1980") and a photo of Grassi on a mountain top. Another, handwritten, copy (by Glen Brook?) is in Whyte Museum of the Canadian Rockies, Rummel fonds, M28/46.

81 Whyte Museum of the Canadian Rockies, Link fonds, M60/23, Glen Brook to Dr Link, 14 March 1973.

82 Brown, contribution to "Our Favourite Places," 29 May 2009, http://www .theglobeandmail.com/life/travel/our-favourite-places/article4248809/ ?page=3.

83 Whyte, *Tommy and Lawrence*, p. 9.

84 Tom George Longstaff, MD, AC, FRGS, FZS (1875–1964), was an English doctor, explorer, and mountaineer. One of his articles, "Across the Purcell Range of British Columbia," appeared in the 1911 issue of the *Canadian Alpine Journal*. He took part in the 1922 Everest expedition as medical officer, and published his observations "Some Aspects of the Everest Problem," in the *Alpine Journal* (England), reprinted in the *Canadian Alpine Journal*, 13 (1923): 31–9. He served in both the First and Second World Wars and was listed as chairman of the Alpine Club (England) in the *Canadian Alpine Journal* through the 1930s.

85 Whyte, *Tommy and Lawrence*, p. 72. The episode was told to Whyte by Dr E.M. Mitchell of Victoria. Mitchell's letter, dated 8 December 1980, is in Whyte Museum of the Canadian Rockies, Jon Whyte fonds, M88 II.C. files 16-18.

Epilogue

1 Information about Mount Lawrence Grassi was provided by Ronald Kelland of the Historic Resources Management Branch, Province of Alberta. The peak was named in 1991 at the request of the Association of Canadian Mountain Guides (1989) with the support of the Alpine Club of Canada and the town of Canmore.

2 The 1927 naming of Grassi Lakes is discussed in detail in chapter 4. In 1998 a group styling itself "Ghosts of Lawrence Grassi," based in Canmore, completed a trail to the summit of Ha Ling Peak, the northern-most of the three peaks on Ehagay Nakoda (Buchsky, "Theft of Wheelbarrow").

3 Parker, "There Lives a Man of the Mountains," pp. 8–9.

4 The report of the Bow Corridor Eco Advisory Group is available at http://www.stratalink.com/corridors/wildlife_corridors_report.htm; for the housing subdivision see http://www.canmorealberta.com/maps/three-sisters-peaks-of-grassi.

5 Nancy Wolfer (Tony Minoletti's granddaughter), conversations with the authors, Calgary, 2010. Tony Minoletti's career as a chimney sweep in Italy is discussed in chap. 2.

6 Lizzie Rummel, without Lawrence's knowledge and with the assistance of his friends, led a campaign to grant Lawrence the award (Whyte Museum of the Canadian Rockies, Rummel fonds, M28/46.).

7 The letter was written on the stationary of the School of Dentistry, University of Alberta, Edmonton, and mailed on 15 February 1939 (Grassi fonds, M45).

8 Hayes was a former president of Canmore Mines Ltd and had made many climbs with Lawrence.

9 Kariel, "Hut Construction," pp. 134–5. Kariel wrote: "Although it took only ten months from deciding to build the hut to its dedication, eight years of prior planning were required to reach that stage" (p. 135). Mount Clemenceau is "rarely climbed," according to Chic Scott (conversation with the authors, 2010), but is in Kariel's view an "awe-inspiring location when a storm from the west sweeps up the Cummins River to engulf the entire ridge and towering Mt Clemenceau in thunder, lightning, and pouring rain" ("Hut Construction," p. 135).

10 The Lawrence Grassi Hut on Mount Clemenceau no longer appears in the ACC list of huts maintained by the club. The facts concerning the hut's fate were confirmed by a letter to the authors from Nancy Hansen of the ACC in December 2014, stating that the hut was closed after an inspection in 2006 and was decommissioned and removed in September 2008.

Appendix

1 14 August 1916.

2 10 November 1913.

3 Grassi fonds, M 45 1/11, Caterina Grassi to Lorenzo Grassi, 13 October 1925.

4 Grassi fonds, M 45 1/11, Caterina Grassi to Lorenzo Grassi, 1 December 1932

5 Whyte Museum of the Canadian Rockies, Archives and Library, Grassi fonds, M 45 2/21, Angiolina Grassi to Lorenzo Grassi, 1 May 1956.

6 See chapter 2, note 54, for a brief discussion of this Grassi family tragedy.

7 This and the following letter from Grassi to his family in Falmenta were retrieved from the Grassi family collection, Falmenta, Italy, 2008.

8 Caterina Grassi appears to be offering her son the alpine *cascina* property – which she held and which was known in the family as *monte Baro* – as a surety for the money she requires from his savings account. See below, note 68, where Virginia reported this landholding to her brother after their mother's death. In present-day usage the name of the mountain is written as *Barro*.

9 "Rico" is a short form of "Enrico," the name of her son-in-law.

10 The meaning here is not clear. She may be referring to a banknote sent to her that was enclosed in one of Lorenzo's letters to Enrico. Much of the letter has to do with money Enrico borrowed (cf. letter of 28 April 1923) for which she demands some sort of commitment for repayment from her son-in-law on behalf of her son. The fact that Enrico and his family are "in the mountains" seems to provide Caterina with a free hand to express herself more frankly about her son-in-law.

11 The mention of the "mountains" refers to the practice of seasonal trans-humance, or relocation to higher elevations in the mountains circling the Cannobino Valley. This practice allowed farmers to exploit these areas for upland pastures for their animals, for producing hay, milk, cheese, and so forth.

12 She is probably referring to trips to and from the hospital. This travelling would have involved journeys to Cannobio itself, facilitated to some extent by the building of the road to Falmenta from the valley bottom in 1921.

13 The name suggested by Virginia Grassi seems to be a variant of the name "Giovanni" or a variant of a local place name, "ä Välégä du Giuanun" (see *Atlante Toponomastico del Piemonte Montano: Falmenta*, p. 251). Her husband, Enrico, was known by the nickname "U Giuvanun," perhaps so called because of where he lived. Alternatively, the name could mean "the young one." Virginia's request that her brother use this name reflects a fear that his letters might not reach her. It also supports the notion that she and her family were not living with her mother in the Giuseppe Grassi house. Virginia's concern about letters reaching her might have stemmed from the realization that in Falmenta it was difficult to distinguish one Grassi household from another for postal delivery.

14 The municipal tax may have been owed on the Giuseppe Grassi house and therefore "owed in common" in the sense that Lorenzo and his sister were the heirs and joint owners of their father's property.

15 Lorenzo Grassi to Caterina Grassi, 4 December 1924, letter retrieved from Grassi family collection, Falmenta, Italy, 2008.

16 This is a discussion about the division between Lorenzo and Virginia of the family property left to them by their father: half was bequeathed to Virginia and half to Lorenzo. As Virginia's husband, Enrico clearly has an interest in the inheritance, and he is not comfortable with the idea of dividing the house itself in half for the reasons he states.

17 The term used by Enrico translates literally as "indecent," but it is obviously used here to mean rundown or ruinous.

18 It is not clear whether this reference to lack of space for beds refers to his own house or to the Giuseppe Grassi house, where space might have been limited because some of the rooms were in disrepair.

19 Roughly twelve to sixteen dollars a year, according to the exchange rate Enrico Grassi provides in this letter.

20 The *carabinieri* are the Italian federal police force.

21 Italian men were required to perform military service – a minimum at the time of two years – after they turned eighteen. Lorenzo Grassi turned eighteen in 1908, and received his notice to present himself in March 1910. He was inducted in August 1911 but served for only a few months before being released. Caterina's phrase "regularize your position" may refer to his limited service and to the need to complete his term. See chapter two, note 27 for the source documents for his conscription.

22 We do not know whether Caterina's description of Lorenzo's letters as arriving only once a year is, at this point in time, accurate. She may simply be using this as a convenient phrase rather than describing them as "occasional."

23 Enrico had also become an emigrant, albeit as a migrant worker in nearby Switzerland. Caterina later indicates (M45 1/19) that he has found work in or near Lucerne.

24 This letter is out of chronological order; rather than listing by date we have listed letters by archival accession number.

25 The condition of dwellings in Falmenta – in particular those in the village's alpine territories – suggests depopulation, an indication of the difficult economic conditions locally.

26 The Ginesco farmhouse is part of the Giuseppe Grassi family holding Enrico discussed in an earlier letter to Lorenzo Grassi concerning dividing the property between Lorenzo and Virginia. This was the *cascina* attached to the main property in Falmenta itself. Virginia is asking her brother whether he intends to purchase her half of this portion of the family holding.

27 Virginia somewhat playfully, and perhaps even with a tinge of sarcasm, reminds her brother about one of the important components (often even a

staple: hence the sarcasm) of the local diet and economy. Chestnuts were dried for preservation and no doubt utilized when other foodstuffs were scarce or unaffordable.

28 This appears to be a second reference to the question of addressing mail correctly. (For the first, see above, note 13). In the following sentence Virginia also seems to suggest that her mother is best addressed by both her maiden name and her local nickname; her suggestion may be rooted in fear that Lorenzo's letters could be going astray, given their infrequency. And this concern over the correct address again supports the claim that Virginia and her family are not living in the Giuseppe Grassi house with her mother.

29 The fascist government of Italy on 19 December 1926 passed a law that imposed a bachelor tax on all unmarried men aged twenty-five to sixty-five years, except for clergymen, soldiers, and those who were disabled. The intention was to increase the Italian fertility rate. This tax was calculated by age (thirty-five liras for men aged twenty-five to thirty-five years, fifty liras for those aged thirty-five to fifty, and twenty-five liras for those aged fifty to sixty-five) and also varied according to income.

30 This is the incident on Mount Bastion (see chapter 3) in which Lorenzo Grassi carried Dr R.G. Williams down the mountain after Williams injured his leg.

31 We do not know the identity of this woman.

32 As in this instance, Caterina Grassi sometimes signs herself as Caterina Testori because of her status as a widow.

33 Lorenzo Grassi to Virginia and Enrico Grassi, 5 December 1928, letter retrieved from private collection, Grassi family, Falmenta, Italy, 2008.

34 The Ginesco landholding is the *cascina* or summer pasture property of the Giuseppe Grassi family farm. It would appear also that an earlier discussion from Enrico Grassi, Lorenzo's brother in law, about dividing Virginia's and Lorenzo's family holding has been "resolved" with his brother in law's decision to buy another house.

35 From the next letter it is clear that Lorenzo does not answer this letter.

36 Caterina went ahead with the assessment despite her son's failure to reply; see M 45 1/21.

37 Solduno, Locarno, Switzerland; Giacomina was Caterina's sister, so one of Lorenzo's maternal aunts. See chapter 2, note 74 for a letter from Solduno to Caterina Grassi from her nephew, Domenico Grassi.

38 We can only assume that Lorenzo's mother left out a zero in this figure.

39 Caterina Grassi here seems to assume that her son will purchase his sister's share of their joint inheritance in the family holding, and this might

be the context for her reference to purchase documents she is not able to have drawn up.

40 The implication is Angiolina has in the past received some correspondence from her uncle and godfather.

41 In the Grassi fonds this letter is placed near the end of the letter collection, as having been written in 1938, which is not possible because Caterina Grassi died in 1935, as reported in M 45 2/11.

42 Emilia (Cerutti) Zanni, married to Giovanni Zanni, emigrated with her son and her brother, Pietro Cerutti, the latter of which climbed with Lorenzo Grassi in the late 1920s; see chapter 3.

43 The word used is *miseria*.

44 The Feast of St Lawrence is celebrated on 10 August.

45 This curious form of sign-off, as well as her salutation, is so phrased because she is writing for both herself and her husband.

46 This note by Angiolina was included in the letter of the same date sent by her mother.

47 It is difficult to know how frequently Grassi's family in Falmenta learned about his welfare through visits by emigrants returning to the valley. On this occasion, the Cerutti family were in contact with Grassi (see chapter 3). Lorenzo had climbed in the Rocky Mountains with Emilia's brother Pietro Cerutti. See also below, M 45 2/3, for a return visit to Falmenta by Agostino Grassi, who was in contact with Lorenzo Grassi in Alberta.

48 Grassi's niece refers to the Great Depression, which has affected not only Falmentines overseas but also those whose emigration was closer to home, including her father, who had been a sojourner in the vicinity of Lucerne, Switzerland.

49 The term used by Lorenzo's mother is *indecente*, "ruinous."

50 The word, as in the letter by Caterina Testori of 6 August 1931, is *miseria*.

51 Although Angiolina says she sent one photograph to Lorenzo, there are two photographs in the Grassi fonds of Virginia and her three daughters, M45-2 and M45-3; one of these is reproduced in fig. 22. Agostino Grassi, mentioned both by Angiolina and by her grandmother in a previous letter, is discussed in chapter 3.

52 This is translated from the term *mamma grande* in the original.

53 See above, M 45 1/21, Caterina Grassi to Lorenzo Grassi, 12 December 1929.

54 The main road had been built along the valley bottom in the last quarter of the nineteenth century. In this letter Virginia reports that as a type of make-work project this road has been extended up the hillside to reach Falmenta itself.

55 Italy's fascist government moved gradually to restrict emigration in the 1920s. Together with increasing restrictions on emigration was the effort to redistribute the Italian population internally. The *Comitato permanente per le migrazioni interne* (Permanent Committee on Internal Migration, CPMI) was created in early 1926. Its task was to coordinate the transfer of unemployed workers from the north to those areas in the south where they were needed for public works, to cultivate reclaimed land (*bonifiche*), and eventually to fill jobs created by the attendant growth of private business initiatives.

56 See above, M 45 1/7, for the use of this name, probably to provide the family household with a distinctive address in the village. The matter of distinguishing the address is also raised in M45 1/14.

57 That is, she will die. What Virginia is struggling to describe probably was a combination of health problems related to Caterina's arthritis, coupled with her heart condition. The water retention problem was also probably caused by other undiagnosed conditions, including perhaps kidney failure.

58 Caterina's meaning here is not clear.

59 Virginia leaves out the verb in this clause. An alternate meaning is "Don't forget Virginia because you, Lorenzo, don't have anyone else in the world."

60 The term *stallo* translates as "animal enclosure" but it is not clear where Caterina Grassi could have been moved, presumably for fresh air – perhaps into one of the porticos of the house at ground level; see the photograph of the Grassi house in fig. 21.

61 This Latin phrase, slightly misquoted by Virginia, comes from the Catholic doxology. It is from the Gloria Patri: "Gloria Patri, et Filio, et Spiritui Sancto. Sicut erat in principio, et nunc, et semper, et in saecula saeculorum. Amen." (Glory to the Father, and to the Son, and to the Holy Spirit. As it was in the beginning, and now, and always, and to ages of ages. Amen.)

62 This reference number does not reflect the chronological sequence of this letter. To be in correct sequence this should be listed as 45 2/10, on the basis of both the date and the content.

63 This is Caterina's response to her son's written suggestion that his sister should use his savings in Italy to deal with their financial difficulties. Virginia's letter to her brother requesting money – the $20.00 he has forwarded – has not survived in his letter collection. It is interesting that Caterina insisted on reading the letter from Lorenzo herself and that she replies through her daughter that she is unable (or unwilling?) to withdraw money from her son's accounts for her daughter.

64 No letter survives documenting this request from Virginia for three thousand liras) from her brother.

65 The clause was left out.

66 Presumably this means that Virginia had the will registered for probate purposes in the municipal office.

67 Caterina Grassi held property in her own right, which was not uncommon for Italian women. "*Monte Baro* [*sic*: Barro] property" may refer to a *cascina* holding in the Monte Barro alpine region where Falmentines had alpine pastures (Bergamaschi, *Conoscere la Valle Cannobina*, p. 126). She also had the use or benefits of income (usufruct; see following note) from her husband's property, which she and Enrico had rented out.

68 Under Italian inheritance law usufruct is the right to enjoy the fruits (income and other benefits) of someone else's property for a given period of time. It may be that because Virginia and Enrico had moved into their own property and had not determined what would happen to the property they had inherited from their father, the income from the latter property, which Caterina had rented out, went to her. In the Grassi family papers in Falmenta there is an official record for the transfer of this usufruct from the deceased Caterina Testori to the children "Grassi Virginia and Lorenzo of the deceased Giuseppe Antonio." The property was described as five plots (*appezzamenti*) of pasture/grass land, three plots "a Geslido," one cultivated, and a house or dwelling with six rooms and "*due cascine.*" The total value of the usufruct was given as 251.25 liras and was recorded at Cannobio on 28 March 1935.

69 Virginia may have had to pay 150 liras to have the will registered or probated.

70 The term Virginia used was *capitale*, which means "capital" in the technical sense as in English, but colloquially it also means "a huge amount." When Caterina dealt with Lorenzo's money, she mentioned post office accounts and bank accounts (savings bonds?). Virginia presumably is referring to the same arrangement but using different terms.

71 The emigrant who is departing was Emilia (Cerutti) Zanni, sister of Pietro Cerutti; see chapter two, notes 28 and 39.

72 There is no date on this letter but it was probably written in 1937. In January 1938 Virginia reported receiving a money order "in December" (1937) from her brother that she exchanged for 1,887 liras (M45 2/16, Virginia Grassi to Lorenzo Grassi, 4 January 1938). The letter contained no date, but was clearly written after the preceding two, to which Lorenzo had apparently not replied. It does not begin with Virginia's usual "Dear brother…"

73 According to Enrico Grassi, writing on 2 March 1925 (M45 1/10), the exchange rate then was roughly twenty-three to twenty-four liras to the dollar, so on this occasion Lorenzo sent his sister around eighty dollars.

Perhaps this was money that was sent in response to her request for "at least one hundred dollars" (M 45 2/13).

74 In other words, Angiolina's marriage was planned for when she would have been about twenty-two years old.

75 One of these photographs, that of Angiolina and her fiancé, is preserved in the Grassi fonds (M45 2-16) and is reproduced in fig. 23.

76 No doubt this is a reference to the 1,887 liras Virginia, in her letter to her brother dated 4 January 1938 (M 45 2/16), reports that she has received.

77 Virginia is saying that the man previously in charge of the post office, by the name of Lorenzo, has died. A daughter is now the clerk, and the man who has replaced Lorenzo is named Giovanni Grassi. Falmenta's post office was in Ponte di Falmenta, a *frazione* or hamlet of the neighbouring municipality of Cavaglio Spoccia.

78 On our copy of this letter, obtained from the Grassi collection in the Whyte Museum, no reference number has been assigned.

79 Cunardo is a town in the province of Varese, in the Lombardy Region. Angiolina died at Luino in the same region (across Lake Maggiore from Cannobio) on 14 January 1997.

80 The expression mistakenly used by Angiolina is *le precedenti* (the preceding ones).

Bibliography

Archives Consulted

Whyte Museum, Archives and Library, Banff, Alberta: Alpine Club of Canada
  fonds; Lawrence Grassi fonds; R.R. (Tommy) Links fonds; Lake O'Hara
  Trails Club fonds; Liz Rummel fonds; Trono family fonds; Sydney Vallance
  fonds; Jon Whyte fonds
Falmenta, Piedmont: Parish Registers (Marriages, Births, and Deaths), Parish of
  San Lorenzo; Falmenta Municipal Registers (Marriages, Births, and Deaths)
Glenbow Museum and Archives, Calgary, Alberta: Thomas B. Moffat fonds;
  Canadian Youth Hostelling Association fonds; Joe Clitheroe fonds
Thunder Bay Historical Society, Thunder Bay Museum, Thunder Bay, Ontario
Library and Archives Canada/Bibliothéque et Archives Canada, Ottawa,
  Ontario: J.S. Woodsworth fonds

Books, Articles, and Other Resources

Albera, D., and P. Corti, eds. *La montagna mediterranea. Una fabbrica
  d'uomini? Mobilità e migrazioni in una prospettiva comparata (ss. XV–XX)*
  Cavallermaggiore: Gribaudo, 2000.
Alexander, Rob. *The History of Canmore*. Banff: Summerthought, 2010.
Allan, H.W. "Chairman's Report re: Club House." *Canadian Alpine Journal*, 19
  (1930): 156.
Appleby, Edna Hill. *Canmore: The Story of an Era*. Canmore: Author, 1975.
Atlante toponomastico del Piemonte montano: Falmenta. Edited by Regione
  Piemonte. Turin: Università degli Studi di Torino, 2007
Beers, Don. *The Wonders of Yoho*. Calgary: Highline, 1993.

Bercuson, David J., ed. *Alberta's Coal Industry, 1919*. Calgary: Historical Society of Alberta, 1978.

Bergamaschi, Cirillo, ed. *Conoscere la Valle Cannobina: Studi e Ricerche di Autori Vari*. 2nd ed. Verbania: Alberti Libraio Editore, 2004.

Buchik, Pat, and Graham A. MacDonald. *Field Town Site, Yoho National Park: Built Heritage Resource Description and Analysis*. Calgary: Public Works and Government Services Canada, 1997.

Buchsky, Johnny. "Theft of Wheelbarrow Halts Trail-Building Effort." *Calgary Herald*, 1 October 1998, p. B8.

Christensen, Lisa. *A Hiker's Guide to Art of the Canadian Rockies*. Calgary: Glenbow Museum, 1996.

"Club Proceedings and Club News." *Canadian Alpine Journal*, 25 (1932): 202–6.

Conway, Lorie. *Forgotten Ellis Island: The Extraordinary Story of America's Immigrant Hospital*. New York: Smithsonian Books/Collins, 2007. Harper Collins EPub Editions (Kobo), 2010.

Cruise, David, and Allison Griffiths. *Lords of the Line*. Toronto: Penguin, 1996.

Dresti, Silvano, "Emigrazione." In *Conoscere la Valle Cannobina: Studi e Ricerche di Autori Vari*, 2nd ed., edited by Cirillo Bergamaschi, pp. 249–59. Verbania: Alberti Libraio Editore, 2004.

"Dr. R.G. Williams." *Canadian Alpine Journal*, 46 (1963): 128.

Drinnan, A.W. "Turret Mountain." *Canadian Alpine Journal*, 16 (1926–27): 51–4.

Drinnan, Nan. "Corrigendum." *Canadian Alpine Journal*, 65 (1982): 71.

– "Lawrence Grassi: 1891–1980." *Canadian Alpine Journal*, 64 (1981): 70–1.

Ferrari, Ornella. "Il Paese." In *Atlante toponomastico del Piemonte montano: Falmenta*, edited by Regione Piemonte. Turin: Università degli Studi di Torino, 2007.

Fleming, Margaret. *History of Lake O'Hara*. 4th ed. Banff: Lake O'Hara Trails Club, 1989.

Forestell, Nancy. "Bachelors, Boarding-Houses, and Blind Pigs: Gender Construction in a Multi-Ethnic Mining Camp, 1909-1920." In *A Nation of Immigrants: Women, Workers and Community in Canadian History, 1840s–1960s*, edited by Franca Iacovetta, Paula Draper, and Robert Ventresca, pp. 251–90. Toronto: University of Toronto Press, 1998.

Fox, Karen, and PearlAnn Reichwein. "Margaret Fleming and the Alpine Club of Canada: A Woman's Place in Mountain Leisure and Literature, 1932–1952." *Journal of Canadian Studies*, 36, no. 3 (2001): 35–60.

Fynn, Val A. "First Ascents of Mt. Barbican 10,100 Feet and Mt. Geikie, 10,854 Feet." *Canadian Alpine Journal*, 14 (1924): 60–6.

Gadd, Ben. *Bankhead: The Twenty Year Town*. Banff: Friends of Banff National Park, 1989.

Glisan, R.L. "Expedition to Lake O'Hara." *Canadian Alpine Journal*, 1, no. 2 (1908): 20.

Grossutti, Javier. "Emigration from Friuli Venezia Giulia to Canada." http://www.ammer-fvg.org/_Data/Contenuti/Allegati/eng/en_grossutti_canada.pdf. Accessed 24 January 2014.

Harney, R.F. "A Case Study of Padronism: Montreal's King of Italian Labour." In *If One Were to Write a History…: Selected Writings*, edited by Pierre Anctil and Bruno Ramirez, pp. 143–72. Toronto: Multicultural History Society of Ontario, 1991.

– "The Commerce of Migration." In *If One Were to Write a History…: Selected Writings*, edited by Pierre Anctil and Bruno Ramirez, pp. 19–36. Toronto: Multicultural History Society of Ontario, 1991.

– "Men without Women: Italian Migrants in Canada, 1885–1930." In *The Italian Immigrant Woman in North America*, edited by Betty Caroli, R.F. Harney, and Lydio Tomasi, pp. 79–102. Toronto: Multicultural History Society of Ontario, 1978.

Henshaw, Julia, "The Mountain Wildflowers of Western Canada." *Canadian Alpine Journal*, 1 (1907): 97–102.

Heron, Craig. *Booze: A Distilled History*. Toronto: Between the Lines, 2003.

Hickson, J.W.A. "Alpine Accidents 1927." *Canadian Alpine Journal*, 16 (1926–27): 175–7.

Kain, Conrad. "The First Ascent of Mt. Robson, the Highest Peak of the Rockies (1913)." Translated by P.A.W. Wallace. *Canadian Alpine Journal*, 6 (1914–15): 22–8.

– *Where the Clouds Can Go*. Surrey, BC: Rocky Mountain Books, 2009 [1935].

Kariel, Herb. "Hut Construction at Mt. Clemenceau." *Canadian Alpine Journal*, 65 (1982): 134–5.

La Force, Gina. "Modernization, Canadian Nationalism, and Anglo-Saxon Mountaineering." *Canadian Alpine Journal*, 62 (1979): 69–83.

"Laurence Grassi." *Canadian Alpine Journal*, 20 (1931): 191.

Lavallée, Omer. *Van Horne's Road: The Building of The Canadian Pacific Railway*. Calgary: Fifth House, 2007.

"Lawrence Grassi, Canmore Guide, to Join Climb." *Calgary Daily Herald*, 16 June 1936, p. 9.

Leonard, Richard M. "Can Mt. Waddington Be Climbed?" *Canadian Alpine Journal*, 23 (1934–35): 31–6.

MacCarthy, A.H. "The First Ascent of Mt. Louis." *Canadian Alpine Journal*, 8 (1917): 69–74.

Manry, Kathryn. *Skoki: Beyond the Passes*. Banff: Rocky Mountain Books, 2001.

Marcella, Jeanne, ed. *A History of Jackfish*. Terrace Bay: Terrace Bay Public Library, 1986.

Marty, Sid. *Switchbacks: True Stories from the Canadian Rockies*. Toronto: McClelland and Stewart, 1999.

McNaught, Kenneth. *A Prophet in Politics*. Toronto: University of Toronto Press, 2001.

Menard, Louis. "Diversity." In *Critical Terms for Literary Study*, 2nd ed., edited by Frank Lentricchia and Thomas McLaughlin, pp. 339–45. Chicago: University of Chicago Press, 1990.

Mills, Allan G. *Fool for Christ: The Political Thought of J.S. Woodsworth*. Toronto: University of Toronto Press, 1991.

Moffat, T.B. "Malcolm D. Geddes." *Canadian Alpine Journal*, 16 (1926–27): 169–73.

"Mt. Inglismaldie (9725)." *Canadian Alpine Journal*, 22 (1933): 195–7.

"Mt. Ishbel." *Canadian Alpine Journal*, 22 (1933): 197.

Neave, Ferris. "Climbing at Banff." *Canadian Alpine Journal*, 18 (1929): 90–4.

"Notable Climbs at Alpine Meet." *The Calgary Daily Herald*, 9 August 1926, p. 13.

Oltmann, Ruth. *Lizzie Rummel: Baroness of the Canadian Rockies*. Calgary: Rocky Mountains Books, 2002.

Parker, Elizabeth. "The Alpine Club of Canada." *Canadian Alpine Journal*, 1 (1907): 4–6.

Parker, Elizabeth. "Report of the Secretary." *Canadian Alpine Journal*, 1 (1907): 123–6.

Parker, Pat. "There Lives a Man of the Mountains." *The Hoodoos Highlander*, 14 February 1979, pp. 8–9.

Patillo, Roger W. *Lake Louise at Its Best: An Affectionate Look at Life at Lake Louise by One Who Knew It Well*. Aldergrove, BC: Amberlea, 2008.

Patton, Brian, and Bart Robinson. *The Canadian Rockies Trail Guide: A Hiker's Manual to the National Parks*. Rev. ed. Canmore: Devil's Head Press, 1978.

Perry, Chris, and Joe Josephson. *Bow Valley Rock*. Calgary: Rocky Mountain Books, 2000.

Petrosina, Cecilia, ed. *Chilò: Falmenta si racconta*. Casalserugo: Nuova Grafoticnica, 2007.

Piovesana, Roy H. *Italians of Fort William's East End, 1907–1969*. Thunder Bay: Institute of Italian Studies, 2011.

Pole, Graeme. *The Spiral Tunnels and the Big Hill*. Hazelton, BC: Mountain Vision, 2009.

Potestio, John. *The Italians of Thunder Bay*. Thunder Bay: Institute of Italian Studies Lakehead University, 2005.

Pozzetta, George E. "The Mulberry District of New York City: The Years before World War One." In *Little Italies in North America*, edited by R.F. Harney
and J. Scarpaci, pp. 7–40. Toronto: Multicultural History Society of Ontario,
1981.

Pucci, Antonio. "Thunder Bay's Italian Community, 1880s–1940s." In *The
Italian Immigrant Experience*, edited by John Potestio and Antonio Pucci,
pp. 79–102. Thunder Bay: Canadian Italian Historical Association, 1988.

Ramirez, Bruno. "Brief Encounters: Italian Immigrant Workers and the CPR,
1900–30." *Labour/Le Travail*, 17 (Spring 1986): 9–27.

Reichwein, PearlAnn. "Mountaineers and Mountain Parks: Reflections on
History, Epistemology, and Cultural Landscapes." Paper presented at
Canadian Parks for Tomorrow: 40th Anniversary Conference, 8–11 May
2008, Calgary. http://hdl.handle.net/1880/46945.

Reichwein, PearlAnn, and Karen Fox, eds. *Mountain Diaries: The Alpine
Adventures of Margaret Fleming, 1929–1980*. Calgary: Historical Society of
Alberta, 2004.

Reisenhofer, Glenn. "Yamnuska's Secret: A Wondering." *Canadian Alpine
Journal*, 89 (2006): 90–2.

"Report of Upper Yoho (1914)." *Canadian Alpine Journal*, 6 (1914–15): 181–92.

Ricker, Karl, and Ann Morton. "How Many Routes on 'The Finger'?" *Canadian
Alpine Journal*, 46 (1963): 85–90.

Riva, Walter. *Survival in Paradise: A Century of Coal Mining in the Bow Valley*.
Canmore: Canmore Museum and Geoscience Centre, 2008.

Robinson, Zac. "The Golden Years of Canadian Mountaineering: Asserted
Ethics, Form, and Style, 1886–1925." *Sport History Review*, 4 (2004): 1–19.

Sampson, H.E. "President's Address." *Canadian Alpine Journal*, 25 (1932):
206–8.

Sandford, R.W. *High Ideals: Canadian Pacific's Swiss Guides, 1899–1999*.
Canmore: Alpine Club of Canada and Canadian Pacific Hotels, 1999.

– *Yoho: A History and Celebration of Yoho National Park*. Canmore: Altitude, 1993.

Sandilands, Catriona. "Where the Mountain Men Meet the Lesbian Rangers:
Gender, Nation, and Nature in the Rocky Mountain National Parks." In
This Elusive Land: Women and the Canadian Environment, edited by Melody
Hessing, Rebecca Raglon, and Catriona Sandilands, pp. 142–62. Vancouver:
University of British Columbia Press, 2005.

Scott, Chic. *Pushing the Limits: The Story of Canadian Mountaineering*. Calgary:
Rocky Mountain Books, 2000.

Vallance, Sydney. "Lawrence Grassi." *Canadian Alpine Journal*, 60 (1977): 67–9.

Wait, N.A. "Grassi of Canmore: A Miner Who 'Did His Thing' and Gave
Alberta a Heritage of Beauty." *Canadian Golden West*, 4 (1969): 24–5.

Wheeler, A.O. "Honourary President's Address." *Canadian Alpine Journal*, 25 (1932): 208–11.

Whymper, Edward. *Chamonix and the Range of Mont Blanc*. London: John Murray, 1902.

Whyte, Jon. *Tommy and Lawrence: The Ways and the Trails of Lake O'Hara*. 2nd ed., edited by Chic Scott. Lake Louise: Lake O'Hara Trails Club, 2010.

Wilson, L.C. (Jimmie). "The Club House, 1929–1959." *Canadian Alpine Journal*, 42 (1959): 112–15.

Woodsworth, J.S. "Study Groups and Holidays." *Weekly News* (newspaper of the Independent Labour Party, Manitoba), July 1927.

– "The Trail Maker." *Jewish Post* (Winnipeg), 23 September 1927.

Index